THE INTERPRETED WORLD

THE INTERPRETED WORLD

An Introduction to Phenomenological Psychology

Ernesto Spinelli

SAGE Publications
London • Newbury Park • New Delhi

First published 1989

SAGE Publications Ltd
28 Banner Street
London EC1Y 8QE

SAGE Publications Inc
2111 West Hillcrest Drive
Newbury Park, California 91320

SAGE Publications India Pvt Ltd
32, M-Block Market
Greater Kailash – I
New Delhi 110 048

British Library Cataloguing in Publication data

Spinelli, Ernesto
  The Interpreted world: an introduction to
  phenomenological psychology.
  1. Phenomenological psychology
  I. Title
  150.9′2

ISBN 0–8039–8114–7
ISBN 0–8039–8115–5 Pbk

Library of Congress catalog card number 89–60698

Typeset by Fakenham Photosetting Ltd, Fakenham, Norfolk
Printed in Great Britain by Billing and Sons Ltd, Worcester

Contents

This text is dedicated to
Philip K. Dick
a writer of phenomenological marvels
and to
Maggi Cook
who allowed me access into her world

Preface

Of the various regrets in my life, one that comes back to haunt me, on occasion, is my, now long-ago, choice not to pursue philosophy as my area of academic specialization.

Ironically, it was an introductory course in philosophy which led me to psychology. Unlike what we might now expect to make up the ingredients of an undergraduate-level introductory philosophy course – a touch of Plato, a smattering of Aristotle, some Kant for the sake of confusion, and a hint of Nietzsche just to flavour the whole concoction – in place of all such, I was made to read Freud.

If this strikes the reader as being somewhat unusual, I must clarify that I sat this course in 1968 – a time when the unusual was taken for granted.

In any case, having been presented with the writings of one of the very few true geniuses in my profession, I was beguiled into becoming a student of psychology. I was not a brilliant student; far from it, in fact. Often uninterested, frequently disappointed, I don't know to this day why I persisted. Still, persist I did, even if, always at the back of my mind, there remained a hint of a serious gap, a missing element, in all that I learned.

Over the intervening years, I've discovered that numerous others seem to have arrived at a similar conclusion. Among them, many of my students (usually the best in their class) have confided in me that they're not really certain why they remain in this field either, especially since the gap between what it claims to offer and what it actually delivers seems unbridgeable.

This text represents my attempt at relieving some of this shared dissonance. As will become apparent, it seems to me that a *phenomenological* perspective in psychology offers the possibility of reconsidering many established psychological issues and concerns in ways which are both original and illuminating. More importantly, perhaps, phenomenology seems to bring a breath of fresh air to how we think about 'doing' psychology.

Having taught an introductory course on phenomenological psychology on a yearly basis over the past eight years, I've been rewarded with the newly rediscovered enthusiasm for psychology expressed by the great majority of students who have taken it. Their comments, and the superior standard of much of their submitted work, provided me with the necessary energy and determination to reformulate my lectures into a text which, in its wider accessibility, may invigorate and enlighten a greater audience.

Like most authors, I've found the writing of this book to be a challenge. First, because it is the first extended piece of non-fiction that I've ever attempted. Secondly, and of far greater personal significance, because it has forced me to confront that source of regret – and weakness – that I mentioned earlier.

For, more than any other system in psychology, the foundations of phenomenological psychology are firmly grounded in philosophy. As aware as I am of my philosophical deficiencies, it remains necessary for me to examine and argue a number of important philosophical propositions. I hope that my attempts to present such arguments do not earn me the enmity of philosophers.

To the students and friends who, in their unique ways, have encouraged me throughout the writing of this text, my heartfelt thanks. May they decide that their efforts have been worthwhile.

Introduction

As odd as it may seem to non-psychologists, the study of *consciousness* has held little appeal for twentieth-century psychology. Dismissed as unworthy of scientific examination by behaviourists, devalued in favour of the unconscious by psychoanalysts, reduced to physiological artefact, and remodelled to suit electronic parallels, our species' conscious experience of the world (and of itself, of course) has received short shrift from psychology.

Indeed, for many years, the only authors who treated consciousness seriously and openly, without need to explain or defend their seemingly perverse fascination with the subject, were Continental European philosophers who, in what might have seemed to be their attempts to test the perseverance and mettle of their readers, insisted on presenting their ideas in a language so arcane and rarefied that it made the decyphering of the Dead Sea Scrolls seem like the simplest of tasks. The most ardent (and, arguably, obscure) among such writers were philosophers belonging to an approach that has come to be labelled **phenomenology**.

Initially, phenomenologists took their principal task to be the exploration of subjective experience, not for its own sake, but in order to expose how our consciousness imposes itself upon, and obscures, 'pure' reality so that they might, ultimately, **bracket** (or set aside) conscious experience and arrive at a more adequate approximation of 'what is'. These academic pursuits soon came to be recognized as the principal focus of what has since become the **transcendental** branch of phenomenology. Its main ideas are discussed in Chapters 1 and 2.

An alternative branch – **existential phenomenology**, or **existentialism** – arose as a result of the refocusing on the implications of such issues for the very meaning of existence. As such, the principal task of existential phenomenology became the exploration of the potentials for freedom and the unavoidable limitations inherent in human beings' experience of themselves as beings-in-the-world. I will discuss some of the principal ideas of existential phenomenology in Chapter 6.

Not surprisingly, the concerns of both branches of phenomenology intrude upon most (if not all) of the major subject areas of psychology. The ideas of transcendental phenomenology, for instance, can be shown to have significant impact on a variety of topics centred on the study of **perception**. Chapters 3, 4 and 5 examine various aspects of this vast area.

Similarly, certain key ideas of existential phenomenology have had a major impact upon **psychotherapy**, as I will attempt to demonstrate in Chapter 7.

Although phenomenological psychology is far from being a recent development, and, increasingly, has become an accepted component of both undergraduate and graduate programmes in psychology, psychotherapy and counselling, there still remains a general confusion as to its principal concerns and direction. This confusion is further aggravated by the tendency to lump together phenomenological and **humanistic** psychologies as though they were one and the same system. While it is true that both share similarities in their realms of discourse, and that humanistic psychology is indebted to an overwhelming degree to certain principal tenets of phenomenology, there are also major differences between these approaches. I will attempt to clear up some of this confusion in Chapter 8.

More generally, in spite of criticisms from representatives of the remaining major contemporary psychological systems, the phenomenological approach can both clarify and expose the (often hidden) biases and assumptions within these systems, and in their practical applications, and may well provide the means towards the development of a more unified psychological science. Chapters 9 and 10 provide a more detailed discussion of these issues.

There exists a wealth of literature on both transcendental and existential phenomenology as *philosophical* systems. These writings are often of obvious importance to phenomenological psychology. Nevertheless, as well as being a source of strength, the link between phenomenology as a philosophical system and phenomenological psychology has helped to minimize the latter's impact upon psychology. Phenomenological philosophers are notorious for the obscurity of their language and the convoluted manner in which they express their ideas (Heidegger, for example, is a perfect case in point), so that, at first, it may seem that phenomenology's central arguments are not likely to be easily grasped, or correctly understood, by non-philosophers. More to the point, any psychological applications of these ideas might, as a result, be seen to be of limited and dubious value.

This text seeks to present the relevant philosophical arguments in a manner which is accessible to non-philosophers and which directly relates them to psychological concerns. In order to achieve this aim, I have attempted to keep this text as jargon-free (or 'reader-friendly', as some might say) as possible and have sought to provide both experimental studies and clarificatory examples drawn from everyday experience in order to illuminate potentially difficult arguments which might otherwise be easily misunderstood by readers new to the subject. I realize that, in doing so, I run the risk of irritating those who are more advanced in their understanding of the principal concerns of the area, but I hope that such readers will see their necessity and tolerate (or simply skip) them.

All this is not to suggest that there exist no relatively recent texts which deal adequately with phenomenological psychology. Misiak and Sexton's *Phenomenological, Existential, and Humanistic Psychologies: A Historical Survey* (1973) achieves exactly what its title suggests, and Shaffer's *Humanistic Psychology* (1978), though obviously focusing on the humanistic approach, provides excellent summaries of a number of phenomenological issues and of the main ideas of some of its key theoreticians.

Similarly, a number of reliable texts already exist dealing with existential phenomenology's applications to psychotherapy. In addition to the established classics in this field, such as Boss's *Existential Foundations of Medicine and Psychology* (1979), Binswanger's *Being-in-the-World* (1968), Frankl's *Psychotherapy and Existentialism* (1967), May's *Existential Psychology* (1969), and Laing's *The Divided Self* (1960), two texts in particular, Yalom's *Existential Psychotherapy* (1980) and van Deurzen-Smith's *Existential Counselling in Practice* (1988) provide particularly clear introductory accounts of this aspect of phenomenological psychology.

Last, but by no means least, a remarkable series of papers delivered at a symposium at Rice University and published as *Behaviorism and Phenomenology* (edited by T.W. Wann, 1964) remains an excellent example of serious (if erratic) attempts to explore areas of convergence and divergence between these philosophical and psychological systems.

At the same time, however, it seemed to me that there still remained a need to present phenomenological psychology's unique focus and approach to a representative number of key psychological issues in a clear and systematic manner so that its distinctive characteristics could be more accurately understood and assessed. Many writers, for example, have assumed that phenomenological psychology dismisses experimental findings and takes, in general, an anti-experimental stance. This is far from being the case – as I will seek to demonstrate.

Although the issues I will discuss might well be informative to a general readership, this text is principally aimed at both psychologists and those who apply various aspects of psychology in their profession. As such, as well as being of possible value to introductory courses which deal specifically with phenomenological psychology, or which examine the various contemporary systems in psychology, many (if not all) of its topics should also be of use to trainee and practising therapists and counsellors, as well as to members of the various caring professions and to medical and nursing staff. Wherever it seemed both valid and useful, I have employed brief therapeutically oriented examples drawn from my own phenomenologically oriented practice. A possibly realizable personal hope is that this text might open the way for a greater number of courses, or course-sections, whose focus is upon phenomenological psychology.

Though I began this Introduction by referring to the role of 'consciousness' in psychology, I do not wish to mislead the reader into thinking that the sole, or even principal, concern of this text, as was the case with early, now virtually forgotten, introspectionist theories in psychology, lies in the exploration of the components and structures of subjective experience.

Even if the question of consciousness remains the starting point of all phenomenological investigations, the central focus of phenomenological psychology rests, more properly, with the analysis of how all of us arrive at **unique interpretations** of our experience by means of both innate invariants, or limitations, imposed by our biology and experientially derived social constructs and frameworks. Such an approach has, I think, greatly increased the adequacy of our understanding of the great variety of thoughts and behaviours generated by all members of our species.

1

An Introduction to Phenomenological Theory

Pure logical thinking cannot yield us any knowledge of the empirical world; all knowledge of reality starts from experience and ends in it.

A. Einstein, P. Podolsky, N. Rosen

As human beings, we attempt to make sense of all our experiences. Through our mental acts, we strive to impose meaning upon the world. In our awareness and acceptance of this immense capacity, we are led, ineluctably, to an underlying issue which poses perhaps the most basic of all philosophical questions: What is real? At first, the answer to such a question might seem to be absurdly simple to provide, and indicative of the unnecessarily pedantic obscurity of much that passes as philosophical enquiry.

A typical reply to such a question might proceed in the following manner: If I look around my room, I see (among other objects) books, a desk, a chair, a pen. Similarly, I can look out of my window and observe people walking down the street, other houses, flowers, shrubs, trees and so forth. All these things are real to me in that I believe them to be independent of my consciousness. If I were to die suddenly at this moment, I assume that these objects would continue to exist since I view them as having an existence which is separate to my own. Their physical properties and their independent existence lead me to declare them as being real.

This theory of reality, which the vast majority of us in the West take to be so patently obvious that we imagine it to be not theory but fact, has led us to posit the existence of an **objective reality**. The notion of an objective reality adopts the view that there are real objects in the world that exist independent of our conscious knowledge or awareness of them. In addition, it argues that we have direct access to them through our senses. Whether organic or man-made, they exist as separate entities, separate structures. What we perceive as being 'out there' *is* actually there; it is objectively real.

Like much of modern philosophy, the system known as phenome-nology questions this viewpoint in an attempt to clarify it. It asks us first to consider the possible assumptions and biases which have led us to our conclusion so that we may be more certain of its accuracy. As a result of such probing, representatives of scientific fields as diverse as neurophysiology, sociology, theoretical physics and psychology have arrived at an intriguing, not to say disturbing, conclusion.

Stated simply, this conclusion argues that true reality is, and will forever remain, both unknown and unknowable to us. Instead, that which we term reality, that is, that which is experienced by us as being reality, is inextricably linked to our mental processes in general, and, in particular, to our in-built, innate capacity to construct meaning.

This view is the starting point to phenomenological enquiry.

The Origins of Phenomenology

The term 'phenomenology' is partly derived from the Greek word *phainomenon* (plural *phainomena*). *Phainomenon* literally means 'appearance', that is, that which shows itself. Philosophers generally define 'phenomena' to mean 'the appearances of things, as contrasted with the things themselves as they really are'. The world, as we experience it, is a phenomenal world.

Immanuel Kant, the most influential of the post-Classical Western philosophers, took as the cornerstone of his philosophical speculations precisely this contrast and argued from it that our mind cannot ever know the thing itself ('the noumenon', to employ Kant's terminology), but can only know it as it appears to us – the phenomenon. As such, the true nature of reality, for Kant, was not only far from being obvious, it was beyond our ability to understand and to experience directly.

Although the term 'phenomenology' was coined in the mid-eighteenth century, and several noteworthy philosophers (such as Kant, Hegel and Marx) employed it at various times in the course of their writings, the philosophical school known to us as phenomenology only originated in the early years of the twentieth century.

When Edmund Husserl (1859–1938), its founder, adopted the term, he supplied it with new meaning and significance. Husserl wanted nothing less than to develop a science of phenomena that would clarify how it is that objects are experienced and present themselves to our consciousness. Husserl's hope and stated aim was 'to reform philosophy, and ... to establish a rigorously scientific philosophy, which could provide a firm basis for all other sciences' (Misiak and Sexton, 1973: 6).

In an attempt to fulfil this aim, Husserl developed an approach to investigation which is generally known as the **phenomenological method**. Husserl was not its inventor, nor can it be said that he was the first philosopher to employ it, but he refined and specified its conditions and purpose, and raised the method to the status of a fundamental philosophical procedure which would become the cornerstone of his approach.

As we will see in the following chapter, the method focuses on the data (or phenomena) of consciousness in order to clarify their role in the process of meaning-construction, and, as well, to set them aside – or 'bracket' them – in order to arrive at a more adequate (if still necessarily incomplete) knowledge of reality.

Transcendental and Existential Phenomenology

Husserl's attempts form the basis of one strand of phenomenology – **transcendental phenomenology** – of which he remains the most prominent exponent. However, it would be wrong to identify all of phenomenology as being solely, or even principally, Husserlian. Of equal, if not greater, philosophical and psychological significance is the second major branch known as **existential phenomenology** (or, more commonly, **existentialism**), which was principally influenced by the writings of Husserl's university assistant, Martin Heidegger (1889–1976).

As such, it is more helpful and accurate to consider phenomenology not strictly as a school or doctrine possessing a set body of agreed-upon tenets, but, rather, as a general approach which encompasses a variety of doctrines whose common focus is directed toward the investigation of our experience of the world.

I will consider both strands of phenomenology in the course of this text. For the moment, however, let us remain with the Husserlian transcendental strand since, as well as historically preceding existential phenomenology, it supplies us with the central arguments presented by phenomenologists on the issue of reality.

The Phenomenological View of Reality

As I stated at the beginning of this chapter, the objects which we perceive (including, of course, the people we interact with, as well as ourselves) exist, in the way that they exist, through the meaning that each of us gives them.

For example, the book which you are currently reading appears to you to be real, you see it as being separate, inhabiting a different space to that which you inhabit; it is a concrete entity. In your meaning system, it is 'a book'. But what is it *really*? If, for some inexplicable reason, your vocabulary, your meaning system, were suddenly to be deprived of the meaningful term 'book', what would it be that you held in your hands? What is it that you would be perceiving? It would certainly be 'something', but the definition or meaning given to that 'something' would have as much to do with you, and the meaning system that you employ, as it would have with the thing itself.

Phenomenologists argue that this interpretational process must be acknowledged in our statements about reality. Indeed, phenomenologists suggest that, in our everyday experience of reality, this process is to all intents and purposes indivisible from the reality being perceived. Reality, as far as each of us experiences it, *is* this process.

That our interpretations of reality turn out to be seemingly more or less correct is dependent upon any number of factors. For instance, they may be incorrect only insofar as one culture has provided a different meaning system to that imposed by another culture for the object being perceived.

So, for example, were I a representative from a Stone Age society, who is confronted, suddenly, with an object which you, as a representative of your society, have labelled as being 'a book', it would be highly unlikely that I, too, would label it in the same way. I would certainly perceive 'something', but my interpretation might be that the object was some type of weapon, or a rather unusual stone, or perhaps even a previously unseen food product.

Whose interpretation is the correct one? Whose reality is truly real? For each of us, the object would have a reality that was dependent upon our interpretation of it. As such, to argue the case for a 'correct' or 'incorrect' interpretation of reality is highly misleading. Our conclusions are relative – based as they are upon a number of socio-cultural variables. Ours is a phenomenal reality, and, as such, it remains open to a multiplicity of interpretations.

Nevertheless, though phenomenologists avoid terms like 'correct' and 'incorrect' when considering interpretations of reality, they still recognize that, at times, the meanings construed by individuals will be at great variance with those which (to some degree at least) are shared by others – perhaps even the majority of others.

For example, an individual suffering from what could be termed 'paranoid delusions' might imagine, indeed might be convinced, that the nurse who was coming to provide him with medication is actually about to make an attempt upon his life. Not surprisingly, he might take steps to avoid the danger. This interpretation might be judged as being wrong, or even 'crazy', by the nurse, or by most other people. Would not phenomenologists be shown to be unnecessarily pedantic if they were to argue otherwise?

The Problem of 'Correct' Interpretations of Reality

Phenomenologists deny the possibility of 'correct' interpretations since such would presuppose that we had access to, or knowledge of, an ultimate reality in any given situation. But we do not; our interpretations, far from being certain, remain open to alternatives in meaning. What most of us term a 'correct' interpretation is not based upon external, objective laws or 'truths' that have been universally ascertained. Rather, our judgement is influenced, to a great degree, by consensus viewpoints agreed upon by a group of individuals, or by a whole culture.

If we return to my example of the person suffering from paranoid delusions and deliberate upon the issue phenomenologically, we would note that, like that person, we have also carried out an act of interpretation which led to an imposed meaning upon our experience. We are likely to have assumed, for instance, that our experience is in some way normal, that our perceptive faculties are in some way superior, more in touch with what we have labelled 'reality', than those of the person suffering from paranoid delusions. Our studies, our background, our teachings and lessons as clinical psychologists and therapists, have given us the knowledge to interpret behaviour as being normal or abnormal; it is this knowledge that now makes meaningful for us the extraordinary behaviour of this person. Our stance assumes that our conclusions are not based upon interpretations of reality but are accurate reflections of objective reality.

Phenomenologists would argue that such a stance is likely to prevent useful, constructive communication and interaction with our 'paranoid' patient. Indeed, initially at least, our dismissal of his interpretation would almost certainly lead him to be further convinced of the 'correctness' of *his* stance. This is not to say that phenomenologically oriented psychotherapists would not initiate some form of 'intervention'. However, as I will show, any such interventions would not be based upon mistaken assumptions concerning 'correct' interpretations of reality.

The phenomenological view does not deny that, to some degree, many of us do, indeed, partially share similar interpretations of reality. Important research demonstrating just how much we do share in our mental frameworks and models of experience is available in abundance and is not being discounted nor disputed. I will consider its place in phenomenological theory at a later point.

All that is being argued for now is that, regardless of how singular or generally shared our interpretations of the world may seem to be, they remain *interpretations*.

Meaningless Experience

Any behaviour which at first appears to us as being inexplicable, or meaningless, is disturbing to us; it is a basic aversive stimulus. Its meaning *must* be uncovered so that, in our ability to explain, we can relax mentally. So long as the meaning or explanation we provide for our experience is suitable or acceptable to us as an explanation, it will be able to remove or, at least, reduce the disturbance we experience.

Let me provide an example in order to make this point as clear as I can. Imagine that you are looking at a surrealist painting. Let us say it is that famous painting by Magritte, *Time Transfixed*, which, among other things, depicts a train emerging from a fireplace. Looking at it, the first question that springs to mind might be: 'What is this painting about? What does it mean?'

In an attempt to answer this question, you might construct any number of hypotheses and theories which focus on the symbolic significance of the objects in the painting. You might conclude for example, that the train represented Magritte's penis, that the fireplace in some way evoked memories in Magritte of his mother, and of his relationship with her, and that, therefore, the painting was an expression of a universal Oedipal complex.

Alternatively, you might approach the problem from another angle. You might argue that the painting was, in fact, about the role of perspective in Western art, and that this was Magritte's attempt to explain its rules in the most original of ways.

Whatever the explanation would be (and there have been many forthcoming!), in the end, your conclusions as to the meaning of the painting would be dependent on which interpretations were satisfactory enough to reduce the tension you experienced as a result of your confrontation with meaninglessness.

Let me take things a step further. What would happen if you were unable to provide a satisfactory or acceptable meaning to your experience? Imagine now that, instead of looking at a painting by Magritte, you are standing in front of an abstract painting, and that, like many people, you dislike abstract art. When asked why, you explain that it's because you don't understand it, or because you don't know what it's supposed to mean, or because you can't see why abstract painters don't employ figurative elements with which to make their statements. All you see are colours and vague shapes that have no meaning.

Due to the growing anxiety and irritation that this meaningless experience evokes, you might declare that abstract art is, in some way, less acceptable, or less worthy, than figurative art. Indeed, you might go so far as to declare that it might not be 'art' at all and hence that your inability to find its meaning is because there is no meaning to it to begin with. This conclusion would itself be a meaningful explanation – and, if accepted, would remove or reduce the tension being experienced.

Alternatively, you might conclude that there was, indeed, a meaning to the painting but that you were incapable, at this point in time, of discerning it. The assumption of a currently hidden meaning open to future revelation would be enough to reduce tension at least temporarily.

Meaning, then, is implicit in our experience of reality. We cannot tolerate meaninglessness. Through a variety of in-built species invariants and experientially derived mental frameworks, we attempt to stamp our experiences with meaning. Once again, however, it is important to remember that, whatever the meaning arrived at, it cannot be concluded that it is a true or 'correct' reflection of reality.

Subjective versus Objective Reality

At this point, readers might well be concerned that the phenomenological argument is leading to the conclusion that reality is a purely *subjective* process. That is, that nothing other than mental constructs exists. Is this what phenomenologists conclude?

The recurring controversy concerning the separation between external reality and subjective consciousness, and how the two might interact within each of us, has plagued Western philosophy and psychology for centuries. For some, objects exist independent of the mind; for others, nothing exists except the mind. Psychologists and philosophers have tended to side with one viewpoint or the other. To rephrase this issue phenomenologically, we can say that we are concerned with the difference, if any, between the appearance of things and what those things actually are (that is, 'the things themselves').

Initially, it was the stated aim of transcendental phenomenology to examine, expose and separate any such differences. If phenomenologists could find the true things themselves, that is, the ultimate reality that was separate and independent from our mind, then they could tell us what objective reality truly was. The rallying cry of early transcendental phenomenologists was: 'To the things themselves!' By this, they made it absolutely clear (at least to other philosophers) that their aim was to find the ultimate, true nature of reality.

It should come as no surprise that they were unable to fulfil this aim. Modern phenomenology admits that it cannot tell us what the true nature of reality is, nor will it ever be able to do so. Indeed, it argues that no human-created system – be it scientific or philosophical – will ever be able to. Still, though phenomenologists cannot provide us with an answer to this question, their attempts to clarify and examine experienced, or phenomenal, reality provide a resolution to the continuing debate concerning objective and subjective reality which is, I believe, both simple and elegant.

Phenomenology's Resolution of the Problem of Reality

Answer :

As an example of this resolution, let me pose yet another art-related hypothetical situation. Imagine that you are in an art gallery walking past a series of paintings which hang from one of its walls. Imagine that you are attracted to one particular painting and stop in front of it in order to pay it closer attention. Perhaps you focus upon a certain element that intrigues you, or note the title of the painting, the name of its painter, and so on. You might even say something like: 'This is the painting that I've been meaning to see for years, but have seen only in textbooks, and now I can see the real thing.' Eventually, having satisfied yourself, you move away, and walk on to the next painting.

What happens to the painting? Does it continue to exist as it did when you perceived it? Or is that particular perceived painting no longer in existence?

#1 : ps RM

Phenomenologists would begin to answer the question by pointing out that the painting has physical substance. There is clearly some kind of 'raw matter' which acts as stimulus to our sensory-based perceptions of the painting. At a macroscopic level, we could argue that the painting was made up, to some extent, of the wood that forms its frame, of the canvas, of the oils, the pigment and so forth. This is its raw material. Although what that material might actually be in any ultimate atomic, or sub-atomic, sense remains unknown, whatever reality that painting has lies in this raw stimulus matter.

#2

However, phenomenologists would also argue that the painting that you perceived, indeed the painting that anyone perceives and then walks away from, can never be perceived again in exactly the same way as it was initially perceived. Even though the painting in its raw state continues to exist, insofar as the basic materials that make it up continue to exist, the perceived painting exists in the way it does only at that moment of perception.

What phenomenologists propose, then, is that our experience of the world is always made up of an interaction between the raw matter of the world, whatever that may be, and our mental faculties. We never perceive only raw matter; just as, similarly, we never perceive only mental phenomena. We always experience the interaction between the two.

Each of us, as a representative of our species, develops, both through maturational processes and through social experience, increasingly complex mental frameworks (or 'schemata', as some developmental and cognitive psychologists might label them) through which we interpret the raw stimuli which bombard our senses.

Although, as members of the same species, we share the same psycho-biological limitations which give a common underlying structure to the development of our mental frameworks, nevertheless, each of us adds a number of variables derived from our individual life experiences. Through the combination of the two, each of us constructs a unique interpretation of the world.

To return to my example of the painting you perceived in the art gallery, the viewpoint just outlined would argue that your experience of the painting was unique to you since, among the variables giving shape and meaning to your experience, would be those which pertained to your particular life experiences as an individual. Indeed, should you return to it at another point in time, your experience of the painting would not (could not) be the same as it was in the first instance, since in returning to it you would now be adding to your previous 'schema' for that painting and, through this fresh experience, you'd be altering its previous context and relations.

Our interpretations of the world, therefore, are not only unique, they are also unfixed ('plastic') in their meaning.

The 'Raw Matter' of Reality

Our contemporary scientific guesses as to the ultimate make-up, or reality, of the 'raw matter' of the world are entirely dependent upon our current theories of physics. As advanced as they may be, these theories remain incomplete and undergo continual – and major – revision.

Much to their credit, a substantial number of physicists have pointed out that physics, like all other sciences, is subject to the mental faculties of the individuals who have provided its theories. As such, whatever physics has to say today, or will ever state, about the 'raw matter' of the universe cannot be final or categorical since physics is itself 'tainted' with the subjective biases and limitations of all-too-human theoreticians. This conclusion can be seen to be in keeping with the phenomenological view of reality.

There *is* a physical reality which remains separate from our consciousness, and which, in this sense, can be labelled **objective reality**.

Equally, however, we do not have direct access to that reality, nor can we, in any sense, ever know it as it actually is. All we can do is acknowledge its existence and construct theories that might provide approximations of its nature and mechanics. In the end, however, we are forced to concede its mystery.

Edmund Husserl and the Development of Phenomenology

The acknowledged founder of the philosophical school known to us as phenomenology was the German philosopher Edmund Husserl. Husserl was born in 1859, in Moravia (now Czechoslovakia), which was, at the time, an annexed state of the Austro-Hungarian Empire. Husserl's initial academic interests lay in mathematics and the natural sciences, including psychology. Indeed, while a student at Leipzig, he attended a series of lectures given by Wilhelm Wundt, a leading proponent of experimental psychology, but found them to be distinctly unimpressive; if anything, he emerged from them even more convinced that mathematics was far more worthy of his attention and interest. He continued studying mathematics in both Berlin and Vienna where his dissertation on mathematical problems led to his being awarded his PhD in 1883.

Although he returned briefly to Berlin, by 1884 he was back in Vienna where, under the growing influence of the philosopher Franz Brentano, he began to engage in studies which would interest him for the remainder of his life. Brentano's lectures (which, incidentally, were also attended by the young Sigmund Freud and played a role in the eventual development of psychoanalysis (McGrath, 1986)) revolutionized Husserl's thought. Central to Brentano's philosophy was the key notion of **intentionality**. As I will discuss below, a slightly modified version of this term has become a central assumption of phenomenology.

So influential was Brentano's philosophy upon Husserl, that it is generally acknowledged to be the principal forerunner of the phenomenological movement. Indeed, Husserl specifically declared his indebtedness to Brentano by referring to him as his one and only teacher of philosophy (Husserl, 1965). On a more personal level, Husserl's strong missionary zeal in promoting the ideas of phenomenology was a direct outcome of Brentano's influence (possibly because Brentano had initially trained to enter the priesthood). Though they would eventually part company intellectually (Brentano could not accept – or, perhaps, appreciate – a number of Husserl's ideas), the two men remained friends for life.

Husserl was appointed Full Professor of Philosophy at the University of Freiburg in 1916; he would remain there until his retirement in 1929. During these years, and for the remainder of his life, Husserl wrote extensively on phenomenology and gave lectures on it in London, Prague, Vienna and Paris. His principal assistant at Freiburg was Martin Heidegger, who later succeeded him in the post and who would himself provide important contributions to phenomenological theory. Husserl died in Freiburg, in 1938.

Phenomenology's Fundamental Issues

In his attempt to explore and examine how we construct our reality, Husserl focused on two fundamental issues: the notion of **intentionality** as the basis to all mental experience, and the **noematic and noetic foci of intentionality** as 'shapers' of our experience.

Intentionality

For Husserl (Husserl, 1931a; 1931b) the basis to all our meaning-based constructs of the world lay in the fundamental relationship which he labelled 'intentionality'.

The term 'intentionality' is taken from the Latin *intendere*, which translates as 'to stretch forth'. As it is employed by phenomenologists, intentionality is the term used to describe the fundamental action of the mind reaching out to the stimuli which make up the real world in order to translate them into its realm of meaningful experience. In other words, intentionality refers to the first, most basic interpretative mental act – that of 'translating' the unknown raw stimuli of the real world, which our senses have responded to, into an object-based (or 'thing'-based) reality.

Franz Brentano first coined the term 'intentionality' in order to clarify his assertion that a real physical world exists outside our consciousness and that, as such, all consciousness is always directed towards the real world in order to interpret it in a meaningful manner (Brentano, 1973).

Husserl adapted Brentano's idea by arguing that, for human beings, consciousness is always consciousness *of some thing* in that the most basic interpretative act of human consciousness is to experience the world in terms of objects, or things. For instance, if I am conscious that I am worried, then I am worried about some thing; if I am confused, I am confused about some thing; if I react, I react to some thing; and so forth. Even if I did not know what the specific 'thing' was, my attention would focus upon the eventual identification of 'some thing'.

We have no idea whether 'things in themselves' truly exist. All we can say is that, as human beings, we are 'programmed' to interpret an object-based or 'thing-based' world. Whatever sense we make of the world is intentionally derived. Our earliest, most primitive relations and interpretative interactions rely upon the object distinctions we establish and build up over time.

The process of intentionality points out that, as humans, we never have direct access to, or knowledge of, the real world as it is. Since ours is an object world, it can be stated that, even at the most basic level of consciousness, an interpretative act has occurred. Through intentionality, the sensory data at our disposal, which respond to the unknown stimuli emanating from the physical world, undergo a basic, unavoidable 'translation' or interpretation that leads us to respond to the stimuli as if they were objects.

When phenomenologists speak of intentionality as 'the mind stretching forth into the world' and translating its stimuli into phenomenal objects, they are presenting (in spite of the scientific awkwardness of their language) an argument which is both profound and, unfortunately, not always easy to grasp. Perhaps a simple example will clarify their point.

Imagine that you are directing your attention to an object, say, a television set. As we have already seen, the meaning you have given to that object, the functions you ascribe to it and so forth are dependent upon various experiential socio-cultural variables through which you have 'set' your mental framework, or schema, for 'a television set'. As such, your 'knowledge' that what you see before you is 'a television set' is not the straightforward result of your direct access to external reality, but rather has come about through a complex of interpretations linked to your experience of, and dealings with, the world. The object 'a television set' is a phenomenal object.

As such, you might now rightly ask: Well, what is this object (which I have labelled 'a television set') really? If I were capable of setting aside, or bracketing, all the additional meanings and functions that I've invested upon it, what would be left? Unfortunately, your question cannot be answered in any complete or final sense. Phenomenologists argue that it will never be possible for us to know the 'ultimate reality' of any object, be it 'a television set' or whatever else, precisely because we are limited by the intentional relationship through which we experience an object world. The very question '*What* would be left?', in its reference to 'some thing', makes clear the intentional boundaries in our experience.

Through the term 'intentionality', then, phenomenologists point out a basic *invariant* relationship that exists between the real world and our conscious experience of it. Unable to bracket this relationship, we are forced to acknowledge, through it, the undeniable role of interpretation which lies at the heart of all our mental experience.

Noema and Noesis

The phenomenological notion of intentionality points out that we carry out a basic (and invariant) interpretational step of translating the unknown stimuli of the world into things, or objects. Intentionality, then, can be seen to focus consciousness initially on some *thing* in the world (regardless of what that 'thing' may actually be in its real state).

Husserl suggested that every act of intentionality was made up of two experiential foci, or 'correlational poles' (Ihde, 1977: 43), which he labelled **noema** and **noesis** (Husserl, 1929, 1931a, 1931b, 1948). 'For what is experienced, as experienced, he used the term *noema* or noematic correlate, and for the mode of experiencing . . . he used the term *noesis* or noetic correlate' (Ihde, 1977: 43). Noema, then, refers to the *directional* element of experience; it is the object (the *what*) that we direct our attention towards and focus upon. Noesis, on the other hand, is the *referential* element of experience; it is the mode (the *how*) through which we define an object. As Ihde points out: 'This internal correlation within experience may seem trivial and obvious – if I experience at all, I experience something and in some way' (Ihde, 1977: 43).

As a simple example of the different emphases given by the noematic and noetic constituents, consider the following situation. Two individuals are attending a political rally. They both hear a speaker presenting a speech dealing with nuclear disarmament and taking the stance that unilateral disarmament would be a serious and dangerous error. The first individual agrees with the speaker's sentiments and claps loudly and enthusiastically at the conclusion of the talk. The second individual, sympathetic to unilateral disarmament, becomes increasingly irritated by the arguments being presented and boos the speaker at the end of the speech.

The **noematic focus**, that is, the what of the experience, is made up from the content, or argument, of the speech heard by each individual. The **noetic focus**, on the other hand, contains those referential elements dealing with how each individual's various cognitive and affective biases add further elements of meaning to the experience. Together, the noematic and noetic foci lead each individual to interpret the experience of the political rally in a different and unique manner, and, as a consequence, to respond to it in their disparate ways.

There is a tendency within psychology to obscure or minimize the significance of this correlation either by focusing exclusively upon the noematic focus or by minimizing the unique experiential variables which add to any individual's noetic focus. This may be due to the fact that although we can, in theory, distinguish between the noetic and noematic foci, in practice the two are not fully distinct from one another. None of us can approach any experience in our life, past or present, without instantaneously evoking both foci. For instance, were I to ask you to remember any experience from your past, whatever it was that you remembered would not be merely the events contained in that experience, that is, its items (the noema), but, in addition, the way you experienced them (the noesis).

Conc. # 1

As a result of clarifying the noematic and noetic foci in all intentional acts, the phenomenological assertion that all experiences are, at best, only partially sharable should become clearer. Shared biological and socio-cultural variables may well provide a partial similarity in separate individuals' experiences. Nevertheless, the foci (particularly the noetic focus) retain individually determined variables which limit the extent to which any experience can be said to be shared between individuals.

#2

Although phenomenologists stress the unique and unsharable differences in each individual's experience of the world, this stance should not be seen to be either explicitly or implicitly minimizing or invalidating the great number of important studies dealing with the shared features of human experience. Such studies clarify the innately determined species frameworks which 'set' the structure of our experience and demonstrate the power of socio-cultural factors in influencing the development of mental frameworks, or schemata, which come very near to incorporating socially shared attitudinal variables to our experience.

#3

Nevertheless, phenomenologists are at pains to point out that although there may well be a substantial degree of 'sharability' in our experiences, there remain a variety of factors which, ultimately, point to the uniqueness in each individual's experience. To employ an analogy from nature, although the structure of all snowflakes is determined by the same six rules, each emergent snowflake retains a unique design. It is simply because experimental research in science (and in psychology in particular) has tended to focus upon the study of shared features and has either dismissed or diminished the importance of the unshared variables in experience that phenomenologists emphasize the latter in their studies. It is not because unique factors in themselves hold greater significance; phenomenologists are simply redressing the balance, and, in so doing, are increasing the adequacy of our theories.

All mental acts, then, can be seen to be intentional. Our consciousness is always object-directed or of 'some thing'. This most basic of interpretative acts always contains two foci – the noematic focus which directs our experience towards 'some thing', and the referential, or noetic, focus which provides the mode through which we experience 'some thing'.

Consider, as an example, this very book which you are currently reading. Through intentionality, the (primarily) visual and tactile sensory responses to the unknown 'raw matter' are experienced in terms of 'some thing' or object. Through the noematic and noetic foci, that object is not only further interpreted as 'a book', but is also referentially defined in any number of ways (for example, the book is easy/difficult, interesting/boring, important/insignificant, and so on). As a phenomenal object, the book each of us experiences is a product of both shared and unshared variables; each of us experiences a unique approximation of what it really is.

The concept of intentionality, and its noematic and noetic foci, led Husserl to the development of a specific approach designed to clarify the interpretational factors contained within every experience. This approach has since become known as the phenomenological method. Just what the phenomenological method consists of and what its implications may be for psychologically related issues is the principal concern of the following chapter.

2

The Phenomenological Method

*The idea had occurred to me that maybe what we see is not real.
That it is somehow – I don't know what the alternative to 'real'
is. . . . There's a state of things being semi-real.*

Philip K. Dick

Husserl's analyses led him to conclude that our experience of the
world is a unique intentional construct containing both directional
(noematic) and referential (noetic) foci. On this basis, he argued, it
was to be the principal task of phenomenology to find the means to
strip away, as far as possible, the plethora of interpretational layers
added to the unknown stimuli to our experience in order to arrive at a
more adequate, if still approximate and incomplete, knowledge of
'the things themselves'. In order to achieve this aim, Husserl proposed a **phenomenological method** of investigation which could be
applied to all analyses of experience. This method became the primary basis for all conclusions arrived at by transcendental
phenomenologists.

Though clearly of central importance to phenomenology in
general, its primary value to phenomenological psychology differs
slightly from the original function ascribed to it by Husserl. Husserl
sought to employ the method in order to strip away the variants of
experience and so to arrive at a clearer understanding of its invariants. Phenomenologically oriented psychologists (among others
who seek to apply a phenomenological orientation to their respective
fields), on the other hand, apply the phenomenological method for
the principal purpose of identifying and clarifying the variables, or
variants, of experience so that they may be more adequately
controlled in the variety of studies undertaken by the different
systems in psychology, and, also, so that their role in influencing (and
limiting) the interpretations and conclusions arrived at by psychologists may be made more explicit.

Because this text deals with the phenomenological orientation
within psychology, my account of the phenomenological method
focuses on this latter concern. Whatever its primary goal, however,
the phenomenological method is carried out in much the same way. It

is composed of three distinguishable, though interrelated, steps (Ihde, 1977; Grossmann, 1984).

Step A: The Rule of Epoché

The first step has become known as the rule of epoché. This rule urges us to set aside our initial biases and prejudices of things, to suspend our expectations and assumptions, in short, *to bracket* all such temporarily and as far as is possible so that we can focus on the primary data of our experience. In other words, the rule of epoché urges us to impose an 'openness' on our immediate experience so that our subsequent interpretations of it may prove to be more adequate.

For example, imagine that you are about to meet someone for the first time and that you have been told certain things about this person by others so that, even before your meeting, you have built up a number of expectations and reservations about the person. Chances are that your eventual initial experience of that person will have been already 'set' and constrained by these biases. And, as is often the case under these circumstances, your judgements and conclusions about the person may well turn out to be both inadequate and imbalanced.

On the other hand, were you to follow the first step of the phenomenological method, you would attempt to bracket these biases as far as was possible for you so that you had more of an open mind about the person and so that your subsequent conclusions would be based more upon your immediate experience of the person rather than upon prior assumptions and expectations.

Although it may well be impossible for us to bracket all biases and assumptions, we are certainly capable of bracketing a substantial number of them. In addition, even when bracketing is not likely or feasible, the very recognition of bias lessens its impact upon our immediate experience.

Step B: The Rule of Description

The second step in the phenomenological method is known as the rule of description. The essence of this rule is: 'Describe, don't explain'.

Having 'opened up to the possibilities' contained in our immediate experience as far as is possible through the rule of epoché, we are now urged not to place another type of limitation upon our experience by immediately trying to explain or make sense of it in terms of whatever theories or hypotheses we may tend towards.

Instead, the rule of description urges us to remain initially focused on our immediate and concrete impressions and to maintain a level of analysis with regard to these experiences which takes description rather than theoretical explanation or speculation as its point of focus. Rather than step back from our immediate experience so that we may instantly 'explain it', question it or deny it on the basis of preconceived theories or hypotheses which stand separate from our experience, the following of the rule of description allows us to carry out a concretely based descriptive examination of the subjective variables which make up our experience.

What value might there be in adopting this step? As an example, consider the hypochondriac who, worried over his health, immediately responds to any variety of somatic experiences by imposing (often incapacitatory) misinterpretations which are dependent upon the medical hypotheses at his disposal. From a phenomenological perspective, a hypochondriac is an individual who has failed to apply the rule of description because, rather than seek to describe his somatic experience in concrete terms, he jumps to abstract, disease-model explanations and theories which provoke levels of anxiety which may well be as debilitating as his hypothetical illness.

While it can be argued that no description is altogether free of explanatory components and hence that the rule of description aspires to an ideal which cannot be achieved, nevertheless it seems reasonable to me to argue that explanations may be seen to run along a continuum ranging from 'concrete descriptive' to 'abstract theoretical'. The former are derived from and specific to any immediate sensory-based experience; the latter are conceptual generalizations which seek to explain or make an experience meaningful within the boundaries of a set theory or hypothesis.

Step C: The Rule of Horizontalization (the Equalization Rule)

The third step in the phenomenological method is known either as the rule of horizontalization or, alternatively, as the equalization rule. Having stuck to an immediate experience which we seek to describe, this rule further urges us to avoid placing any initial hierarchies of significance or importance upon the items of our descriptions, and instead to treat each initially as having equal value or significance.

In the act of simply reporting in a descriptive manner what is consciously being experienced while avoiding any hierarchical assumptions with regard to the items of description, we are better able to examine an experience with far less prejudice and with a much greater degree of adequacy.

In a sense, phenomenologists urge us to treat each bit of initial experience as if we have been given the task of piecing together some gigantic jigsaw puzzle without the prior knowledge of what image the completed puzzle depicts. In such a situation, it is clear that we cannot say from the outset that any one piece of the jigsaw is any more important or valid than any other, and so, initially at least, if we are to succeed in our task, we must treat each piece as having equal significance. In the same way, phenomenologists argue that if we are to embark on any worthwhile attempt to make sense of the gigantic jigsaw puzzle that is our mental experience of the world, we must avoid making immediate misleading hierarchically based judgements.

The Practice of the Phenomenological Method

Taken together, the three steps outlined above make up the phenomenological method. As I will argue in subsequent chapters of this text, when applied to psychological concerns the method provides significant contributions and important clarificatory insights. For the moment, however, to ensure that the reader has understood the phenomenological method, I want to provide two straightforward examples in order to demonstrate how it might be applied in any experience.

As my first example, I will outline a personal experience from my pre-phenomenological past which demonstrates the problems that might be encountered when not applying the phenomenological method.

A number of years ago, a friend phoned me up in a state of deep distress. She explained that she'd just broken up with a long-standing boyfriend, was feeling miserable and wanted a shoulder to cry on. I, dutifully, obliged. Towards the end of our conversation, I happened to remind her that we'd both been invited to a mutual friend's party that night and that going to it might be the best thing for her. She said she'd think it over, thanked me and hung up.

I thought no more about her until that night when, upon entering the apartment where the party was being held, I saw her sitting in the middle of a small group of close friends. I couldn't hear what she was saying, but her facial expression and her body movements suggested to me that she was in a highly agitated state. Certainly, everyone around her seemed to be closely monitoring her every word and action. Suddenly, the girl erupted into a series of excited, spastic movements, grimaced and let out a loud wail. As I moved closer to her, I noticed that she'd begun to shed tears. Now thoroughly convinced that she was, once more, deeply upset, I rushed to her side, hugged her close to me, and offered words of condolence and endearment which I hoped would allow her to regain control of herself. Imagine my shock when, in response, the girl looked up at me with some surprise and indignation and asked whatever was the matter with me and just what was I going on about. Looking round at the others in the circle, I noticed for the first time that most of them also had tears streaming down their faces and that, more importantly, they too were looking at me as if they couldn't make sense of my behaviour.

Eventually, the situation was straightened out. I discovered that, contrary to my initial assumption, the girl had not become emotionally upset once more, but, rather, had just finished telling the group a particularly funny joke which had sent her, and most members of the circle, into paroxysms of unrestrained laughter which, not unexpectedly, had provoked tears.

What had I done to misinterpret events to such an extent? First, I had 'biased' my initial sighting of the girl with my preconceptions and hypotheses as to how she must be feeling under the circumstances – in other words, I'd failed to bracket my beliefs and assumptions. Secondly, I'd sought out an immediate explanation for the general behaviour I observed her enacting. Rather than pay closer attention to what she was actually doing, I'd formulated a theory – based on my assumptions – that made sense of her behaviour. Thirdly, I'd singled out certain variables – those which fitted my theory – and bestowed on them significance and importance, while, at the same time, I'd neglected to consider or had minimized other variables, such as the fact that other members of the group had responded to the joke's denouement in ways highly similar to the girl's, because these did not fit my interpretation of events.

Had I, instead, followed the steps of the phenomenological method and bracketed my beliefs and assumptions, restrained myself from applying impulsive explanations and, instead, concentrated on the immediate data of experience, and treated each, initially, as having equal value or significance, I might well have arrived at a different conclusion – and prevented myself from suffering unnecessary embarrassment.

As a second example, I want to focus on how the phenomenological method can influence interpretations of inner experiences. Consider the following situation. You are on holiday in the country. After a very pleasant evening meal at a local restaurant, you start to make your way home. Walking down the deserted country lane, you come to a stretch of road with overhanging branches; because of the abundance of vegetation on either side of the path, it is particularly dark. Half-wishing you weren't alone, you quicken your steps. Suddenly, you hear a noise. Is it the sound of footsteps following you? Could it be some wild animal? Have you really stopped believing in ghosts and ghouls? Or is the noise simply the sound of twigs and leaves being displaced either by the wind or by your own footsteps?

What would you do were you to follow the phenomenological method in order to make sense of your experience?

First, you would attempt to set aside any immediate biases or beliefs which might predispose you towards any one particular meaning or explanation of the event. Instead, you would, for the time being, remain open to any number of alternatives, neither rejecting any one as being out of hand, nor placing a greater or lesser degree of likelihood on the options available. Initially, you'd be open to all possibilities.

Secondly, in having opened yourself to all possibilities, your focus of attention is forced to shift away from theoretical explanations (since, for the moment, no one explanation is more adequate than any other), and, instead, must attend to the items of your immediate experience so that, through them, you might eventually have the possibility of putting your options to the test. As such, your task becomes one of describing the events of your experience as concretely as possible. For example, you might note that there is a wind tonight and that it is strong enough to be felt passing through your hair; you might also note that there are plenty of dry, fallen leaves upon the path and that the sound they make when being stepped on is reminiscent of the sound that initially startled you; equally, you might note that the stillness of the night allows you to make out the laughter and even some of the words of people who are still in the restaurant. Item by item, then, you build up a store of concrete information based upon your immediate experience.

Thirdly, having collected together a sufficient variety of items, it remains necessary for you to avoid placing any greater or lesser significance or value on each of them and, instead, to treat each, initially, as having equal importance. If you did not do so, you might 'skew' your eventual conclusion so that it proved to be far less adequate than it might have been. In other words, the sound of distant voices, for instance, is initially no more significant a clue than is the crackling sound of dry leaves.

Once you have followed the three steps, you are able to arrive at an explanation of your experience whose adequacy (or 'correctness') rests upon data closely derived from your immediate experience and not upon abstract, biased speculation. Your explanatory conclusion may emerge all at once, as in insight learning, or, alternatively, may come about slowly through the process of elimination of one possible explanation after another on the basis of its ability to make sense of each accumulated item of experience. Whatever the case, in the following of the phenomenological method, the eventual explanations or conclusions we arrive at, as well as any subsequent action we might initiate, can be seen to be more adequate (or, loosely speaking, veering towards correctness) in that they are primarily based upon data derived as closely as possible from direct experience.

The phenomenological method seeks to avoid the imposing of set beliefs, biases, explanatory theories and hypotheses upon our experience either at the very start of any examination or before it becomes useful to do so. Clearly, there can be no fixed point at which we can say that enough data have been accumulated and theories can now be initiated. Indeed, it is likely that some degree of theoretical speculation exists in even the most 'descriptive' accounts of experience. Nevertheless, this limitation does not diminish the power of the phenomenological method. For the concern is not so much that we theorize, but that we typically fix upon *a* theory and derive our explanations and subsequent actions from its (often inadequate) conclusions.

In general, the application of the phenomenological method allows all experiences to be considered as initially valid. Phenomenologists have labelled this consequence the **inclusionary/exclusionary rule** (Ihde, 1977: 36–7). This rule states that in our exclusion of any initial judgements and biases, we are including an openness, or receptivity, in all our experiences.

Similarly, the following of the phenomenological method forces us, in the initial stages of investigation, to treat all experiences as being equally real or valid, so that they may be exposed to examination. This **equal reality rule** (Ihde, 1977: 37) can only be applied temporarily since it has no fixed end-point and, as such, all investigations must, at some point or other, set a pragmatic limit to its application. Nevertheless, in being willing to follow this rule to some extent, investigators reduce the likelihood of imposing unnecessary judgements or biases on their initial observations. In doing so, they increase the adequacy of their conclusions.

The practice of the phenomenological method, at the very least, minimizes our tendency to rely exclusively upon any one theory throughout the whole of our investigation. Equally, in its claim to lead us not to correct or final conclusions, but, rather, towards increasingly adequate approximations or probabilities, it allows for a theoretical flexibility and 'open-mindedness' which is in keeping with the ideology – if not the practice – of science.

Upon consideration, it should become evident that the phenomenological method reveals important weaknesses in the various systems of contemporary psychology. Since each system is committed initially and primarily to a specific theory and/or methodology, its tendency is to fix upon those variables which it deems to possess significance *because* they validate its theory and/or methodology and to minimize the significance of those variables which suggest inadequacies and limitations in the theory and/or methodology. I will discuss this point at greater length in later chapters.

Consequences of the Phenomenological Method

Husserl initially developed the phenomenological method in order that it might be applied as a means of resolving a number of fundamental philosophical issues. A discussion of many of these lies outside the scope of this text. Nevertheless, the use of the method led to several consequences which have direct relevance for a variety of psychological concerns. It is to these that we must now turn our attention.

Straightforward versus Reflective Experience

If we analyse the manner in which we experience any event from a phenomenological standpoint, we discover that, typically, each of us first experiences the event and then follows the experience with an attempted explanation or description of it. The differences between the two experiences are so rarely considered that we commonly assume them to be part and parcel of a unitary experience.

However, through the process of 'bracketing' experience in order to carry out the phenomenological method, we are led to a singular and inescapable discovery: in the process of any experience taking place, no explanation or description can be given; it is only *once the experience has occurred* that we may both describe and explain it to some degree of adequacy. Nevertheless, the experience itself, as it takes place, stands outside the realm of description or explanation. We cannot describe any experience as it occurs, but only after it has occurred.

For example, were I to state: 'Tell me what is happening to you right now,' you would note several important invariants in your attempted response to my question. First, whatever your response, the event it alluded to would have already occurred. The 'now' experience you report is already a past event. No matter how much you tried, you could not experience an event and describe your experience of it simultaneously.

Further, whatever your response, it would be both partial and incomplete. You could not ever tell me *everything* that you had experienced in that 'now' moment for several reasons. First, at any point in time, your senses are being bombarded by so many different stimuli that the vast majority would remain below your threshold of awareness. Secondly, even if it were possible for you eventually to become aware of each of these stimuli, it would probably take you the rest of your life to report them – and, even then, your report would almost certainly remain incomplete. Thirdly, you might not have the knowledge or vocabulary to describe all of your experiences. As such, whatever description you gave as your answer would never be as complete as the experience itself.

Phenomenological enquiry makes a clear distinction between the experience as it occurs and our interpretations of that experience. The former is commonly labelled **straightforward experience**, while the latter is usually referred to as **reflective experience**.

Straightforward experience is action-based; it is the activity of experience itself *as it occurs*. As such, straightforward experience is both timeless and ineffable. It is timeless because it always functions in the 'now' of any event. Time only enters when we attempt to describe or explain the experience. Equally, straightforward experience is ineffable since it cannot be talked about directly; any statement of description or explanation occurs subsequent to the experience and is limited by the amount of explanation/description that is practically possible.

On the other hand, when we make various attempts to describe or explain what has been experienced, we enter the realm of reflective experience. Reflective experience requires some kind of system of communication, relies upon notions of time, and is therefore open to measurement. It is through reflective experience that we formulate meaning and construct the various hierarchies of significances contained within those meanings. In doing so, we eliminate from our interpretations of experience any number of variables that form our straightforward experience on the grounds that they are unimportant or unnecessary to communicate or are incommunicable simply because we are unaware of their existence or do not possess the language to describe them. Reflective experience allows us to communicate only a minute part of the sum total of any experience.

The more commonly employed psychological term 'attention' might help the reader to grasp the idea being presented. When we attend to an event, we are carrying out a hierarchy of significance through which we decide, on any number of grounds, just what is and is not of significance in our experience. We focus on certain items of experience and exclude others from our focus of attention.

Any theory that we care to formulate (including, of course, phenomenological theory) is the result of reflective experience since it is an attempt to provide some hierarchy of significance to any straightforward experience.

The Phenomenological 'I'

In distinguishing between straightforward and reflective experience, we are led to yet another intriguing implication derived from the phenomenological method. This is concerned with our notion of 'I' – our experience of self.

Typically when we think about the 'I' in experience, we often start from the assumption that the 'I' is the primary means to an experience, that the 'I' must be present in order for us to experience anything. Our very language is infused with such assumptions. We say, for instance, that 'I had this experience', or that 'I am now experiencing this', and so forth.

Although it is typical for us to assume that the 'I' must exist so that any experience can occur, phenomenologists question this assumption. They point out, for example, that one can note that in a great many experiences the 'I' becomes a conscious presence only once the experience has been completed. This is particularly apparent when we are involved in intense and/or repetitive behaviour. In activities such as jogging, gardening, carpentry, typing and so on which require repetitious physical movements and an increasing focus on the actions themselves, the subjective experience of 'I' diminishes to the point where there seems to be no 'I' there at all. Indeed, all that there seems to be is the activity itself, just 'the process of doing' wherein any sense of 'I' is temporarily lost.

If we consider sexual intercourse, which is both an intense and largely repetitive activity, there is, once again, the commonly reported experience of a temporary loss of any ordinary sense of 'I'. For a period of timeless time, at the very height of intensity during the act, all 'everyday I'-related (that is, self-conscious) experience seems to disappear. For some, there is the experience of a total loss of self as a result of an experienced 'merging' of the lovers' selves so that there is simply the action taking place. For others, the 'I' seems to become all-encompassing such that the distinction between 'I' and 'not I' (self and others) loses all meaning. In this case, the 'I' seems to become everything, unlimited – and, hence, undefinable.

It is only once the action has been completed that the 'I' comes once more into focus and begins its assessment of what has just occurred.

Husserl noted how minimal self-consciousness is during such experiences (Ihde, 1977: 44–52). On further reflection, he realized an odd paradox: when we consider the most astounding, the most vital, the most involving experiences in our lives, those times when we felt the most 'alive', we find that here, too, the 'I' is minimally self-conscious; indeed, during such times there seems to be little, if any,

'I'-related experience. It is only once the experience has ended, when we return to it in order to give it qualitative and descriptive meaning, that the 'I' takes centre-stage. Prior to this, however, it is difficult to state with any certainty that any subjective experience or awareness of 'I' exists.

As a result of the phenomenological method, we are led to an inversion of the typical view we take concerning the role of 'I' in any experience. Whereas we tend to assume, in a common-sensical manner, that the 'I' initiates our experience of things, transcendental phenomenologists posit that in the realm of straightforward experience there is no obvious 'I', certainly not at a conscious level. It is only when we reflect upon our experience, when we begin to analyse and attempt to make sense of it, that the 'I' appears and takes its central place as the (seeming) originator of experience.

This major reanalysis of the role of 'I' in our experience will be explored further in Chapter 5.

'I' and 'not I': The Relationship between Self and Others

The analysis of the phenomenological 'I' has an immediate implication for the relationship between self and others, since it would seem that the phenomenological argument leads us to question whether any intentionally constructed object (including, of course, self and others) truly exists *as a separate and distinguishable entity* which is independent of one's conscious experience of it. That is to say, if our notions of self and others are intentional constructs, it would seem that they, too, cannot be viewed as being experientially independent of one another. Just as the 'I' is a product of reflective experience, so, too, must be 'others' (or, as phenomenologists prefer, 'not I'). Such a conclusion, of course, once again runs counter to our everyday assumptions.

Phenomenological theory argues that each of us can be described as a **being-in-the-world**. We are all beings-in-the-world in the sense that we all share an intentionally derived conscious experience of the world and ourselves, through which we make various distinctions such as those relating to notions of 'I' and 'not I'. Although we are all similar in the sense that we are all beings-in-the-world, each of us *experiences* being-in-the-world in a unique and unsharable way.

Since 'I' and 'not I' are intentional constructs, we cannot say what 'I' and 'not I' actually are in themselves. Each has a basis in material reality, but our experience of 'I' and 'not I' is not a direct experience of 'the things themselves', but of 'things as they appear to us' – we experience *phenomenal* versions of 'I' and 'not I'.

I will attempt to clarify this issue further in Chapters 4 and 5, where I will consider phenomenology's stance on the perception of others and the perception of self in greater detail. For now, what can be stated is that each of us, through intentionality, certainly 'constructs' others – in the sense that we each experience others from a unique and ultimately unsharable viewpoint.

If, for example, I experience you as being intelligent or unintelligent, as female or male, as black or white, or as whatever other defining characteristics I might wish to apply, all such characteristics can be seen to be products of *my* intentional interpretation of you – and *not* of objective 'factual' statements relating to aspects of your being.

The example of interpersonal attraction should make this argument obvious. What makes someone attractive to someone else is the result of a unique set of intentionally derived conclusions. The physical features and characteristics that one person focuses upon as being significant determinants of someone else's attractiveness are (thankfully!) open to a great deal of individual variation within which any one conclusion cannot be said to be 'more correct' than the other.

However, the phenomenological argument does not end here; there is another implicit, and perhaps far more significant, issue concerning the status of others.

Upon consideration, it becomes evident that each of us requires the existence of others in order that we may be able to define ourselves. Restated phenomenologically, we would say that the 'I' requires the existence of the 'not I' in order for it (the 'I') to have any meaningful phenomenal reality. In other words, I can only know who I am by comparing some assumed aspect of myself to that which I have interpreted as existing in others. I cannot, for instance, state whether I am male or female, short or tall, intelligent or unintelligent, overweight or underweight, attractive or unattractive, without undertaking some kind of explicit or implicit comparison between those aspects as perceived in myself and in others.

Phenomenologists argue that the variables 'I' and 'not I' are inseparable in that each is equally necessary for the definition of the other. A world in which no separation between 'I' and 'not I' existed would be a unified, identityless world. Several theoreticians (primarily oriented within the psychoanalytic school (Greenberg and Mitchell, 1983)) have argued that, at some point in our early development as human beings, some such 'split' in this unified pre-self-conscious world occurs and leads us to the development of an identity (an 'I') through the (defensive) comparisons we make with the newly constructed others (the 'not I's') in our world. This argument, compelling as it is, nevertheless remains open to debate and is difficult to substantiate in any empirical manner. Whether it is ever likely to be 'proven' or 'disproven' is doubtful.

Nevertheless, the phenomenological contention that at *some* point in time (be it anywhere between the moment of fertilization and some time during our infancy) each of us develops notions relating to our concept of 'I' as a result of our interactions with items of our experience which we have categorized as being examples of 'not I', remains unchallenged.

Phenomenological Invariants

The mutual definitional dependency between 'I' and 'not I' is a specific example of a more general phenomenologically derived fixed and unchanging rule, or invariant, of experience known as the **figure/ ground invariant** (Ihde, 1977, 1986; Grossman, 1984). I will have much more to say about this invariant in the following chapter, which deals with the perception of objects in more detail. For now, I merely wish to bring the notion of invariants to the reader's attention.

Many of the insights and conclusions arrived at by phenomenologists that I've outlined in this chapter reveal a number of basic invariants to our experience of the world. Intentionality and its noematic and noetic constituents are examples of experiential invariants.

Of the two main branches of phenomenology, it is transcendental phenomenology which places particular emphasis upon the examination and analysis of that which remains once the various biases of reflective experience have been 'transcended', or bracketed, as far as is possible. It employs the phenomenological method in order to arrive at those invariants of experience which (in much the same way as do proven mathematical equations) provide the fixed-rule boundaries which govern all investigations concerned with human experience. Since experiential invariants cannot be removed or bracketed, it is through their discovery that we become aware of the ultimate limitations to our ability to experience 'things in themselves'.

Phenomenological Investigation: a Summary

Phenomenology, like all Western philosophical systems, is concerned with the relationship between the reality which exists outside our minds (objective reality) and the variety of thoughts and ideas each of us may have about reality (subjectivity). How these two variables interact with each other is both the most fundamental and the oldest of philosophical issues.

Phenomenology presents a unique perspective on this problem; it argues that we experience the phenomena of the world, rather than its reality. All phenomena experienced by human beings are constructs, formed as a result of the invariant process known as intentionality. Through the inseparable correlational foci of intentionality – noema and noesis – we interpret the make-up of our phenomenal world and imbue it with unique, constantly altering (or plastic) significance and meaning. Even the being whom we think we are, the 'I', undergoes this continual revolution.

Each person's experience of the world undoubtedly contains commonly shared variables. As members of the same species, we have the same innately determined biological mechanisms designed to allow specific interactions with the world. One basic shared – or invariant – mechanism is that we interpret the unknown material stimuli of the world as 'things' or objects. Similarly, various socio-cultural influences tend to 'set' us into mental frameworks, or schemata, which limit the parameters of our experience. Nevertheless, as a result of the unique experiential variables in each of our lives, no individual experience can be fully shared by any two people. In this sense, each of us experiences a unique and solitary phenomenal reality.

At its most basic level, phenomenology presents itself as a science of experience. Experience, from a phenomenological perspective, includes within it all mental phenomena, such as wishes, memories, percepts, hypotheses, theories, etc. By employing a specific approach – the phenomenological method – phenomenologists attempt to arrive at increasingly adequate (though never complete or final) conclusions concerning our experience of the world. Similarly, through this approach, phenomenologists are able to describe and clarify the invariant structures and limitations that are imposed upon our experiences.

Such interests, of course, impinge upon psychological territory. What place is there for a phenomenologically derived approach to psychology? What would be its primary concerns and identifying characteristics?

Phenomenological Psychology

The place to be assigned to psychology in the phenomenological system was a problem that deeply concerned Husserl (Husserl, 1948). However, as much as he was convinced that psychology and phenomenology had a great deal to contribute to each other, Husserl remained a severe critic of contemporary schools of psychology, admitting an inability to follow their literature and revealing a lack of familiarity with the experimental approaches to psychology being initiated in North America and Great Britain.

This conflict led Husserl to revise his views on the contributions and relationships between psychology and phenomenology several times and revealed his uncertainty as to the place of either approach with regard to the other (Misiak and Sexton, 1973: 12–5). Eventually, it became obvious that the only resolution to this problem was for him to develop an alternative, radical psychology. Husserl's lecture notes dating from the years 1925 to 1928 reveal the growing emphasis he placed on this problem. Calling his new system at first 'rational psychology' or 'eidetic psychology', Husserl eventually settled on the term 'phenomenological psychology'.

Husserl argued that the goal of phenomenological psychology was the application of the phenomenological method to psychological enquiry. As such, he theorized that any experimental studies from other psychological approaches could be accommodated to his developing theory. In translating phenomenological philosophy into a psychological system, Husserl 'loosened' some of the aims and strictures which formed the central emphases of his 'transcendental' system.

As is now generally agreed (Giorgi, 1970; Misiak and Sexton, 1973; Shaffer, 1978), phenomenological psychology is principally concerned with the application of the phenomenological method to issues and problems in psychology so that an individual's conscious experience of the world can be more systematically observed and described. Any conscious act – such as perception, imagery, memory, emotion and so on – falls under the scrutiny of phenomenological investigation. In keeping with the rules of the phenomenological method, the focus of such a psychology is placed on the description (and acceptance) of current experience as a result of 'bracketing' as many assumptions, suppositions, theoretical explanations and habitual psychological biases as possible.

In its broadest sense, phenomenological psychology is distinguished by its central concern with the issue of personal, subjective experience. It can be contrasted with those psychologies which admit only the study of objectively observed behaviour or which place their focus of interest on theoretical unconscious mechanisms.

Unlike other approaches, phenomenological psychology does not seek to invalidate the findings of other schools of thought; indeed, many phenomenologically oriented psychologists avoid formally defining it as a 'school' of psychology in the strict sense of possessing separate canons, hypotheses and interests to the other psychological schools. Most commonly, phenomenological psychology is presented as an *orientation* taken towards the examination of central psychological issues via the use of a specific methodology known as the phenomenological method.

Defining Characteristics !

In keeping with the general conclusions arrived at by previous authors (see, for instance, Misiak and Sexton, 1973; and Shaffer, 1978), I would propose that phenomenological psychology contains a number of specific defining characteristics.

→ Phenomenological psychology places the analysis of our conscious experience of the world as its primary goal. Further, its focus of interest lies in the exploration of all human experience (from its subjective origins to its behavioural manifestations) without recourse to implicit or explicit reductionist or associationistic assumptions, nor by 'the exclusive restriction of the subject matter of psychology to behavior and its control' (Misiak and Sexton, 1973: 41).

→ Instead, broadly derived from phenomenological philosophy, phenomenological psychology attempts an unbiased examination of conscious experience, via the application of the phenomenological method, in order to present a description of phenomena which is as free from experientially based, variational biases as is possible. Rather than seek to stand beside, or replace, existing systems in psychology, phenomenological psychology attempts (where possible) to complement them, and, in its application, to clarify or remove such systems' unnecessary and/or divisive biases and assumptions.

→ Though not strictly 'experimental' in its emphases, phenomenological psychology derives much of the data for its conclusions from controlled studies carried out by researchers allied to the more empirically oriented approaches. Nevertheless, as we will see, as it is not uncommon to find many inconsistencies in both the data and conclusions arrived at through experimental research in psychology, phenomenological psychology often reinterprets such findings in order that it may both clarify the sources of such inconsistencies and provide a more 'bias-free' set of hypotheses and predictions. In doing so, it presents unique perspectives on the standard concerns of psychology and paves the way for more adequate, and unified, models of human beings.

Having laid this basic framework, I can now turn the remainder of this text over to specifically psychological issues. As my first area of investigation, I want to consider the perception of objects.

3
The Perception of Objects

If the doors of perception were cleansed, everything would appear to man as it is, infinite. For man has closed himself up, till he sees all things through narrow chinks of his cavern.

William Blake

Although the study of perception was once considered to be an area of investigation which could rely almost exclusively on neuro-biological data in order to advance and extend its theories, it has now become evident that such a view is no longer tenable. Richard Gregory, one of the acknowledged experts in the scientific study of perception, pinpointed the current problematic state of research on object perception in his book *Mind in Science*:

> It is an amazing thought that all our sensations and experience, and so knowledge, come from signals running to the brain down tiny cables; that the brain does not receive light, sound or touch, or tickle, but only patterns in space and time of electrical impulses which must be read – decoded – before they can have reference to the world of objects. (1981: 202)

How the brain translates these electrical impulses into meaningful perceptions, what in-built mechanisms for translation (if any) the brain possesses and what their limitations may be are key issues of perceptual research. As I will seek to show in this chapter, a phenomenological analysis of object perception may clarify many current concerns and help to inform future research.

There have been three major, if conflicting, traditional approaches to the study of perception: **stimulus theory**, which seeks to find a physiological basis to, or correspondence with, every perceptual act; **Gestalt theory**, which emphasizes innate properties and tendencies in perception; and **inference theory**, which applies an empiricist perspective to studies of perception.

The stimulus school argues that 'for each type of perception ... there is a unique stimulus or type of stimulus information. Thus there is no need to postulate such mechanisms as unconscious inference or spontaneous neural interaction to explain perception' (Rock, 1984: 12). Instead, the stimulus school seeks to find correlations between subjective sensations and external physical stimuli without having to posit intervening mental variables. In spite of the forceful arguments made in its favour by proponents such as J.J. Gibson (1950), this approach has been found to have limited explanatory value and, as we shall see, many experimental findings in perception pose serious problems for its wholehearted acceptance.

The Gestalt approach has been heavily influenced by philosophical conclusions first presented by Descartes (who argued that the mind possesses an innate knowledge of form, size and other properties of objects) and later extended by Kant (who theorized that the mind imposes its own subjective conceptions of time and space upon sensory data). Gestaltists were among the first scientifically oriented theoreticians to posit the notion of an *organizational* element in perception (Kohler, 1929; Koffka, 1935). They argued that, unlike sensations, which are chaotic and unrelated to one another, perceptions are characteristically organized into wholes or units which are qualitatively different from the sum of their parts. Rather than assume that the organization of perception is somehow learned over time, the Gestalt approach theorized that our perceptions are organized at birth 'on the basis of innately given laws that govern unit formation ...' (Rock, 1984: 11). While this theory has been very useful for the understanding of perceptual constancies and illusions, research has shown that it is, at best, only partially correct in its stance in that some amount of perceptual organization can be shown to be the result of learned experience (Rock, 1984).

Modern-day inference theories of perception have been derived directly from the writings of British empiricist philosophers such as Locke and Hume. Locke, for instance, argued that perception was, in essence, reflection; the characteristics of perception were 'out there' in the world, not within us. The mind was seen to be a kind of blank slate which received experiential impressions. As Locke himself wrote:

> Let us suppose the mind to be as we say, white paper, void of all characters, without any ideas. How comes it to be furnished? Whence comes it by that vast store which the busy and boundless fancy of man has painted on it with an almost endless variety? Whence has all the materials of reason and knowledge? To this I answer in one word: from experience, in that all our knowledge is founded, and from that it ultimately derives itself. (Locke as quoted in Gregory, 1981: 339)

For many empiricists, perception was to be regarded as the passive acceptance of selective knowledge from the external world. However, as with the other schools, there exists a multitude of experimental evidence on both human and other laboratory animals which demonstrates the error of this viewpoint. Perceptual studies reveal inferential and predictive processes to be central in all acts of perception (Gregory, 1981; Rock, 1984); we do not merely react to sensory signals by rigidly associating them with past experiences; our interpretational processing is far more complex than that.

In keeping with the conclusion arrived at by Irvin Rock in his recent valuable overview of theories of perception (1984: 13), it can be argued that each school, on its own, contains serious inadequacies. As I will argue in this chapter, the phenomenological approach to perception presents a position which goes some way to reconciling various aspects of the three schools summarized above and, in particular, unifies much of the data arrived at by followers of the Gestalt and inference schools. Before considering phenomenology's views, however, I must first clarify some more basic issues.

Sensation and Perception

There has been some confusion in the past, especially among students not well versed in perceptual theories, in clarifying the distinction between sensation and perception.

Not all of human behaviour takes perception as its starting point. Reflexive responses, for example, have been shown to be direct reactions to external stimuli (Gibson, 1950). Such responses require no mediation, no learning, no conscious awareness. It is only when mediating processes *influence* responses that the issue of perception arises. The differences between sensory and perceptual processing are clearly delineated by Hebb:

> *Sensation* may . . . be defined as the activity of receptors and the resulting activity of afferent paths up to and including the corresponding cortical sensory area. *Perception* is defined as the activity of mediating processes to which sensation gives rise directly. Sensation is in effect a one stage process. Perception normally requires a sequence of stimulations. (1966: 257)

Inference in Perception

It is now generally accepted that the brain receives sensory information in the form of electrical signals which are carried by nerve fibres conducting at speeds close to that of sound. If, as was originally supposed, perceptions were the result of direct access to, and stimulus selections of, the physical world, then research in object perception would not need to posit the existence of any 'mediating processes'.

That such processes *are* considered is because it has been demonstrated that the progress from sensory input of physical stimuli to the perceptual analysis and reaction to such inputs requires a sequence of neuro-psychological 'interpretations'. Any act of perception depends upon a variety of inferences derived from the neural signals. Such inferences may be more or less adequate, but *never* complete, or completely true.

Just one (if important) experiment which demonstrates the inferential aspects of perception was reported by Heron et al. (1956). Heron and his associates instructed subjects to peer into a tachistoscope (an instrument which allows visual material to be presented for very brief periods of time) and to gaze at a point in the centre of the screen. Subjects were then informed that letters would appear on the screen for a brief period (1/100th of a second) and that their task was to report as many letters as could be recalled. Different groupings composed of four letters were presented. Some groupings occurred to the left of the fixation point, some to the right, and some were centred on the fixation point. These positional variations were random and subjects were given no advance warning as to upcoming positions. Results revealed a consistency in the ordering of reports *regardless of the position of the letter patterns*. The selected order was: top left, top right, bottom left, bottom right – in other words, the order one must adopt in order to read English properly.

Significantly, subjects perceived the groupings of letters in this order even though the individual letters were presented instantaneously. Accurate reports were highest for those letters which appeared at the top-left position (about an 80 per cent level of accuracy) and lowest for letters appearing at the bottom right position (about a 40 per cent level of accuracy). In addition, subjects' experiential reports pointed out that the top-left letter was perceived as being more vivid than the top-right one and so on down the line.

There was no objective reason why subjects should perceive one letter as being more vivid than another, just as there was no objective reason why the top-left letter should be reported first and most correctly under nearly all circumstances. After all, when the groupings were arranged to the left of the fixation point, the right-hand letters became the nearest to the fixation point. Followers of the stimulus school would have predicted that, in this circumstance, the right-hand letters would be reported first and most correctly. But the data obtained failed to confirm this prediction; subjects still reported the top-left letters first and most accurately.

The authors concluded that the perceptual process itself had imposed an order on the sensory input in a way that was obviously linked to the past experience of reading English. Confirmatory (if reversed) findings were reported by Mishkin and Forgays (1952), who carried out the experiment with subjects who were skilled readers of Hebrew, a language properly read from right to left.

Perception, then, is best understood as a mediating process activity. Although a perceptual act may seem to have occurred instantaneous to sensation, experimental investigation reveals that a complex serial ordering of events takes place. Such research has demonstrated convincingly that the same sensory stimulus gives rise to completely distinct perceptions and that different stimuli can give rise to the same perception (Rock, 1984). Such results run counter to any hypothesis which presents perception as nothing more than a complex sensation.

As an example of the same sensory stimulus giving rise to variable perceptions, consider the **ambiguous figure** in Figure 1. This figure is often seen either as a bird bath or vase, or as two faces. No eye movement is required in order to perceive both figures. Simply by fixing one's eye on the black space between the two noses, or at the centre of the vase, the reader will find that a seemingly spontaneous reversal of images will occur.

Figure 1   *Rubin's vase/faces ambiguous figure*

The sensory process itself cannot account for this phenomenon. Extensive research in the area of ambiguous figures reveals both the fallibility of perceptual processes and the great degree of error that such processes are capable of. Indeed, studies of ambiguous figures are among the major means at the disposal of researchers to develop an understanding of the kinds of inference and assumptions on which perception depends and from which we develop various schemata

which influence future perceptual experiences (Neisser, 1967, 1976; Eysenck, 1984).

I will return to ambiguous figures later in this chapter. For now, I use them merely as particularly clear examples of the conclusion that variability is a general property of perception. Even relatively superficial consideration of everyday perceptual processing leads us to the same conclusion. In fixing upon any point in our immediate environment we may note how variable is our perception in its shift from one detail to another or from one perceptual range to another. While it may be proper to argue that the sensory input sets limits on what may be perceived, nevertheless within these limits perceptual variability can be pronounced.

On the other hand, the various **perceptual constancies** that have been demonstrated and analysed by researchers in the field provide indisputable evidence for our ability to maintain the same perception without regard to any changes in sensory stimuli. The phenomenon of **brightness constancy** provides an important example of a situation where the stimulus varies while the perception remains the same.

Brightness constancy is best understood when we consider that, for example, a white object will still appear to be white regardless of whether it is in bright light or in dark shadow. That it *should* remain white seems, at first, such an obvious expectation that the oddity of this perceptual phenomenon escapes us until we begin to ask ourselves how this event could possibly take place.

The amount of light reflected by an object will determine its colour (as perceived by us). The greater the amount of light reflected, the whiter the object will appear to us to be; similarly, black objects are such because of the small amount of light that they reflect. And yet, to refer to an oft-quoted example, although a chunk of coal lying in the sunlight reflects much more light than a nearby strip of white paper lying in deep shadow, our perceptual experience reveals that the coal still looks black, and the paper white.

What influences our perception is our dependence on contrast. The coal may be reflecting a good deal of light, but it reflects much less than do the objects which appear around it. Under experimental conditions where contrasting variables have been controlled, the coal will appear to be bright silver. Equally, a sheet of white paper in a contrast-controlled, dark environment will look dark grey (Rock, 1984).

The social chaos that would ensue if brightness constancy was not a part of our perceptual make-up is worth thinking about: cars left in car parks would not be so immediately identifiable, room colours would be constantly shifting, so many actions whose simplicity or speed depends principally on brightness constancy would need to be relearned. Thankfully, most of us can take brightness constancy (and any of the remaining constancies) for granted. What is important, however, is what it reveals about perceptual processing. The 'hard data' we receive through our senses, and the 'meaning' we construct from them, make plain once again the inferential elements in perception.

Like phenomenologists, the great majority of perceptual psychologists conclude that each of us experiences an *interpreted* world and not one directly accessible via our senses. In addition, when we begin to consider the wide range of variations within an individual's perceptions of the world, the phenomenological argument that each of us experiences a *uniquely* interpreted world becomes (alarmingly) obvious. To quote a conclusion arrived at by the philosopher Immanuel Kant which has since become a perceptual truism: 'We see things not as *they* are, but as *we* are'.

If the primary function of sensation is to react to stimuli, the primary function of perception allows us to impose a logic and order on the chaos of the thousands of sensations that bombard our senses. Even though our eyes detect lights and colours, and our ears react to tones of different loudness, pitch and timbre, we do not see or hear the world as a random array of light, dark, and colours, nor do we hear random tones of different loudness and pitch. Instead, perception allows us to make sense out of all these sensations.

Innate Biases in Perception: Wholeness and Organization

Is it possible that organisms may have developed perceptual processes which incorporate species-shared rules? There seems to be no logical or biological objection to this so long as it is understood that the rules still provide for wide degrees of flexibility.

All species may have developed in keeping with the rule we've labelled 'evolution', but the near-infinity of species-determined variables allowable within the confines of this rule demonstrates its interpretational possibilities. One such likely rule for our species, as I discussed in Chapter 1, is that our perceptual world is composed of objects, *things*. The 'blooming, buzzing, confusion' that William James supposed must be our earliest experience of the world has not been entirely borne out by experimental research (Rock, 1984).

It also appears to be the case that, in the act of experiencing the world, our species not only experiences 'things', but also organizes 'things' into forms which make up meaningful wholes (Koffka, 1935). In the course of organizing our perceptions into something mean-

ingful, we have a strong tendency to unify our experience. For example, if we look at a tree, we don't see its various constituents – its trunk, branches, leaves and so on – and from these conclude that we are seeing a tree; we see the whole 'thing'. We unify the constituents into a meaningful whole which we label 'a tree'. Similarly, if we drink from a cup of tea, we do not note the wide variety of taste and touch sensations that the action brings forth; we unify them into a meaningful whole which informs us we are 'drinking tea'.

Indeed, so pervasive and taken-for-granted is this construction process that we become aware that it is a process only when it breaks down. Numerous scientific studies of various forms of agnosia (the inability to attach meaning to sensory impressions) provide compelling reminders of just how vital this unifying process is (Luria, 1969; Miller, 1978).[1]

An intriguing, if somewhat extreme, case which demonstrates the fundamentality of this idea is reported by Oliver Sacks in his book *The Man who Mistook his Wife for a Hat* (1985) – an important text which presents a radical challenge to one of the most entrenched axioms of classical neurology.

In the case of Dr P, the man who mistook his wife for a hat, Sacks presents an unforgettable example of a man who has lost his ability to construct objects as 'whole things'. Dr P found himself increasingly incapable of seeing faces. His incapacity led him to make false judgements which led to unusual behaviour. Genially Mr Magoo-like, when in the street he might pat the tops of water hydrants and parking meters, taking these to be the heads of children, or he would amiably address carved knobs on furniture, and be astounded when they did not reply.

Nevertheless, Dr P's musical powers, which were extensive, remained as dazzling as ever. His problem became truly apparent only when he developed diabetes. Aware that diabetes could affect his eyes, Dr P consulted an ophthalmologist, who, after conducting a series of tests, concluded that there was nothing the matter with Dr P's eyes, but that there *was* trouble with Dr P's visual cortex. Referred to a neurologist, Dr P went to see Dr Sacks.

In one test, Dr Sacks opened up a copy of the *National Geographic* magazine, and asked Dr P to describe some pictures in it. Dr P's responses were very curious. His eyes darted from one thing to another, picking up tiny features, such as any striking brightness, colour or shape that attracted his attention, but he failed to see the images as 'wholes'. He had no sense whatever of landscape or scenery.

Similarly, when presented with a real glove, Dr P eventually posited that it was a continuous surface, infolded on itself, which appeared to have five 'out-pouchings' (a word invented by Dr P). Again, when asked whether, now that he'd given a description of the object, he could say what it was, Dr P queried whether it could be a container of some sort.

At the same time, when he was tested on platonic solids, he was perfectly capable of distinguishing cubes, duodecahedrons and more complex abstract shapes. These clearly presented no problems. Dr P's perceptual problems were with the *concrete world*, not with abstractions. It was this phenomenon which stood neurological theory on its head.

Significantly, he had lost the emotional constructive element that gives deep meaning to one's world. When asked to describe the story of *Anna Karenina* for example, Dr P could remember incidents without difficulty, and had an undiminished grasp of the plot, but he completely omitted visual characteristics, visual narrative or scenes. He remembered the words of the characters but not their faces, and though, when asked, he could quote, with remarkable and almost verbatim accuracy, the original visual descriptions, these were quite empty for him, and lacked sensorial, imaginal or emotional reality. It was a case of complete visual and internal agnosia.

The case of Dr P points to the fundamental and innate ability to interpret the world in a meaningful and holistic manner. So obvious is this ability that it becomes apparent only when we are confronted with evidence of its loss. Even so, Dr P's somewhat fanciful attempts to make sense of his world, in spite of his agnosia, further reveal how deep-seated is our need to extract meaning – regardless of how inadequate it may be.

Gestalt psychologists working during the first quarter of this century were the first to stress the features of wholeness and organization as being primary and irreducible aspects of human perception. These tendencies of perception, they argued, were universal and classifiable into several factors, principally: **similarity** (the tendency to perceive items of the same size, shape or quality as groups or patterns, rather than as dissimilar elements); **proximity** (the tendency to group together perceptually items that are physically close to each other; **continuity** (the tendency to avoid or deny perceptual breaks in the flow of a line, design, or pattern); and **closure** (the tendency to close or complete an incomplete pattern).

There is a substantial amount of experimental evidence in favour of the conclusion that many of our perceptual processes incorporate inherited rules or biases. There is no question here of any necessary allegiance to a Lamarckian-based system which posits the inheritance of particular experiences, or of ancestral knowledge and skills. Rather, what has been inherited is, like functionally appropriate structures such as hands, likely to be the result of trials and errors of natural selection which, over time, have become incorporated into the genetic code.

In addition, Wolfgang Kohler, one of the major figures in the Gestalt school, provided experimental evidence that animals learn to respond to *relationships* between stimuli, as well as to specific stimuli. He was among the first to demonstrate, for example, that a chicken can be taught to avoid a dark-grey square, and to approach a medium-grey square. If, after learning this, the chicken is presented with a medium-grey square, and another square of lighter grey, it will go to the lighter-grey square. It was evident that the chicken had learned to respond not to the stimulus, but to the *relationship of one stimulus being lighter than another* (Kohler, 1929).

The organization of sensations is a fundamental perceptual process. In general, there are three basic types of perceptual organization. The first, **form perception**, as I've discussed above, refers to how stimuli are organized into meaningful shapes and patterns. A second type of perceptual organization deals with **depth and distance perception**. This relates to our ability to organize the world into three dimensions, in spite of the fact that our retina records only two-dimensional images. A related issue, here, is how we perceive depth in a two-dimensional picture. A third aspect of perceptual organization deals with **perceptual constancies**.

Perceptual constancies refer 'to our ability to perceive objects as relatively stable in terms of size, shape, and color despite changes in the sensory information that reaches our eyes' (Crider et al., 1986: 98). It could be said that perceptual constancies are innate perceptual biases or illusions.

In his review of perceptual constancies, for example, Rock (1984: 36–43) concludes, on the basis of currently available experimental evidence, that **shape, spatial and lightness constancies** seem to be unlearned, direct perceptions. Rock also points out that there exists a fair degree of suggestive evidence that form perception is innate. Direct evidence might be obtained from individuals who were born blind and later gained their sight (Rock, 1984: 140), but such data do not exist as yet.

The next-best type of evidence comes from studies with animals who have been deprived of normal vision in some way. Hubel and Wiesel's (1962) work on detector mechanisms seemed to suggest a means to study these possible effects. However, these data are also open to question since subsequent discoveries on detector mechanisms have shown that the animals' earliest environmental experiences influenced the kinds of detector mechanisms developed (Rock, 1984: 141).

Some fairly strong evidence that form perception is present at birth at least in some animals comes from Fantz's (1961) studies of the vision of newly hatched chicks, where it was found that three-day-old chicks showed clear preference for pecking at round-shaped objects on an innate basis. Human infants also show preferences for particular shapes and colours (Rock, 1984: 143).

Zimmerman and Torrey obtained evidence that form perception is present in infant monkeys (Rock, 1984: 144). Such findings were supported by research carried out by Sackett (Rock, 1984: 145), who demonstrated that six-week-old infant monkeys reacted differently to pictures of other infant monkeys or to those of monkeys in a threatening stance. These various studies strongly suggest that something similar is likely to occur in humans.

It is also likely that distance perception is present from the very beginning of human life. Studies of depth perception (such as those reported by Gibson and Walk (1960) on visual cliff phenomena) demonstrate that a capacity for depth perception in humans is likely to be innate. However, as Rock points out, this doesn't mean that learning plays no role in development of depth perception: 'We appear to be born with the axiomatic "assumption" that we are localized within a three-dimensional spatial world. . . . But we learn to use additional cues and learn to interpret given cues with greater precision after birth' (1984: 88–9).

On the other hand, **size perception** is probably a learned constancy. The issues here are somewhat complicated due to the fact that innate capacities need not be present at birth. The now-famous experiments carried out by T.G.R. Bower (Rock, 1984: 39–40) at Edinburgh University provide evidence that size constancy is present at birth. Unfortunately, experimental variations of Bower's work which have been carried out in Australia don't match his findings (Rock, 1984: 40).

The different results may be due to *distance* variations which might influence infants' responses. Rock argues that even if Bower's conclusions were replicated, this doesn't rule out the possibility that size constancies may be the result of experience, since these constancies might develop very quickly in the first few weeks of life, as has been demonstrated by Heller's experiments on size constancy in rats (Rock, 1984: 41). Human infants may demonstrate innate size constancies under *dynamic* conditions (that is, when the infant subjects are motionless while attending to moving objects), but they seem to develop size constancy for *static* conditions (when the perceived objects are at rest) as a result of experience.

That there are a number of important innate factors in human perception seems beyond doubt. However, it would be wrong to conclude, as does the Gestalt school, that the basis for all perceptual processing is innate. Experience, too, plays a major role in human perception.

Interpretative Variables in Perception: the Effects of Past Experience

So prevalent is perceptual processing in our experience of the world that it becomes justifiable to ask whether any instances of pure sensation exist in human experience. No matter how unusual or novel a stimulus such as an odd noise may be, our common response is immediately to associate it or identify it with something that is already familiar to us. On the basis of the schemata built up from past experience, we infer its meaning and react to the perceived stimulus. If the previous experience recurs frequently, our interpretative schema becomes so fixed that our response becomes one of habit.

It is probable that the vast majority of our daily sensory experiences are perceived in an habitual manner, based on repeated previous experiences. In practice, many of our daily activities consist of responses to familiar cues or symbols. For instance, we smell coffee percolating and visualize breakfast being prepared; the young child hears the garage door open and concludes that mother has just come home and bedtime is near. In reacting to such cues we have, more accurately, trained ourselves to jump to conclusions, from partial yet familiar stimuli from the past.

But does this imply that *only* past experiences determine our perceptions of objects? Phenomenologists, while not denying the importance of past experience, consider it to be just one of several variables influencing perception.

In general, we may say that whatever object each of us perceives at any given time depends on the nature of the actual stimulus, our previous experience, the background or setting in which the object exists, our feelings of the moment, and our general prejudices, desires, attitudes and goals. Such a conclusion is, of course, entirely in keeping with the phenomenological notion of intentionality.

Interpretative Variables in Perception: the Effects of Selection

When experience affects perception, it does not do so by molding the stimulus to conform to how things were seen in the past. It is not entirely a top-down process. Rather . . . *something* was first perceived bottom-up, on the basis of certain principles of organization and without recourse to experience. Once the initial perception occurred, if what was seen was similar in some respect to objects seen in the past, those memories were accessed and they played a role in the further processing of the stimulus input. A useful term to characterize effects of this kind is *enrichment*. The perception is enriched by, though not entirely determined by, memories of earlier perceptual experience. (Rock, 1984: 132)

An interpretational variable in perception based upon past experience is our *expectation* of what to perceive. This phenomenon is often referred to as the **perceptual set**. One of the earliest and most vivid demonstrations of perceptual set is a picture originally published in *Puck* magazine in 1915 and reproduced below in Figure 2. Whether we first perceive a young society woman or an old crone can be influenced by what we see before it. If we see a picture that is clearly a young woman before we see the ambiguous figure, we see the ambiguous figure as a young woman. If the same image is preceded by a picture of an old woman, we first perceive the ambiguous figure to be an old woman. Through our perceptual set, we perceive objects in a particular way on the basis of *previous* information.

Figure 2   *Old woman/young woman ambiguous figure (from an original drawing in Puck magazine, 1915)*

Closely related to perceptual set, however, is the **perceptual context**. In the perceptual context, other stimuli that are *present at the same time* affect our perception of a stimulus. An example of this has been provided by Coren, Porac and Ward (1978) which I reproduce in Figure 3. It is likely that you read the message in that figure as: 'My phone number is area code 604, 876–1569. Please call!' However, if you look more closely you will realize that the word 'is' and the number '15' are identical, as are the letters 'h' in 'phone' and 'b' in 'number', and 'd' in 'code' and 'l' in 'call'. Your different interpretations of these identical stimuli are due to the context within which you read them.

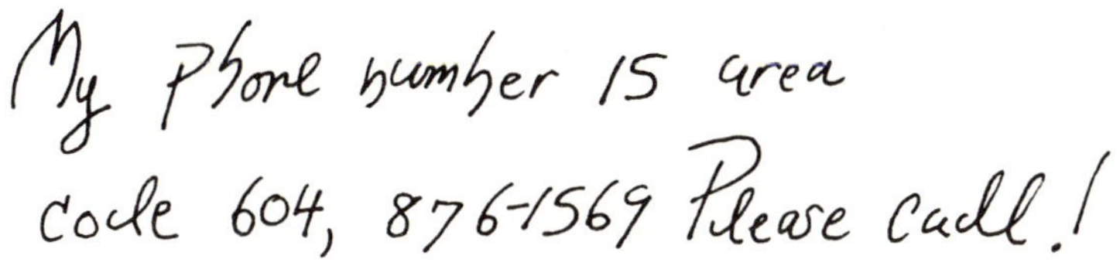

My Phone number 15 area code 604, 876-1569 Please call!

Figure 3   *An example of perceptual context (Coren et al., 1978)*

Another factor that can affect our perceptions is our current **motivational state**. One of the first evaluations of the effects of motivation on perception was carried out by R.N. Sanford (1935), who studied the effect of hunger on the perception of ambiguous figures. Sanford presented certain figures to ten children, both before and after they had eaten. In each case he asked the children what the figures looked like. The children responded that the figures looked like food, twice as often *before* they had eaten as after.

All of these interpretative factors allow us to construct our perception of objects through our **selective attention** to certain stimuli over others. One of the most famous studies of selective attention is the so-called 'cocktail party phenomenon' (Crider et al., 1986: 153), which many people have experienced. Imagine that while engaging in social chit-chat at a party, you happen to overhear a much more interesting conversation originating from another part of the room. As you politely try to keep up with your own discussion, you find your attention returning again and again to the other conversation. Unable to follow both conversations at the same time, your attention shifts back and forth between the two until you somehow manage to rid yourself of your partner or, as is more common, your conversation comes to an embarrassing stop.

This phenomenon has been studied under experimentally controlled conditions (Moray, 1959). Typically, subjects wear headphones which play a different message into each ear and are told to attend only to the information coming from one of the speakers and, in order to ensure that they are following instructions, to repeat, or shadow, the attended information as they hear it. Through extensions of such studies, it has also been found that the shadowing abilities of subjects become seriously impaired when the information coming from the unattended speaker deals with sexually explicit messages or mentions their names (Nielsen and Sarason, 1981).

Phenomenological Theory and Object Perception

On the basis of this, admittedly brief, overview of some of the major concerns and conclusions arrived at by experimentally oriented studies on object perception, we can see that human perception, based as it is upon both innate and experiential variables, is primarily an interpretative process. This conclusion, of course, is in keeping with the phenomenological conclusion. Are there are further similarities worthy of our consideration? And, perhaps more importantly, is there anything of value that phenomenology might add to the understanding of human perceptual processing?

In considering the general issues involved, phenomenologists initially point out that all acts of perception have a particular orientation or **directional focus**. If I say that I am perceiving any particular object, what I imply is that I am directing my attention on to something.

As I stated earlier, it is important to remain aware of the fact that the number of stimuli that the brain responds to at any moment in time is vast in relation to the amount that enters conscious awareness. Neurophysiological studies have pointed out that one of the main functions of the brain is to 'filter', or select, incoming stimuli so that only a fraction of them become consciously perceived (Bergson, 1907).

We can gain a hint of how pervasive this filtering process actually is by simply recording and playing back a monologue or a conversation on audio tape. While recording, we are only conscious of the sounds that are of significance to us, such as the voice or voices that hold our attention. Other sounds remain unnoticed unless there is something about them – their volume perhaps, or repetitiveness – which intrudes upon our attention. When we play back the tape, however, we are likely to hear any number of irrelevant sounds that we had previously remained ignorant of. Almost magically, we can now clearly make out a whole cacophony of sounds remarkably similar to those of cars honking in the street, people shouting from other rooms, fingers scratching at skin or clothing, breathing, wheezing – all manner of noises captured and preserved as carefully as those which we'd attended to!

Of course, what has occurred is that the microphone picked up the sounds and translated them on to magnetic tape on the basis of 'filtering' mechanisms which are far less complex than those employed by our brains. The microphone's filtering is limited to factors relating to sound levels; that is the only 'meaning' that the different sounds have to it. But the human brain filters sounds on the basis of a wide number of variables – of which sound level is but one – in order to select out those variables which require our conscious attention.

Figure/Ground Invariance

In arguing for, and analysing, this act of orientation, phenomenologists soon realized that a second basic invariant of perception could be considered. Through the process of attending to stimuli, we are confronted with the perceptual invariant commonly labelled the **figure/ground phenomenon**.

In all acts of perception there is a focusing upon the object of our attention (the figure) and the receding away from our awareness of all the momentarily extraneous stimuli (the ground). As with the directionality of our attention, the figure/ground phenomenon is an essential component of our ability to employ selective attention. If, for example, I focus my attention upon my desk, I can only do this if I make the desk my figure, and make everything else in my vision its background. If I don't see the distinction between the two, I can't actually arrive at any object-based perceptual conclusions.

We can only perceive a world full of 'things' *because* we employ a figure/ground distinction. Otherwise, our ability to perceive boundaries and limitations, startings and endings, even gaps between things, would not be possible. The mind organizes patterns of sensations into particular figure/ground differentiations. This view was initially hypothesized in 1921 by Edgar Rubin (Rock, 1984: 113–15) and is fundamental to all perception. We typically tend to perceive as *figure* those regions that are *surrounded, smaller, symmetrical, and vertical or horizontal.*

The figure/ground relations seems to be an innately based, fundamental invariant in the human perception of objects, as is borne out by studies with individuals who are born congenitally blind and who, subsequent to medical operations, become capable of vision only later in their lives (Rock, 1984). Although the figure/ground relation is initially independent of experience, experience enhances and clarifies this relation so that its variability increases as a result of perceptual learning. Nevertheless, *any* act of orientation *depends upon* a figure/ground perspective.

In most cases, we assume the perspective to remain static. That is, there will be no spontaneous figure/ground shift which occurs independent of our perceptual set of expectations. The great interest on the part of perceptual psychologists in ambiguous or reversible figures is largely because such images *do* allow for a seemingly spontaneous figure/ground shift. Studies of ambiguous images such as those illustrated earlier in this chapter provide researchers with keys towards an understanding of the shifting process between figure and ground and of the many general features of human perceptual processes.

As a result of varying elements of the figure/ground of ambiguous images, we can construct radically different perceptual images to the ones we may have initially perceived. Indeed, the very *meaning* of the images alters as a result of a shift in our figure/ground perspective.

It is not easy to state what principle of organization is at work here. The most commonly accepted theory of reversal is Kohler's **satiation or fatigue theory** (Kohler, 1929), which argues that each perceptual organization is determined by a separate neural event in the brain. If one ongoing neural event becomes satiated, the brain will resist its further occurrence. When resistance fully blocks that neural event, there is a switch to another neural event. Some evidence supports this theory (Hochberg, 1970) and reversals are said to take place spontaneously after about fifteen seconds of viewing.

Rock (1984), however, remains sceptical about this argument. His own work at Rutgers University shows that reversals *don't* occur if subjects remain unaware that the figure is ambiguous. Most studies tell subjects in advance that there are two images to be found, thereby incorporating an important, if rarely considered, 'demand character' into the experiment, since subjects will have been 'set' to assume that a reversal will occur.

However, Rock's experiment demonstrated that when these 'demand character' instructions were not given in a traditional experiment employing the vase/faces figure (see Figure 1), high-school subjects failed to report reversals after over a minute, if at all, and that those who did report reversals did so only once or only a few times during the whole of the experimental period (Rock, 1984: 122). When traditional instructions were given at the start of the control study, however, reversals occurred as they were 'supposed to'. As Rock concluded:

> Merely thinking about the alternative not being perceived at any given moment may suffice to lead to perceptual reorganization in which it *is* perceived. In short, the explanation of reversal in the case of informed observers may have more to do with a shifting memory reference than with neural fatigue. (1984: 123).

Ihde's Phenomenological Study of the Hallway/ Pyramid Illusion

One particularly illuminating phenomenological argument which focuses on ambiguous images has been presented by Ihde in his book *Experimental Phenomenology* (1977). I will attempt to summarize some of the intriguing aspects of his analysis.

Consider the following example. Suppose a group of observers are shown (for the first time in each subject's life) the 'hallway/pyramid illusion' as represented in Figure 4. When each member of the group is asked 'What do you see?', the response is divided. One group, Group H, say that what they see is a hallway. The other group, Group P, assert that what they see is a cut-off pyramid. Let us suppose that the two groups are stubborn in their belief so that each group sees *only* either the pyramid or the hallway. Within this initial framework for analysis, we may say that the noema of each group is fixed, or literal-minded.

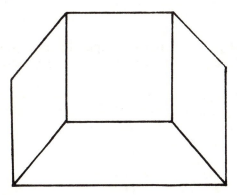

Figure 4   *The hallway/pyramid illusion (Ihde, 1977)*

In addition, although the noema perceived by each group is different, each group can argue that its perceptual conclusion is valid since each claim is open to repeated experiential verification. Ihde labels this ability to return again and again to one's previous perception in order to fulfil one's previous claim as **apodicticity**. As such, at this first stage of investigation, each group maintains its literal-minded position apodictically.

Now, let us move on to the second level of investigation. Let us say that certain members from each of our first two groups somehow realize that *both* perceptual claims are valid. These individuals have ascended to the second level of investigation and can be seen to belong to a new group – Group A (for ascendance).

Members of Group A are in an ascended position over those in Groups H and P insofar as their ability to see both claims is more comprehensive and, in this sense, superior to the ability to see only one claim. In addition, Group A members can still employ apodicticity for each perceptual claim; they do not lose this ability. However, in being able to return to both claims apodictically, the superiority, or significance, of one claim over the other begins to fade.

Since Group A's noema now contains two possibilities, phenomenologists argue that Group A's view is more *adequate* than that of the first two groups. Moreover, Group A's apodicticity is irreversible. No member in Group A can return to his first, naive, literal-minded claim. In being able to return to both claims, a viewpoint which argues for the superiority of one claim over the other cannot be maintained; the apodictic significance is now permanently altered.

In order to arrive at this second level of analysis, members of Group A have employed (knowingly or not) the phenomenological method in that they have bracketed their initial biases and assumptions, focused upon their immediate impressions and considered them descriptively, and avoided any immediate hierarchical considerations with regard to the interpreted sensory data.

This suggests that members of Group A have taken a much more active role in arriving at their perceptual conclusions. This view runs counter to the assumptions of many perceptual researchers who argue that the reversibility of the images is spontaneous and requires no active involvement on the part of the perceiver. As I have already noted, Rock's experiments (1984) lead us to question this claim.

I will return to this disagreement later in the discussion. For the moment, let us consider what might result were we *deliberately* to pursue an active role in a consciously determined manner in order to test Husserl's contention that, in doing so, we not only increase the adequacy of our perspective, but also gain a greater richness in our perception. As Ihde demonstrates, in looking at the image actively one can claim that a *third* image emerges. Now, he argues, not only can we perceive both a hallway and a pyramid, but also a headless robot on crutches.

In order to perceive this third image, return to Figure 4. Now, 'flatten' the image so that it is perceived as being two-dimensional rather than three-dimensional. Imagine that the centre square is the robot's body, that the upper diagonal lines are its arms, and that the lower diagonal lines are its legs. The two remaining vertical lines are its crutches, and the bottom horizontal line is the ground. If it helps, add the dotted outline of a head and neck just above the centre square until you have the image of a robot on crutches and then lop off its head in order to return to the reversible figure.

This third alternative, once its appearance has been noted, fulfils the same criteria as do our first two claims. The headless robot claim is apodictic and irreversible in that anyone who has surmised the existence of the headless robot can never go back to a previous claim that only the hallway and pyramid exist. In addition, as I argued earlier, this third claim also increases the relative adequacy of our perceptual stance.

'But', I can imagine some of my readers saying, 'there seems to be something wrong here! Perceptual psychologists using this illusion for their tests have never reported any subjects who've claimed to perceive a headless robot when presented with the image. Whereas the first two claims seem natural – even normal – the third is something that appears to be far less so. There is clearly some trickery or irregularity here. Could it be the case that in the first two variations normal perceptual effects are being noted, while the third is the result of something else?'

This reaction is not unusual. Nearly all of my students react in this manner when the headless robot is introduced to them for the first time. And yet, is there any basis for this reaction? *Is* the headless-robot image any less valid than the previous two? At first, this would seem to be the case.

'The hallway/pyramid figures are obvious,' my students report. 'We see them spontaneously, whereas the headless robot is unusual, we had to be *taught* to see it.' What my students reveal, however inadvertently, is what phenomenologists refer to as a **sedimented** outlook. Their initial perceptions are contained within their beliefs and (psychological) background. They *know* that this particular ambiguous figure reveals two – and only two – possibilities. Even if they'd never seen this ambiguous figure before, its very label, 'the hallway/pyramid illusion', will limit their expectations – and their perceptual openness. After all, the image is not referred to as the hallway/pyramid/headless robot illusion.

Let us consider their contention that there is no evidence of anyone ever having perceived the headless robot spontaneously. Well, certainly, someone (perhaps Ihde himself) *must* have seen the headless robot spontaneously at some point in the past in order for it to be part of our current discussion. So, at the very least, its noematic perception is as possible as (if seemingly less likely than) the previous two interpretations of the image.

As such, there are really only two key points of contention. First, the headless-robot image is novel and seems unusual when compared to either the hallway or the pyramid images. Second, in order to see the headless robot, we had to be taught to see it, whereas the hallway/pyramid images seem to appear spontaneously.

Let us turn our attention to the first point. My students' reaction to the headless robot's novelty is not unexpected. The more sedimented your outlook is towards something, the stronger and more negative is your likely reaction to arguments which suggest alternatives or which extend perceptual boundaries. How many movements within the arts, how many scientific theories and hypotheses have there been, whose novelty and unusual approaches to the issues at hand provoked similar – if not more aggressive – reactions by both experts and lay-persons? It is easy to forget, for example, that most impressionist paintings – which are today so admired and considered by many to be superlative representatives of Western art – were originally derided as being puerile rubbish which attacked the eyes and whose claim to artistic value was an insult to painting (Hughes, 1980).

Novelty implies temporality. With the passage of time and, possibly, with the lessening of the anxiety that externally imposed novelties induce, the novelty may become accepted, even highly valued, and itself become part of a new sedimented framework. Novelty which results from one's own insights or active search is more likely to produce exhilaration than anxiety. In this case, the novelty is likely to be more quickly accepted and treated as having significance equal to if not greater than any pre-insight standpoints.

Even in the case of the headless robot, once having been made aware of it, many students, like myself, can no longer see the hallway/ pyramid images without also seeing the headless robot. Indeed, now our perception of the robot comes as easily, as spontaneously, as do the two earlier perceptions, such that the tendency to ascribe inherently different origins to its appearance seems not only unnecessary, but wrong.

As to the question why there should be so few (if any) reports of the headless robot by subjects in perceptual experiments, it is important, as Ihde reminds us, that in typical psychological experiments on perception,

> Response times are usually limited, and the experiment is deliberately designed to eliminate reflection, critique or extensive observation. This raises the question of what such an experiment reveals. . . . It is possible that an instantaneous glance shows us something basic about perception, isolated from so-called higher, or lower level conscious functions. It is equally possible than an instantaneous glance shows only what is most sedimented in the Noetic context, the context within which perception occurs. (1977: 74)

The polymorphic-mindedness which allows us to perceive the headless robot as well as the hallway and pyramid results from the same sequence of investigation which allowed us to step aside from our initial literal-minded view.

Phenomenologically, the greater the number of apodictic possibilities, the more adequate is our perception. If so, does that suggest that we haven't exhausted the range of perceptual possibilities inherent in the image? So it seems. Given the impetus, my students have been able to come up with an ever-increasing number of apodictic alternatives; where there was once the possibility of only one act of reversibility, the image has now opened itself to multiple reversals. (A personal 'practical' aspect of this increased adequacy is my ability to draw the hallway/pyramid figure relatively much more accurately now that I can also imagine it as a headless robot.)

Still, the persistent critic might argue, all well and good, but having now demonstrated a virtually limitless range of uncommon possibilities, so what?

Putting aside the increased adequacy that polymorphic-mindedness allows, it also seems clear that the process seems central to what is usually referred to as 'creativity'. As Koestler so capably demonstrated in his text *The Act of Creation* (1964), it is precisely this ability to see what is not usually seen, to form unusual connections between seemingly disparate events, that is the basis to all acts of creation, be they artistic or scientific.

Sedimented beliefs may provide (illusory) security and a (seeming) order to our world-views, but it is polymorphic-mindedness which allows for personal and cultural advancement.

If we consider the second common criticism, that of spontaneous reversibility *vs* 'learned' reversibility, we can see that the assumptions being made here are open to debate. The basic contention of perceptual researchers is that, with an increased response time, subjects report that an ambiguous figure will spontaneously reverse itself. Standard accounts of this phenomenon seem satisfied to imply that the phenomenon is in some way a result of passive staring and, thus, requires no mental activity to experience it. Ihde, on the other hand, argues that it is more likely that rather than the stimuli undergoing some mysterious spontaneous reversal, what has occurred is that the initial, sedimented noetic context with which we perceive the picture has now, through time, been able to diversify, to spread, 'to open itself' to other possibilities.

The experiments carried out by Rock (1984), as discussed above, take on particular importance with regard to this debate. Recall that Rock's data provide strong evidence in favour of the conclusion that reversibility only occurs for many subjects *if* they are aware that the figure is ambiguous or reversible. If they see no potential ambiguity in the image, they can sit passively and stare at it for long periods of time and experience no reversibility.

Such evidence places serious doubt on the assumption of a 'natural and spontaneous' process of reversibility. Instead, it suggests a conclusion which is much more in keeping with phenomenological prediction. What it suggests is that reversibility occurs because, in some way, we expect it to, and, as a result, we actively engage in a search for the alternative possibility.

In other words, it is likely that reversibility is a 'learned' process. Through some means or other, those of us who can perceive the image reversal have been taught to do so. On consideration, this conclusion seems plausible. On looking at the hallway/pyramid image once more, we realize that it looks neither like a realistic hallway nor a realistic pyramid. Indeed, as with our headless robot, we must have been taught (in some way or other) to perceive the pyramid image, for example, by being asked to imagine a traditional pyramid and then lop its top off. Some strategy must have been employed at some time in our past to 'set' our perception to 'receive' these two images.

The discovery of a multitude of noetic possibilities in the hallway/pyramid illusion reveals the strength of the phenomenological method. Upon realizing that the noema can be viewed as an open range of possibilities which can be actively noetically interpreted, we see that we have been engaged in a special kind of viewing activity – that which searches for what is not immediately apparent. Regardless of its novelty, any constructed image which is apodictic cannot be dismissed – its 'reality' is no more nor less than the 'reality' of any other apodictic image. Moreover, in the acceptance of increasing apodictic possibilities, our interpretation of the stimuli becomes more and more adequate.

In order for any active viewer to be able to carry out this particular kind of object viewing, we have seen that a suspension of sedimented beliefs via the phenomenological method is required. In suspending such beliefs, according to Husserl, we have 'switched' from a natural attitude to the phenomenological attitude.

Phenomenological Implications for Empirical Research on Object Perception

I have shown that phenomenologically derived findings on object perception vary from those arrived at by more standard psychological investigation. Recall that an ambiguous image like the hallway/pyramid illusion initially appears to naive subjects in one of two variations which, typically, is where standard psychological studies, in their naivety, tend to remain. Should a possible third variation be pointed out, it is usually either dismissed or viewed as being less valid than the expected two. For example, one study that focused on another example of a reversible image (the Necker cube), reported that, although some subjects, rather than perceive a three-dimensional image, claimed to perceive a flat, two-dimensional image, this experience could be dismissed as being a result of fatigue (Morris, 1971).

In contrast to this conclusion, phenomenological investigation demonstrates that, once our sedimented outlook is 'opened up', numerous perceptual possibilities become available which can be repeatedly returned to for experiential verification. Far from being insignificant and unworthy of serious analysis, this polymorphous variability provides us with important empirical and epistemological clues to a more adequate understanding of object perception.

We begin to realize, for example, that once it becomes evident that ambiguous images are open to multiple perceptual variations, the *order of appearance* of one image over the others is not dependent upon a perceptual structure but, rather, is the result of subjective sedimented biases. Once polymorphy is accepted, *any* variation derived from the image can be the first to appear. This conclusion is rarely considered in most psychological theories and (not surprisingly) reveals a reluctance on the part of most researchers in this area to give up sedimented assumptions which are linked to any number of theoretical commitments.

Equally, arguments which suggest that only a limited number of variations (usually one or two) are *natural* perceptions while the others reveal only the workings of an over-imaginative mind fail to stand up to logical analysis since, with continued verification, the supposedly odd variations lose their oddity and become more 'natural'. Once again, such criticisms reveal the strength of sedimentation rather than (as is often claimed) provide evidence of a key characteristic of object perception. If central perceptual structures are ever to be discovered, it is more likely that they will come from clues derived from the applied variations of the phenomenological method than from the sedimented perspectives of empirical studies.

In applying this method, it becomes clear that the number of perceptual possibilities are not limited to 'natural' tendencies, but to 'the topographical possibilities of the thing itself, as an open noema' (Ihde, 1977: 107).

But the phenomenological method as applied to object perception not only transforms our experience, it provides us with a clearer understanding of how perceptual experience occurs. Regardless of how vast and complex may be the field of perceptual possibilities, it is apparent that our experience remains structured. Not all conceivable possibilities emerge, only those that 'fit' within the structural boundaries of the image.

So far in our discussion, like most experimental psychologists engaged in perceptual research, we have depended upon unreal, laboratory-based studies to arrive at our conclusions about object perception. But are such conclusions valid for real-life experiences?

Everyday experiences of object perception are, of course, much more complex and imbued with theoretical difficulties. Far from being initially neutral, the objects we perceive in ordinary activities are charged with emotional significance. Yet here too, as in experimental studies, the meanings we give to objects, or the manner in which we perceive them, reveals a sedimentation based upon the mental frameworks of beliefs and habits generated from past experience.

For example, in perceiving the object which is my computer, I have found that I invariably become increasingly anxious when I approach it; I marvel at the advances in technology that it represents and shudder with dread at the new and unique fears that my erroneous interactions with it might produce. These subjective responses add to, and alter, my perception of the object, bind it to my existence in ways far more significant than the receipt of ownership I possess.

Interestingly enough, some recent experimental work carried out by Langer and Piper (Grant, 1988) confirms some of the points I've made in this discussion. Their research was concerned with demonstrating how familiarity with the functions of a particular object bred 'mindlessness' or an unthinking approach to its categories.

The two experimenters introduced an array of both familiar and unfamiliar objects to students either on an 'unconditional' basis (that is, 'This is a – ') or on a 'conditional' basis (that is, 'This *could be* a – '). What they discovered was that students could find novel uses for both familiar and unfamiliar objects only when the objects had been presented 'conditionally'. The effects of 'unconditional' labelling hindered any creative thinking.

As Langer and Piper point out, it is unfortunately this latter ('unconditional') mode of object presentation that typifies the way we are taught to think about objects both by our parents and by our teachers. Whatever its merits, this mode does not 'cultivate the cognitive flexibility needed to deal with a world that is forever in flux' (Grant, 1988: 16).

The lessons of phenomenology force us to examine and perhaps reconsider our sedimented outlooks towards the real, everyday objects we encounter. We realize that our biases to these are far more fixed, far more difficult to apply the phenomenological method to, than when playing with the possibilities of simpler, more neutral, experimental examples. This insight holds the key to the origins of existential phenomenology. As we will see in Chapter 6, this branch of phenomenology takes as a basic invariant the recognition that all acts, even those as simple as my viewing my computer, or labelling objects, bear direct relationship to all viewers' very existence, and implicate them in their experience.

For the moment, it is enough to point out once again how real-life 'breaks' in sedimented perspectives allow us to be creative, to make discoveries both startling and mundane. In playing with the possible reversals of figure/ground, in realigning dominant and recessive features, in exploring new possible connections, we might conceivably produce revolutionary paradigm shifts. For example, in focusing his attention on light rather than upon objects, Monet produced the series of impressionistic masterpieces centred upon Rouen cathedral. Similarly, in linking together elements as disparate as Charcot's demonstrations of hypnosis, the strange case of Anna O and the behaviour of hysterics, the young Freud formulated his developing theory of the unconscious mind (Gay, 1988).

Commonly, the more radical the shift, the more vociferously antagonistic is the social (and perhaps even personal) resistance to it. As in the typical reaction to being shown the figure of the 'headless robot' for the first time, we convince ourselves that alternative perspectives are somehow wrong or less justified than are our sedimented ones. Cultural relativities – and the clashes between cultures that arise out of such relativities – reveal the resistance to change held within sedimented viewpoints. Phenomenology provides us with the basis for lessening the hold of 'fixedness' on our perceptual frameworks. In doing so, it allows us to approach novel and unusual viewpoints and perspectives with more tolerance and flexibility.

The phenomenological investigation of object perception leads us to the conclusion that the objects we perceive, although certainly 'fixed' by a number of innate, species-specific structural invariants of perceptual processing, retain a plethora of experiential possibilities. In altering noematic and noetic variables in our experience, we 're-create' it in any number of ways. Our willingness to do so expands our experience, opens us to the experiences of others, allows us to lessen the power of personal and cultural sedimented perspectives. In doing so, we realize our intimate subjective involvement in our perceptions and are given the means to explore and understand more clearly how each of us comes to select hierarchically certain possibilities over others.

Such discoveries have major implications for our notions regarding 'self' and 'others', and for our relation to our world. The naive and simplistic boundaries we devise in order to distinguish such notions no longer hold true. The assumed separation between experimenter and subject, or between the data being analysed and the person who analyses them (separations which are commonly assumed by most empirically oriented psychologists) become questionable.

The words to a recent anthem tell us that 'we are the world'; broadly speaking, phenomenology reiterates this statement.

4

The Perception of Others

Who are you?

The Caterpillar to Alice

It is useful to begin this discussion on the phenomenology of the perception of others (or 'person perception' as it is also commonly called) with a brief exercise. Take a blank sheet of paper and write down the numbers one through ten in a column along the left-hand margin of your sheet. Once you have done so, look at the photograph in Figure 5 and, while looking at it, without thinking too hard or too long about your impressions, simply write down the first ten things that come to mind about the person depicted in it.

Figure 5
(copyright:
Martin Smith)

Now, having completed the task, what overall impression would you say you have formed of this man? Would you say that his lifestyle is conventional or unconventional? Would you expect him to enjoy classical music, or rock? What (if any) would you say this man's profession was? Would you think he was congenial? Optimistic? Surly? Cynical? Discontented?

When I asked several of my students to carry out this exercise, the range of responses was quite dramatic. Various students saw the man in the picture as being happy, content, a threat to society, unkempt, free, rebellious, dirty, scary, hairy, poor, relaxed, a liberal, originating from a working-class background, a musician, a busker, a slob, a person who is unattached to material things, an intellectual, cool, cute, attractive, a criminal, a spiritually awakened being and so on.

It is important to remember that, as in the exercise you just carried out, all these impressions were formed simply on the basis of the man's physical appearance and facial expression as represented by the photograph. Nowhere in that photograph are we given the information that would allow us to reach many of the conclusions that I've outlined above. Indeed, we can say with a fair degree of certainty that these various (and often contradictory) impressions were not formed on the basis of what was received directly from the senses. Rather, the impressions were the result of **perceptual inferences** dependent on a number of variables originating primarily from the observers rather than from the photograph.

What such an exercise very clearly points out is that in the area of person perception we are not content with simply seeing and noting the physical characteristics of others. Instead, we go beyond these obvious features and infer their underlying motives, interests, personality traits, psychological state, fears, social status, thoughts and so on.

As with object perception, we form an overall impression of others. In our attempts to organize our impressions of others into meaningful and unified wholes, we mix speculation and inference with direct data. More important than whether the impression that emerges is accurate or truthful, is our concern that it be unified and consistent.

Just as my students (and, most likely, you yourself) built up a unified – if unsubstantiated – impression of the man in the photograph, so is the same process re-enacted in our everyday interactions with others. When we meet someone, we invariably feel the need to find out the kind of person we are dealing with; the formation of an organized, coherent impression helps us know what to expect from a person, and how to act in that person's presence.

Person perception involves numerous cues which dictate the

impressions each of us forms of others and which, combined together, provide us with a total picture of the other person. Although the conclusions reached through such cues and our resulting behaviour are clearly of major significance, for the most part people remain largely ignorant of them and their fundamental role in determining social interactions.

A Summary of Psychological Research on the Perception of Others

The various means by which people form their impressions of others are a main focus of interest to researchers who engage in social psychological studies of person perception. Over the years, such studies have singled out a number of variables which play a key role in determining our impressions. Before we can engage in a phenomenologically oriented analysis of person perception, it is important to summarize briefly the major findings obtained by such research.

The Effects of Physical Appearance
As illustrated through the example of the photograph, a major determinant of our impression of others is formed from their **physical appearance**. This, not particularly surprising, conclusion is supported by a number of experimental studies (Middlebrook, 1980: 116–21). The typical procedure of these studies involves the presentation of photographs containing images of individuals whose physical appearance is varied. Subjects are then asked to rate the images on the basis of a number of traits such as attractiveness, intelligence and so forth. In this way, numerous aspects of physical appearance have been discovered to be remarkably consistent in their ability to influence our impressions.

For example, whether or not the person in the picture wears glasses leads to variations of judgement with regard to the person's intelligence, reliability and industriousness (Manz and Lueck, 1968). As absurd as it may initially sound, people *do* seem to view others through the influences of a variety of cultural stereotypes, so that the equation between the wearing of glasses and intelligence, for example, seems to bear some subjective (though, alas, no empirical) validity, at least among Western subjects.

Equally, the clothes that individuals are seen to be wearing can have significant effects on others' impressions of them. In one experimental study, for example, subjects reached major conclusions concerning a perceived person's personality, occupation, moral order, educational level and personal interests on the basis of clothing alone (Gibbins, 1969).

A third significant physical characteristic influencing our perception of others is the degree of attractiveness perceived in the individual. Studies such as those conducted by Dion (1972, 1977) demonstrate how we tend to assume the best about those we have deemed to be beautiful and the worst about those whom we have categorized as being unattractive.

Such conclusions are not limited to our perceptions of adults. Even nursery-school children considered to be physically unattractive are less liked by their classmates and are judged by their teachers as being more likely to misbehave (Dion, 1977). A related finding has gone so far as to demonstrate that an unacceptable act carried out by an attractive child is typically judged as being less naughty than the same act carried out by an unattractive child (Dion, 1972). And, similarly, Clifford and Walster (1973) demonstrated that teachers, too, are not impervious to such a variable: even when two children obtained the same grades on their monthly report cards, teachers assumed that the more attractive child was still more intelligent and predicted a greater likelihood of that child's going on to college!

When one adds the strong tendency towards self-fulfilling prophecies, the unfair power of the variable takes on unpleasant implications. One study, for example, reported that attractive defendants in criminal trials were likely to be seen as being less guilty and sentenced more leniently than were unattractive defendants (Sigall and Ostrove, 1975).

Numerous other variables in physical appearance such as the amount of body hair on males (Verinis and Roll, 1970) and women's hair colour (Lawson, 1971) have been shown to influence subjects' judgements on variables such as the degree of virility and potency in a male and the level of warmth, intelligence and dependability in women.

Similarly, physical handicaps tend to lead individuals to generalize further deficits in the handicapped such that, for example, people will frequently *shout* instructions to a blind person (Wright, 1960) and will tend to assume that handicapped individuals 'compensate' for their disabilities by striving especially hard in tasks which remain unaffected by their handicap (Ray, 1946).

Body weight is yet another physical variable that has been shown to influence our perception of others. In spite of the fact that obesity is often mainly dependent on genetic and biological factors, obese adolescent girls were judged, in one study, as being undisciplined and self-indulgent (DeJong, 1977).

Obviously, the more information we can glean about someone, the less will be the influence of variables relating to physical appearance. Nevertheless, physical appearance remains a potent factor throughout our perception of others. As studies such as the ones mentioned above easily demonstrate, when we have limited information available, or when we are unduly influenced by first impressions, our biases with regard to physical appearance allow us to arrive at subjective judgements about others which are often as influential as they are illogical.

The Effects of Facial Expressions, Names and Possessions

Along with the many studies carried out on the effects of physical appearance are related ones dealing with **facial expressions**. Such research has yielded some evidence to suggest that certain emotions (namely: anger, disgust, surprise, fear and happiness) may well form a 'common language of facial expression' (Middlebrook, 1980: 129).

Ekman and Friesen (1971), for example, showed photographs of Caucasian individuals to New Guinea tribesmen while reading stories with a specific emotional content to them. When asked to pick the photograph that most closely fitted the emotion of the story being narrated, the choices of the tribesmen correlated very closely to the photographs chosen by a control sample of American college students.

Nevertheless, nearly all studies in this area do not fail to acknowledge the great importance of cultural variations (Middlebrook, 1980: 129). So, for example, should you ever find yourself in Tibet, it would be useful for you to be aware that a Tibetan sticking his tongue out in your direction is not out to make trouble (or 'whoopee', come to that), but is merely greeting you as a friend (Ekman, 1975).

As well as facial expressions, social psychologists have noted several other major factors such as one's name (Marcus, 1976) and one's possessions or brand choices (Woodside, 1972) as further significant perceptual determinants.

Surprising as it may sound, there is statistical evidence available which demonstrates that males with culturally judged unusual names are more likely to suffer from neuroses and psychoses than are individuals with more usual-sounding names (Middlebrook, 1980: 122). There is also evidence to suggest that a person's level of popularity (especially so among children) is at least partly dependent on the desirability of one's name (Middlebrook, 1980: 122). And, to take the argument to an extreme, even the brand of beer that you drink can influence how favourably or unfavourably others might look upon you (Woodside, 1972)!

The Effects of Non-Verbal Behaviour and Voice-Related Variables

Studies have also demonstrated the influences of **non-verbal behaviour** upon our perception of others. The frequency of eye contact (Kleinke et al., 1975), a person's gestures (Neirenberg and Calero, 1971), posture (Mehrabian, 1968) and the extent of personal space that another person allows you (Davenport et al., 1971) are all variables which have been found, under experimental conditions, to affect our perception of others. In many everyday circumstances, it is likely that we employ such variables either to supplement or, in some cases, to override verbal statements.

In situations such as when we speak to strangers on telephones or when we hear announcers' voices on radios, we have the tendency to 'flesh them out' and, in so doing, construct all manner of (usually imaginary) physical and psychological characteristics. Experimental research backs up everyday experience. The speaker's *voice* – its pitch (Duncan, 1974), accent (Ryan and Carranza, 1975), depth (Allport and Cantrill, 1934) and loudness (Duncan and Niederehe, 1974) – has been shown to be a major factor affecting our perception of the speaker, regardless of the meaning of the words being spoken.

The Effects of Dispositional and Biasing Factors

Our **explanations** for others' words and deeds provide further variables which may determine our perception of others. For example, Tesser and his associates (1968) demonstrated that a friend's helpfulness may be attributed either to his or her generosity and concern for you, or to an attempt to get something he or she wants from you. The resulting emotions – pleasure and gratefulness in the first instance, resentment and hurt in the latter – may lead to quite different subsequent interactions. Equally, the consistency of a person's actions (Kelley and Stahelski, 1970) and the consensus of your perceptions with those of others (Wells and Harvey, 1971) have been shown to be determining features in our perception of others.

A whole gamut of variables dealing with **biasing factors** have also been examined by social psychologists for the purposes of seeing how such factors might influence person perception.

The fundamental attribution error, that is, our tendency to underestimate the importance of situational factors and to overestimate the perceived person's dispositional factors (Yandell and Insko, 1977), motivational biases arising from stereotypical preconceptions such as gender bias (Deaux and Emswiller, 1974), and actor–observer differences which arise out of our contrasting views of self and others in that we tend to see the behaviour of others as being a reflection of their character while our own is usually judged as being a reflection of our situation (Jones and Nisbett, 1972), all provide further evidence of the often unsuspected variables which help to shape our perceptions.

The Effects of Social Context and Setting

In addition, there exists a great deal of evidence relating our perception of others to the **social context or setting** where our perceptions are constructed.

In one study, a number of therapists (who are generally acknowledged as having great expertise in observing and interpreting the behaviour of others) were asked to view a videotaped interview session. Although all saw the same tape, some had been told that they would be watching a job interview while others were told that they were viewing a clinical interview. Their subsequent assessment of the interviewee's mental status differed markedly in that the therapists who thought they had been watching a clinical interview judged the person more harshly than their colleagues who thought they had just watched a job interview (Langer and Abelson, 1974).

Such studies point to the conclusion that if we are set to see a particular behaviour in someone else, we may act in any number of subtle ways to influence the enactment of expected behaviour in order to meet our presuppositions.

A study which demonstrates this conclusion was carried out by Snyder and Swann (1978). When their subjects interacted with people whom they expected to be hostile, those people actually began to behave in a hostile manner, whereas those subjects who had expected to interact with friendly people developed a cordial and co-operative relationship with them. This subtle (if influential) enactment of the perceivers' self-fulfilling prophecies points us directly to the perceiver – rather than the perceived – as significant agent for the perception of others.

Effects due to Projectional Variables

More generally, the **halo effect**, that is, the tendency to judge a person as being all good or all bad simply on the basis of one positive or negative characteristic (Thorndike, 1920), has been noted as being a particularly powerful influence on our perceptions precisely because it operates at a level below our consciousness. For example, Nisbett and Wilson (1977b) demonstrated that student subjects' overall reactions to a professor were likely to have been determined by a single personality factor. A professor's mannerisms were generally liked by those students who saw him as being warm or friendly. However, those same mannerisms were strongly disliked and judged as being irritating by those students who saw the professor as being cold and aloof.

One final biasing factor that has been studied is concerned with **implicit personality theories** that each of us develops and acts upon. Such theories are concerned with linking personality traits together in order to predict the presence of other characteristics.

As Schneider (1973) has shown, the basic function of such theories is to sort out the various strands of data that we have at our disposal about someone and reshape them into a meaningful – though not necessarily accurate – whole. This often stereotypical tendency tends to remain quite stable in helping us to formulate our perceptions of others (Passini and Norman, 1966).

Nevertheless, evidence strongly suggests that our evaluations of others are largely determined by the values and standards we set for ourselves. In one study, for example, those subjects who labelled themselves as 'achievement oriented' had a strong tendency to focus on achievement as a major factor in their evaluation of others (Cantor, 1976).

Once again, the implication that much of one's perception of others is confused with the perceiver's own personal biases, aspirations, anxieties and so forth seems beyond argument. Rather than objective analysis, our perceptions of others seem to involve, among other variables, distorting tendencies of projection.

The Effects of Central Traits

Solomon Asch, one of the major theoreticians of modern social psychology, has attempted to explain our tendency to create holistic impressions of others on the basis of what he has termed **central traits**. His research (1952) has demonstrated that such central traits as 'warmth' and 'coldness' exert a greater influence on our overall image than do various other traits.

What factors determine whether a trait is central or not is an unresolved issue in social psychology; whether traits like 'warmth' and 'coldness' causally determine our overall image (Asch, 1952) or whether they simply correlate with numerous other traits remains debatable.

The Effects of First Impressions

Asch has also pointed to the influence of **first impressions** on our interpretations of subsequent traits (Asch, 1952). Various researchers (such as Luchins, 1957) have obtained evidence to support the disproportionate importance given to first impressions.

Why first impressions should have such an influence on our perceptions remains unclear. A phenomenologist might suggest that they are certain to be important if one's approach to others does not follow the phenomenological method and, as a result, fails to bracket and 'democratize' immediate interpretational assumptions. This would suggest that the power of first impressions is not an invariant, but rather a tendency which may be controlled. After all, conflicting data demonstrate that not everyone is so easily swayed by first impressions; individual variations may be due to attitudinal approaches which rely wholly or partly, implicitly or explicitly, on the various 'steps' of the phenomenological method.

Effects of Interactive Variables

A major criticism of a great number of studies of person perception is that such studies are unrealistic, insofar as they are essentially **static** (Middlebrook, 1980: 147). Such criticisms point out the obvious: in real life, perceptions are **interactive**; in our interactions with someone, we are aware that just as we perceive that person, so, in turn, are we being perceived.

As such, our perceptions may be modified on the basis of the other person's reactions to us, and vice versa. Unfortunately for researchers in the field of person perception, the intrusion of these interactive factors in perception greatly complicates the issues and raises key questions on the limitations of 'static' theories and hypotheses. Such factors as image seeking (Goffman, 1967), reactive mechanisms (Merton, 1957), our assumptions as to how others see us (Hawley, 1971) and reciprocal perspectives (Laing et al., 1966), although likely to have major effects on the perception of others, are difficult to manipulate under the controlled conditions set by experimentally oriented research. As a consequence, in many studies, the issues are simply ignored.

Phenomenology and the Perception of Others

The above brief overview of some of the major research findings on person perception demonstrates the great extent of inter-subjective involvement in our perception of others. Our perceptions depend on a variety of physical cues, perceiver-based biases, attitudes, motivations, interactional factors and so forth. Together, they lead us towards a basic, if inescapable, conclusion that, far from being objective, our perceptions of others typically contain variables which more correctly define and describe psychological factors in the make-up of the perceiver rather than point out accurate, universally shared 'facts' about the perceived.

All of these findings, of course, strongly back up many of the central claims of phenomenology.

As with the perception of objects, our perception of others is not the simple response to actual 'stimuli' that activate our sensory awareness of the existence of others. Rather, as research indicates, our perceptions are principally formed from a wide variety of inter-subjective factors determined by cultural, personal and, quite possibly, biologically based variables. In essence, our perception of others results from **interpretational variables** which arise from both the noematic and noetic constituents of intentionality.

That there *are* others 'out there' (whatever they might actually be 'in themselves') is not disputed by phenomenologists; what *is* being stressed as requiring serious consideration, however, is what, how much and in what manner each of us *adds* to what is 'out there' in the process of perception. Clearly, as we have seen, non-phenomenological research has already exposed a large number of these interpretational variables.

Nevertheless, the vast majority of social psychologists, trained in empirically derived systems of research and heavily influenced by either cognitive or behavioural models of man, are likely to have little, if any, knowledge of phenomenology. In order for them to be tempted to consider the phenomenological implications inherent in their field of study, they must be convinced that such implications will add to and clarify central concerns. What, then, can phenomenological theory add to an understanding of person perception?

Firstly, research (summarized above) in the area of person perception demonstrates very clearly that a great deal of interpretation on the part of the perceiver *does* take place. What such studies fail to explain to any significant degree is both how and why such constructions occur at a psychological level.

It is true that there is a fair degree of knowledge at the neurobiological level with regard to the mechanics of perception; but such knowledge tells us little of how each of us arrives at the experience of our world. The gap between neuro-biology and psychology remains – in spite of the many and varied attempts to reduce psychological knowledge to that of biology.

Whether this gap may ever be closed remains debatable. As such, the current situation demands an approach which neither dismisses nor assumes this possibility. In its neutrality, in its search for the invariants of experience which, obviously, must contain biological features (though not necessarily *only* these), phenomenology represents a highly desirable option which can no longer remain unconsidered. In the area of person perception, phenomenology is able to supply us with a theoretical basis which opens itself to both neurological and psychological investigation and which allows for the derivation and testing of new hypotheses.

For example, research on *how* each of us constructs our perception of others immediately benefits from the phenomenological observation that the perceiver's past experience of others plays a major role in any current perception of another. Someone might well remind us, physically or behaviourally, of others or another in our past. Our view of this person will be influenced by such memories and, in turn, lead to biases of perception, be they positive or negative, which have direct bearing on our attitude and behaviour towards the person. Phenomenologists such as Merleau-Ponty (1962, 1964) have pointed to the (likely invariant) tendency we have as human beings to categorize new experiences in terms of their 'fitness' to past ones in order to give the new experience a 'meaning' which rationalizes our subsequent behaviour and attitudes towards it. Such a process clearly allows for learning to take place. Indeed, Piaget's notion of the development of more and more adequate 'schemes' deriving from the interlinked processes of accommodation and assimilation contains an abundance of similarities with this phenomenologically derived perspective. Similarly, the hidden (that is, unconscious) variables considered by psychoanalysts to play determining roles in our conscious interactions with, and perceptions of, others are said to be derived from our earliest experiences.

With regard to the perception of others, we should, therefore, expect to find that a person whom we meet (that is, interpret) for the first time obviously undergoes this 'fitting' process. It is likely that the strength of our 'first impressions' (as demonstrated by Asch and others) is at least partly derived from this same process. If so, it becomes more understandable why first impressions are and remain such strong determinants in person perception.

Nevertheless, as was pointed out earlier, the fact that the strength of first impressions *varies* between individuals, or even within the same individual at different points in time, demonstrates that a naive reliance on the explanatory power of 'past experience' further obfuscates our understanding.

Here again phenomenological theory provides us with potential resolutions which demand further research. For, as well as the effects of past experience, phenomenologists also point to the importance of the perceiver's **current affective state** in the perception of others. The psychological set or state that we are in at any given moment in time may well determine additional biases in our perception or, possibly, even determine which aspects of our past experience will take a major role in the process of construction being initiated.

Our willingness to be more open or closed, more sympathetic or antagonistic to the statements, behaviour and appearance of another is largely dependent upon our current mood. Dominated (and limited) as we may well be by past experience, there remains, nevertheless, a fair degree of flexibility as to the noematic and noetic aspects of the associations being formed and in the subsequent interpretations given to them. This flexibility in perception has not been adequately considered by other psychological systems, which have tended to approach person perception from a fixed standpoint either in terms of the static nature of the designed experiment or in the assumption that our perceptions of others remain (other than under exceptional circumstances) largely unchanged over time.

On the other hand, if, as phenomenological theory argues, our current mood is a significant influence, and our current mood is subject to continuous intentionally derived change, then each time we see the same individual, our perception of that person likewise will alter in some (often – though not necessarily – subtle) ways.

Even when our attitudes seem to remain relatively fixed or much the same as those adopted in the past, it would be naive to assume that this was due to the strength of past experience alone. Our current mood affects how we interpret the various elements that make up our past experiences.

Even the extreme fixedness of irrational beliefs over rational conclusions has been questioned by any number of therapeutic systems; among the most recent to explore this have been behaviourally derived cognitive approaches such as rational–emotive therapy (RET). As RET has shown (Ellis and Whiteley, 1979), beliefs *can* be changed and, in that change, contribute to an alteration of attitude, behaviour and perception.

Once again, we see that, in adopting the phenomenological position, we not only find confirmation of our conclusions from other approaches, we also are able to provide testable hypotheses to clarify the weaknesses and inconsistencies in such research and are better able to provide an adequate understanding of person perception.

If we theorize beliefs, attitudes and/or reactions to stimuli as being essentially fixed, unyielding to change other than by dramatic intervention, we can make no sense of data that point to such changes outside these hypothesized limits. It is only once we have grasped that, even within the limitations imposed by past experience, an interpretational flexibility, based upon current mood, still remains that we can make more sense of the data at our disposal.

But, as well as the influences of past experience and current mood, phenomenologists emphasize the importance of those variables related to our **future expectations** with regard to the person being perceived.

When we consciously perceive someone, that is, when we direct our attention towards someone, we reveal the workings of the selective mechanism that is the primary function of our brain. Out of the unlimited variables that bombard our sensory system and which are interpreted and analysed by our brain, only a minute number are selected to 'filter' into our conscious attention. This selection process is obviously not random; at its most basic, its purpose is to increase the likelihood of survival. But, in agreeing that the mechanism is purposive, then, at some level, each conscious perception must strive towards some desired outcome.

It is on the basis of this purposive element in perception that phenomenologists argue that in our perception of others such variables related to desired outcomes, or future expectations, must be present and must, in some ways, influence our perceptions.

At some level in our perception of another we must, in a sense, each be asking ourselves: 'What do I want from this person?' Though this may seem obvious when our perception is directed towards significant others such as our friends and family, it is important to note that, when duly considered, we can also find its presence in our perceptions of passing strangers. Even if all we may want is to ensure that the perceived person simply doesn't bump into us, we still reveal this expectancy variable.

Let me provide an example which, I believe, contains some commonly shared elements: at times, when I travel to work on the London Underground, I find my attention wandering to my fellow passengers. Upon consideration, I can realize that each perceived person points out a subjectively based 'want'. I may, for instance, want one person's newspaper, another's clothes, hairstyle or physique. I might want that person in a sexual sense, or I might require my perceptions of that person in order to convince myself that my life could be far less dreary than I assume it to be, or in order to be (somewhat masochistically) reminded of how dreary my life appears to me to be today. Whether my brain led me to perceive the individual in response to internal conflicts, boredom or the random movements of my eyes is open to argument; what remains, however, is that once the perceptual process has been initiated, the variable of 'future expectation' plays a role in influencing my perception.

As important as the variable may be to understanding person perception, studies of its influence are uncommon in the literature. What studies there are, unfortunately, usually contain the additional weakness of being static in construction. Interactive perception studies, as mentioned earlier, although clearly more 'naturalistic' in their attempts to study person perception, are notoriously difficult to assess and analyse.

That our perception of others can change in the course of a conversation is beyond doubt; what interests researchers is the discovery of those variables which may influence that change. Our future expectations of someone obviously can and do undergo change in the course of an interaction. Indeed, our future expectations may be a – or even *the* – central variable determining such changes. To my knowledge, interactive perception research focusing on this variable has never been carried out.

Phenomenologists argue that it is primarily through the above-stated variables of past experience, present mood and future expectations that each of us constructs our perception of others. In addition, such variables are always present on all perceptual occasions and, though limited and subject to individual variation as to their openness to re-evaluation and alteration, they are by no means 'fixed' to the point of stasis.

This argument does not deny the influence of sensory data in our constructed perception of others. 'Others', like 'objects', are clearly existentially independent of our inter-subjective constructions of them. However, like objects, what others *really are in themselves* remains unknown.

Clearly, our perception of others is so tied up with inter-subjective factors (both psychological and biological) that, in a perceptual sense, the very existence of perceived others is dependent upon the self-awareness of the perceiver. This is, of course, a reminder of the invariant feature of perception known as the figure/ground phenomenon. Others (the ground, or 'not I') can only exist in my perception once I've constructed a limit to my self (the figure, 'I'); if I saw everything as being 'self', there would, obviously, be no others. However, as paradoxical as it may seem at first, this position would also eliminate the existence of a perceived self.

Far from maintaining a solipsistic position (as has been wrongly argued by many humanistically derived theories: see Chapter 8 for my discussion of this topic), phenomenologists in general and, as we will see in Chapter 6, existential phenomenologists in particular, stress the interdependence of self and other. That self and others exist in a physical sense is accepted by phenomenologists, but our perception of each is a construction largely determined by subjective variables. Indeed, phenomenology does not even assume any ultimate (that is, physically real) separateness of self and other.

To repeat, our perceptions of others typically reveal more about our self as perceiver than provide us with objective data about the perceived other. No 'other' is, in any objective sense, ugly or attractive, full of wrath or love, male or female, sane or insane. All such perceptions are relational and intimately involve the perceiver. As such, each perceiver constructs a unique 'other'. Equally, as I've argued above, each perceiver constructs a unique 'other' *in each act of perception*; within the limitations of human experience, our perception of others undergoes continuous (if at times unaccepted or unnoticed) change.

This last point allows an insight of some therapeutic benefit. To use a simple example, consider a typical problem encountered by marriage guidance counsellors: What was once a stable relationship is now on the brink of self-destruction for no discernible reason other than that one of the partners has expressed a desire to change some aspect of his or her life. Whether it be something of seemingly small significance to the other partner such as a new hobby, a change of dietary habits or the altering of one's political affiliations, or whether it be related to desired changes to the relationship itself, say the wish to form separate friendships or to give expression to unmet sexual desires, the very threat of novelty and change is enough to raise doubts as to the viability of continuing with the relationship.

I have had to deal repeatedly with such situations in my own practice. Typically, the partner at the receiving end of the desired (or instituted) change claims that the other is no longer the same person that he or she has known for years, and why can't he or she go on being the person they used to be? Sadly, incomprehensibly, rather than show willingness to 'reinterpret' one's partner in a mutually satisfactory manner, the more drastic option of jettisoning the relationship is enacted.

In his book *The Art of Loving*, Erich Fromm (1956) addresses this issue from the perspective of what he labels neurotic and non-neurotic love. Put simply, his argument is that when most of us supposedly claim to love someone else, we are loving them in a possessive manner, much in the same way as we might love an owned object (neurotic love). In other words, we are not really loving the person, we are loving what we want them to *do for us* almost as if they were objects under our definitional and behavioural control. And so, when the person makes a claim at his or her independence by expressing a desire for novelty or change, this is experienced as threatening. It is as if the aggrieved partner is saying: 'I didn't sanction this, this isn't part of what I see for you, how *dare* you act in such a way that raises questions as to my control over you? Rather than question my assumptions – and hence my power – I'll discard you. Better to lose my partner than to lose the sense of self-importance I've taken to be as basis to all my interactions.'

Phenomenologically interpreted, neurotic love results when one assumes self to be hierarchically placed above (or below) other, or, to put it another way, when one loves one's self more (or less) than one loves others. Why such a situation should emerge in the first place remains an open question.

Existential phenomenologists, as we shall see, argue that the realization that there is no known 'fixedness' in others, nor even in our perception of others, leads us (both through this conclusion itself and in its even more seemingly dreadful implications) to experience an overwhelming anxiety. Faced with such, we deny our very awareness of our conclusion and seek to reassert our previous position.

It is as if, having seen the image of the headless robot in the hallway/pyramid figure discussed in Chapter 3, we seek to deny our apodictic re-viewing of it. The resulting stress created in the maintenance of this position has been categorized by other psychological approaches as symptomatic of 'neurotic' or 'psychotic' disturbance. As I'll argue in Chapter 7, phenomenologically influenced theorists such as Laing approach it from the stance of 'ontological insecurity' – the fragmentation of self.

To summarize the phenomenological argument concerning the perception of others, we can say that, in our everyday interactions with others, though it may appear initially, and naively, sensible for us to assume that we all perceive the same characteristics in others, both experimental data and our experiential analyses lead us to question this supposedly sensible conclusion.

Phenomenologists argue that, at heart, we perceive different appearances of reality, different phenomena. True, through any number of cultural, psychological and perhaps even biological variables, we learn to apply, if loosely, similar labels to the objects of our world through our language. So, certainly, there must be some common constructive processes or predispositions in humans that allow us to share, to some extent, the phenomenal world that each of us creates.

Nevertheless, our worlds remain separate and distinct. We can only know each other's worlds through communication of some variety; even then, however, our knowledge and perception of each other's experience of the world will remain far from complete. Nor can there be any hope of this situation ever changing. For, if, by some near-miraculous event, I could become you, experience the world exactly as you do, even then, in that act, 'I' would no longer retain what personal psychological variables I possess and employ since those variables would not be a part of you! I/you would experience the world from your perspective which could not be fully communicated to anyone else, myself included.

At best, our communications allow us to produce approximations of each other's experience of the world. While it is certainly the case, as I have attempted to demonstrate, that we can greatly improve the adequacy of our approximations, nevertheless approximations they remain. Our perception of others, once assumed to be fixed and certain – a shared and sharable perception – can now only be seen as a probability which remains dependent upon the quantity and quality of experiential information that has been communicated at any point in time.

In ending my discussion of the perception of others, I want to provide one final, and disturbing, case example to demonstrate how the development of different mental frameworks may lead to major differences in the perception of others. The incident was originally reported by Dr Oliver Sacks, in his book *The Man who Mistook his Wife for a Hat* (1985).

One day, while on his hospital round, Dr Sacks heard a roar of laughter emanating from the aphasia (speech disorder) ward. Curious, Dr Sacks looked into the ward and saw that the patients were watching a televised speech being given by the then President of the United States, Ronald Reagan. The speech was typical in its practised rhetoric, histrionics and appeals to patriotism and gut-level emotions. The patients loved it so much that they were convulsed with laughter. Jarred by their unexpected reaction, Dr Sacks soon realized that, although their aphasia left them incapable of making sense of the meaning of 'The Great Communicator's' words, the patients were taking their cues from the various tones and cadences of his voice and from the inadvertent gestures he made with his body. But, in their inability to understand his words, the patients (unlike the average listener) were able to avoid being beguiled by them. To them, the speech was grotesque, full of falsehood and incongruities, so patently a joke, that the only sensible reaction was laughter.

Here, in the example of the President's speech, we are confronted with the power of the various distortions, biases and misjudgements characteristic of our perception of others. In freely and unthinkingly allowing such to dominate our decisions and judgements of others, we open ourselves to misunderstanding and the carrying out of behaviour which often leads to unpleasant consequences. Worse than this, however, we also leave ourselves open to manipulation by (among others) those who, in making use of these distortions, might well become our political and religious leaders.

It seems that our perceptions of others are intricately and intimately bound up with our perceptions of ourselves. Perhaps, the better we come to know ourselves over time, the more able we become in 'bracketing' the self, as much as is humanly possible, from our perception of others. It is possible that, as infants, our perceptions of others were subject to fewer distortions and biases if only because both the range of experience and the development of self-awareness in early infancy were limited. However, the attempt on the part of adults to bracket out as much of their 'self' as possible from their perception of others would not necessarily return them to an 'infant's' view of the world. Precisely because adults *have had* a far greater number of experiences, *are* aware of themselves as beings distinct from others, and have *expectations* of others which, though quite possibly originating in their attempts to deal with infantile bodily demands, nevertheless are open to whole complexes of (symbolic) expression, suggests that their perception of others would have real and significant differences to that of the infant.

But, how well *do* we know ourselves? On that somewhat leading question, let us turn to the topic of self-perception.

5

The Perception of Self

I – I hardly know, Sir, just at present – at least I know who I was when I got up this morning, but I think I must have changed several times since then.

Alice, in response to the Caterpillar's question

As we have already seen, both the perception of objects and the perception of others are interpretationally derived constructions, which, based upon shifting combinations of variables, remain both unique and 'plastic'.

These conclusions lead us to a somewhat disturbing question: if the process discussed above is applicable to our construction of perceived objects and others, would the same process also hold with regard to any perceptions we might hold about our *self*? If so, this would suggest that the commonly held view that the self remains unitary, relatively stable, and 'fixed' over time is an illusion. Phenomenologically speaking, this suggests that we typically engage in a great deal of **selves-perception**.

Psychological Studies of 'the Self'

As a species, we are terribly interested in ourselves and our place in the world. On the one hand, we strive for a sense of our own uniqueness, wanting to be singled out for recognition, status and love. On the other hand, however, our sense of separateness sometimes gives rise to feelings of isolation and loneliness. Thus, our self-awareness reveals opposing aspects which are often a major source of conflict as to our social needs.

Just as such concerns have been the likely genesis to our greatest cultural achievements, they have also instilled a commonly assumed, rarely questioned bias dealing with the very nature of 'the self'. In the Western world, it is not unusual for individuals to claim, under certain conditions, that they have changed (or been changed). Alternatively, many people worry that they haven't changed sufficiently or at all, that they are 'still the same old person'.

Implicit in such claims lies the basic assumption that somewhere in each of us there resides a *core self*. The oft-asked question, 'Who am I?', becomes sensible to ask only if we assume that there is a basic core self which, for any number of reasons, is being kept hidden, or is failing to find its full and proper expression.

This assumption has dominated Western psychology and has formed the basis of virtually all studies on 'the self'. Indeed, the study of 'the self' has been a central concern of psychology from its earliest beginnings in philosophy right through to its modern-day, scientifically derived approaches (Middlebrook, 1980: 45–7). An important summary of psychological research on 'the self' noted the existence of over two thousand titles on the subject (Gordon and Gergen, 1968).

Psychologists interested in the basic nature and characteristics of 'the self' have typically attempted to measure the individual self concept scientifically, and to relate that concept to everyday behaviour. Yet, in spite of the large number of studies, the psychological understanding of 'the self', and its influence on behaviour, remains far from adequate.

In the early days of modern psychology, when its links with philosophy were still relatively strong and clear, 'the self' was an important theoretical concept. William James (1890), the most influential American psychologist of the late nineteenth and early twentieth centuries, extensively and insightfully attempted to analyse the *properties* of 'the self'. James's concern with 'the self' formed part of his broader concern with conscious experience in general, since, for him, it was the basic goal of psychology to both chart and examine its functions.

The psychological literature of the time focused on studies of conscious experience – including, of course, **self-consciousness**. Due to both the behaviourist and the psychoanalytic influences on psychology, such studies became, over time, increasingly less common; when they did begin to reappear around the latter half of this century, they tended to be written by adherents of the humanistic approaches in psychology and focused primarily upon issues of self-related growth, encounter and transcendence. Only relatively recently has the dominant (if still diffuse) trend in psychology – the cognitive approach – turned its attention to the issue of 'the self'.

The 'Components' and 'Characteristics' Approaches to 'the Self'

Some contemporary psychologists still approach 'the self', as William James once did, by examining its **components**. Typically, however, there is little agreement as to what these components are or which can be ranked as the more significant. For instance, components such as the 'social self', the 'psychological self', the 'ideal self' and so forth all have their adherents and detractors (Middlebrook, 1980: 47–50).

Due to the definitional limitations of the components approach, and to the growing recognition that people tend to think of their 'selves' not in such a segmented fashion but rather as 'a cohesive whole functioning as a single unit, and presenting a single image to those who view it at any given time' (Middlebrook, 1980: 50), several contemporary psychologists have refocused their attention away from the components of the self and on to its various **characteristics**.

Here, too, however, there have been unresolved difficulties both on the level of agreement as to which characteristics are central to a definition of 'the self' and, more importantly, with regard to inconsistencies *within* the defined characteristic. For example, if we consider a commonly held characteristic – that 'the self' is *the originator of its own behaviour* – we are presented with conflicting evidence as to the continuing belief in, or acceptance of, this characteristic in individuals (Middlebrook, 1980).

Under most circumstances, people like to 'own' their behaviour; the decisions we make are commonly seen as originating from within. Over and over again, psychological studies have demonstrated that restraints on subjects' perceived behavioural freedom are experienced as highly unpleasant and produce reassertive responses (Brehm, 1966). For example, in one task-oriented study based upon the assumption of this characteristic, housewives living in either Miami or Tampa, Florida, were asked to express their preferences for certain laundry products. Just prior to the start of the study, the Miami legislature had passed an anti-pollution ordinance which prohibited the sale or use of detergents which contained phosphates. In Tampa, however, this ordinance didn't exist. As had been predicted by the researchers, the Miami housewives, having had external decisions imposed upon them, expressed more positive attitudes towards the forbidden phosphate detergents than did the Tampa housewives (Mazis, 1975).

The results of such task-oriented studies lead to the conclusion that the greater the external pressure we feel being imposed upon us, the less attractive the forced activity becomes, the greater will be our emotional dissatisfaction, and the poorer will be our performance in the task (Middlebrook, 1980: 52). In general, these studies suggest that when we feel we have lost our right to make our own decisions, or are not originating our behaviour, we seek to regain this 'power'.

On the other hand, several important studies carried out by social psychologists provide results which suggest the opposite conclusion to the one above. Research carried out by Zimbardo et al. (1972) and Milgram (1974), among others, demonstrates that many people are willing to *deny* their role in decision-making, and do not feel themselves to be the originators of their behaviour, *when the results of such decisions are perceived as being unpleasant.* Under these circumstances, individuals tend to invent excuses which serve to reinforce their denial of any decision-making.

I will consider Milgram's and Zimbardo's studies more fully later in this chapter. For the moment, however, I merely wish to point out that such differing results lead us to question the constancy of this assumed characteristic of 'the self'.

These conflicting results go some way towards clarifying data obtained from studies dealing with the phenomenon known as **learned helplessness** (Seligman, 1974, 1975). Learned helplessness refers to the state certain individuals induce in themselves when feeling trapped in situations that provoke high levels of anxiety. Under such a condition, these individuals become convinced that no relationship exists between their behaviour and the unpleasant circumstance. Learned helplessness has been shown to weaken any motivation to alter or escape from the upsetting situation and to disrupt the individual's learning ability (Seligman, 1974). Under extremely stressful conditions, it can induce severe mental and/or physical illness and even death.

A study carried out in a nursing home in the Midwest of the United States demonstrates this all too well. The subjects in the study were fifty-five women (all aged sixty-five years and above, with an average age of eighty-two) who had all been recently admitted to the home. Seventeen of these women had applied to enter the home as a result of external family pressure and felt that they'd had no choice in the decision. Nearly all (sixteen) died within ten weeks of their admission. On the other hand, of the thirty-eight women who stated that they felt they had had a choice in the decision, only one had died during the same period. The trained staff in the home couldn't explain the differences on any medical grounds (Ferrare, 1962). However, it could be argued that the observed differences were due to differing stances taken with regard to the assumed characteristic of 'the self' as originator of one's behaviour.

Related research by Rotter (1966) theorized individual differences in beliefs concerning personal control on the basis of 'internal/external' dimensions. Certain individuals believe that there is a strong link between what they do and what happens to them (internals, or 'originators' of behaviour), while others deny or minimize this link and explain events on the basis of fate, luck or chance (externals, or 'non-originators' of behaviour).

In addition, the disparity in our self-awareness brought about by such variables as our shifting focus upon either internal or external variables (Duval and Wicklund, 1972) points to the influence of far more complex mechanisms as determinants of self-awareness.

On the basis of the conflicting data, a phenomenological critic might reinterpret these diverse findings as being indicative not of an assumed 'characteristic' of 'the self' but, rather, as evidence for the powerful influence of held beliefs (which are, themselves, open to constant revision) in self-perception. In other words, a phenomenological perspective leads us, once more, to acknowledge the power of the interpretational element in determining our self-concept.

Rather than clarify or enlighten our understanding of 'the self', the components and characteristics approaches adopted by some social psychologists turn out to be far from precise and reveal various internal inconsistencies within each which deny the possibility of allowing anything other than superficial and broad generalizations.

Interactionist Approaches to the Self

A far more satisfactory and useful approach to the study of 'the self' has been that employing an **interactionist model**. This view argues that our awareness of our self emerges as a result of a series of interactions that we undertake with others throughout our lives.

Virtually all contemporary theorists in this area agree that our self-concept results primarily from our attempts to compare and contrast ourselves to those who, in some way, matter to us. There have been various interactionist studies carried out which, though differing in their emphasis as to which interactive influences are the most significant, nevertheless have much in common with each other. There is general agreement that parents and family (Coopersmith, 1967; Wylie et al., 1979) and reference groups (Hyman, 1942; Mannheim, 1966) are central influences on the developing self-concept.

Interactionist approaches have been most productive when focusing on the motivations underlying social comparison. While a common motivation variable might be accuracy (Festinger, 1954), research has also indicated that attempts at self-aggrandizement (Jourard, 1964) – especially by those individuals whose self-esteem is particularly low (Jourard, 1964) – are equally important motivational variables.

Interesting as many current studies on 'the self' may be, the area remains somewhat fragmented. Is it possible that there exists a gap, or perhaps an unstated bias, in psychological attempts to understand 'the self' which has prevented a more adequate analysis?

The Phenomenological Notion of 'Multiple Selves'

If we initiate a phenomenological enquiry, we are immediately led to question a common (if rarely stated) assumption about 'the self'. This is the notion that there is a unitary core self which exists throughout each individual's life, and through which one can study components, characteristics, social determinants and so forth.

To the Western mind, this assumption seems to be so correct and obvious that any alternative argument appears to be distinctly dubious and unworthy of consideration. However, even within the area of social psychology, there are a number of theorists who have suggested that 'the self', far from being unitary, is, more accurately, *a series of selves*, each of which appears and interacts with its environment according to the circumstances that have arisen and whose function is to maximize approval from others (Sorokin, 1947; Harré and Secord, 1972).

Gergen (1971) has summarized a series of experiments which support the argument for 'multiple selves'. In one such study (Gergen and Wishnov, 1965), subjects were first required to rate their self-esteem. One month later, half of the subjects were given the task of describing themselves to partners whose manner and appearance characterized them as being highly egotistical, while the remaining half carried out the same task with 'humble' partners who confessed to several of their own weaknesses.

The analysed data showed that the partners' character influenced the subjects' self-ratings. Those subjects who had been paired with the egotistical partner rated themselves highly favourably while those paired with the humble partner were more self-critical. In order to assess the authenticity of these ratings (especially as there was some disparity with their original self-assessments), the subjects were then asked how honest and open they had been during the exchange. Over two-thirds of the subjects replied that they had been completely honest, and denied any divergence from their earlier assessments.

In attempting to make sense of these results, the investigators hypothesized that 'habitual and unconscious modes of relation to others' (Middlebrook, 1980: 51) caused the changes in self-esteem assessment. The evidence seemed to suggest that an 'individual is not a single self, but many selves, which change somewhat as the individual shifts from situation to situation. In short, we become what the situation demands' (Middlebrook, 1980: 51).

On the other hand, a critic of the 'multiple selves' argument might respond that, more plausibly, the subjects had lied, and that they had done so not out of any conscious desire to fool the experimenters, but because they, like most individuals, had a tendency habitually to deceive themselves.

Is it possible that the notions of 'self-deception' and 'several selves' might be reconciled?

The Phenomenology of Self-Deception

Psychoanalytic theory points out several mechanisms of distortion, denial and repression in everyday life (Freud, 1960). In addition, there exist numerous experimental studies which provide evidence for unacknowledged self-deception (Middlebrook, 1980). Such studies have tended to confirm the conclusion that, under most circumstances, we base our conclusions not upon accurate self-analysis, but, rather, from the biased standpoint of self-created theories we've developed concerning ourselves and our behaviour.

Phenomenologists would not hesitate to agree with such a conclusion and would point out that this was an inevitable result of the failure to follow the phenomenological method. At the same time, phenomenologists would point out that the findings obtained from self-deception studies are highly reminiscent of those reported in studies of post-hypnotic suggestion.

While hypnotized, a subject may be given a suggestion to carry out an unusual action at the appearance of a specific stimulus (Marcuse, 1959). Then, having been told to forget the instruction upon awakening, the subject emerges from the hypnotic state unaware of the instruction. At the appearance of the stimulus, however, the subject reacts in the instructed manner.

When subjects are asked to explain why they acted in the way that they did, they typically attempt to come up with the most reasonable and rational-sounding explanation for what is, quite often, highly irrational behaviour and, more, will stick to this argument until they are made aware of the true reason for their behaviour. For example, having to explain why she suddenly jumped out of her seat shouting 'Fire! Fire!' when no evidence of any fire is available, a post-hypnotic subject is likely to explain that she suddenly felt hot, or that she'd smelled smoke, and that she'd arrived at the wrong – though far from irrational – conclusion that led to her behaviour.

Taken in tandem with self-deception studies, the behaviour of post-hypnotic subjects points to the premise that there exists an invariant human tendency to create meaning from our experience. In both cases, subjects seek to make sense of their utterances and behaviour. That the chosen 'meanings' were false didn't truly matter; they had still served the basic purpose of relieving the tension and anxiety generated by the lack of explanation (that is, the meaninglessness) of their behaviour.

Indeed, in everyday life, when we find ourselves carrying out actions (usually of a highly charged or emotional nature) that, under ordinary circumstances, we would have prevented ourselves from carrying out, our typical answer to this behaviour is to say something along the lines of 'I don't know what came over me' or 'I just blanked out'.

These explanations seem to be suggesting that 'the self' who is usually in control *somehow temporarily lost control*, or was denied such, by another force of either internal or external origins. Such explanations once more point to the tendency that we have of thinking in terms of a basic core self, which, under most circumstances, remains in charge of awareness and both categorizes and unifies experience over time. This theory is so basic to our everyday thinking about ourselves that we hesitate to 'bracket' it.

But what might emerge were we to attempt to do so?

The Phenomenon of 'the Self'

Recall that, through the analysis of intentionality, as discussed in Chapter 2, Husserl was led to the phenomenological conclusion that the 'I' is the *result of*, and not the source or cause of, conscious experience. Straightforward experience leads to (limited and biased) reflective experience; it is only while reflecting upon experience that any conscious sense of 'I' (or 'the self') emerges.

This argument leads us to view the 'I' as being an impermanent construct. Each act of intentionality-based reflection, of necessity produces a new and unique interpretation of 'I'. In that act of reflective construction, we rely on both the external stimulus and the primary subjective variables of past experience, present mood and future expectation *as interpreted relative to the external stimulus*.

In other words, at each point of self-reflection, the self-concept that emerges is the result of the prior intentional act; but no one intentional act is entirely identical to any other since both the physical and perceptual variables will have altered on each occasion. As such, 'the self' that we interpret and believe in at any given moment in time is both temporary and, at best, a partial expression of an infinity of potential interpreted selves.

That each of us may be compelled to 'make up' a self-concept, perhaps as a result of yet another invariant in human experience, is not being disputed here. It may well be the case that the development and maintenance of a notion of 'I' is an innate property of human beings. Certainly, there are any number of good evolutionary reasons why this should be so. Phenomenologists do not question this assumption. What they *do* question, however, is the notion that the self-concept, once developed (at some indeterminate point in our existence), remains fairly fixed and permanent over time.

Is there any suitable evidence to back up the phenomenological stance on the self? I believe that there is. Three broad areas which might be usefully pursued are those of variations in proprioception, psychologically compelling situations and multiple personalities. I will briefly consider each separately.

Variations in Proprioception
Towards the end of the nineteenth century, Sherrington (1947) coined the term 'proprioception' in order to make plain the basic 'sense' through which each of us defines our relationship with our bodies. It is only through proprioception that we feel that our bodies are our property, that they in some way belong to us, and that they are therefore under our operation. This is such an automatic assumption on our part that any assumed alternative to this viewpoint seems inconceivable. And yet there exist numerous examples from medical literature that question this assumption.

In his book *The Body in Question*, which is itself based on a highly successful British television series, Jonathan Miller (1978) reports a number of such cases. Injuries suffered as a result of a stroke can sometimes wipe out recognition of either the whole body or, more commonly, of one side of the body, and thereby impair our sense of proprioception. To quote Dr Miller:

> If one half of the felt image is wiped out or injured, the patient ceases to recognize the affected part of his body. He finds it hard to locate sensations on that side, and although he feels the examiner's touch, he locates it as being on the undamaged side. He also loses his ability to make voluntary movements on the affected side, even if the limb is not actually paralysed. If you throw him a pair of gloves and ask him to put them on, he will glove one hand and leave the other bare, and yet he had use of the left hand in order to glove the right. The fact that he could see the ungloved hand, doesn't seem to help him, and there is no reason why it should: he can no longer reconcile what he sees with what he feels. That ungloved object lying on the left may look like a hand, but, since there is no felt image corresponding to it, why should he claim the unknown object is his?
> Naturally he is puzzled by the fact that this orphan limb is attached to him, but the loss of the felt image overwhelms that objection, and he may resort to elaborate fictions in order to explain the anomaly, fictions which are even more pronounced if the limb is also paralysed. He may claim, for example, that the nurses have stuck someone else's arm on while he wasn't looking; he may be outraged by the presence of a foreign limb in his bed,

and ask to have it removed; he may insist that it belongs to the doctor, or that prankish medical students have introduced it from the dissecting room; one patient insisted that his twin brother was attached to his back. (1978: 15–17)

A more detailed, and dramatic, account of total proprioceptive loss is given by Oliver Sacks in his book *The Man who Mistook his Wife for a Hat* (1985).

Just prior to an operation to remove the gall bladder, Christina, a twenty-seven-year-old woman, was placed on a routine antibiotic. Later that same day, Christina found herself no longer able to stand up unless she fixed her attention upon her feet. She also became incapable of holding anything in her hands (which seemed to take on a life independent of her own), and was unable to sit up without slumping. In sum, she had begun to lose all control over her own body. Her face now expressionless and slack, her jaw fallen open, her words slurred, she reported, with a dispassionate voice, that she felt herself to be disembodied.

Subsequent tests on her parietal lobe functioning revealed that, though undamaged, the lobes were not responding to bodily messages; she'd effectively lost her proprioceptive sense.

Christina now had the task of learning to compensate for this loss through her use of her sense of vision. Over time, Christina learned to recover some of her control over her body; visually monitoring her behaviour, allowing the time for the compensatory mechanism to replace the lost original, her body movements gradually became more natural, and she was discharged.

Even so, Christina continued to feel disembodied; her sense of proprioception never returned. Her ability to control and bring a 'naturalness' and fluidity to her movements remained dependent upon her use of vision. Even when she saw her 'old' self in home-movies, the recognition remained emotionally neutral; she could no longer affectively identify herself with the person she saw.

Just as confounding as the total or partial loss of proprioceptive sensation is the reverse of this phenomenon, best known as the 'phantom limb' effect.

It is a common experience for individuals who have lost a leg or an arm as a result of accident or surgery to report that they still 'feel' sensations in that now missing limb (Miller, 1978). Even the knowledge and acceptance of the fact that the limb has been severed from their body neither reduce their experience of 'phantom pains' nor prevent them from continuing to have a proprioceptive 'image' of the limb. Nor is such an image stationary: 'The phantom limb may seem to move, it may curl its toes, grip things, or feel its phantom nails sticking into its phantom palm' (Miller, 1978: 20). Over time, the phantom limb seems to recede, like a telescope, until only its extremities – the fingers or toes – somewhat disturbingly continue to make their unseen presence felt. This phenomenon suggests that 'it is as if the brain has rehearsed the image of the limb so well that it insists on preserving the impression of something that is no longer there' (Miller, 1978: 21).

The odd effects of proprioceptive impairment lead to the conclusion that the relationship between 'the self' and its physical body is by no means as straightforward as one might have assumed; rather, the relationship reveals the naivety of most theories of 'the self'. Once again, the phenomenological prediction of an elastic interpretational process in the self-concept seems borne out by research. Our image of our bodily self, therefore, is not a reflection of what is truly there, in a physical sense, but is, more accurately, the reflection of what we *believe* to be there.

This view is further borne out from studies carried out on individuals who suffer from anorexia nervosa. When tested under experimental conditions, it has been found that such individuals, although as capable as non-sufferers of describing and physically outlining the dimensions of a body other than their own, consistently overestimate the dimensions of their own body, perceiving it as being far greater in size than outsiders do (Hilgard et al., 1987). As a result of these distorted perceptions, their avoidance of food for dietary purposes makes sense to the anorexic, if to no one else.

Of related interest are those incidents where our notion of 'self' seems to extend beyond the limits of our bodies. Specific persons or objects can often become so closely associated with one's self that anything which happens or is done to them is experienced as though it were happening to one's self. As an everyday example of this, consider your reaction when your car bumper hits the bumper of another car. Typically, people tighten their teeth, assume a 'scrunched-up' posture, make statements like 'Ouch! I really felt that!', and so on. Regardless of logic, both their behaviour and their experience is indistinguishable from that arising from direct injury to their own bodies (Middlebrook, 1980).

When such data are pieced together and analysed, we are forced to conclude that the self-concept is, principally, a phenomenological construct whose boundaries are by no means defined or limited by the material extension of our bodies. We may reject parts of our bodies as not belonging to us, we may persist in 'owning' parts of our bodies that no longer exist, we may take objects or people that are clearly separate from our bodies and convince ourselves that they are inseparable from our sense of self, and we may have highly distorted perceptions of what our bodies look like. All these beliefs are *independent* of the actual physical boundaries and dimensions of our bodies.

The Phenomenology of Psychologically Compelling Situations

It is common for self-theorists to speak of psychologically compelling situations which may drastically alter an individual's self-concept. Sudden unexpected aversive changes in one's ordinary environment, such as finding oneself in the middle of a riot, or caught in an earthquake, or, alternatively, being suddenly imprisoned, kidnapped or brainwashed are said to be so psychologically confusing, or compelling, to certain individuals that they behave in a manner suggestive of a dramatic change in personality. It is as though, in psychologically compelling situations, such people cease being their usual, or normal, selves for a period of time.

One of the most important studies of this effect was carried out by Zimbardo and his associates in 1972 (Middlebrook, 1980: 66–8). In order that he might measure the psychological consequences of both imprisonment and the guardianship of prisoners, Zimbardo set up an experiment in which twenty-one North American male undergraduate students, previously tested to ensure their 'normality' via clinical interviews and personality questionnaires, were paid to become subjects in a simulated prison study.

Half of the subjects were randomly designated as prisoners, while the remaining half were assigned as guards. Although there were certain ethical limitations placed on the simulated prison environment constructed by the researchers, it included many significant similarities with real instances of imprisonment:

> The prisoners were unexpectedly picked up at their homes by a city policeman in a squad car, and taken to the station house where they were searched, handcuffed, fingerprinted, and booked, and then taken blindfolded to the simulated jail. There they were stripped, issued a uniform, given a number, and put into a six by nine foot barred cell with two other convicts. There were no windows in the cells, and the prisoners could be continuously observed by the guards. Toilet facilities without showers were in a nearby corridor. After ten o'clock at night, all toilet privileges were denied, so that the prisoners had to use buckets if they wished to relieve themselves. No clocks or any other personal effects were permitted. To perform routine activities such as writing a letter, or smoking a cigarette, the prisoners were required to get permission from the guards. . . .
>
> The setting was highly realistic for the guards, too. They were given billy

clubs, whistles, handcuffs and the keys to the cells – all symbols of their power. They were told that they should maintain 'law and order' and that they would be responsible for any difficulties that might develop. Sixteen prison rules, including one that prisoners must address each other by their ID number only', were provided, and the guards were told to enforce these to the letter. (Middlebrook, 1980: 67)

Significant changes in the behaviour, thought processes and emotional reactions of the majority of the subjects were noted within a week of the study's initiation. Many of the prisoners had already become 'servile, dehumanized robots who thought only of escape, of their individual survival, and of their mounting hatred of the guards' (Zimbardo et al., 1972: 3). Similarly, the guards began to abuse their power over the prisoners. They invented petty, meaningless and rarely consistent rules which they insisted the prisoners follow.

For instance, they required the prisoners to engage in tedious and useless work (such as moving cartons back and forth or picking thorns out of their blankets) for long periods of the day and night; they made the prisoners sing songs, or laugh, or refrain from smiling, on command; they encouraged the prisoners to curse and vilify each other publicly. Almost any indignity became acceptable as far as the guards were concerned. As one of them subsequently wrote:

> I was surprised at myself, I made them call each other names and clean the toilets out with their bare hands. I practically considered the prisoners cattle. I kept thinking 'I have to watch out for them in case they try something.' (Zimbardo et al., 1972: 9)

What had originally been intended as a two-week experiment had to be stopped after only six days: four of the prisoners had had to be released because of strong signs of either severe emotional depression or acute anxiety attacks; one other prisoner was taken out of the study when he developed a psychosomatic rash over his entire body; some of the guards showed increasingly brutal behaviour.

In order to explain these disturbing findings, Zimbardo and his associates argued that the changes were due to the demands of the psychologically compelling situation; the persistent role-enactment temporarily created different beings.

An even more famous series of studies which, although not usually examined from the standpoint of 'psychologically compelling situations', nevertheless bears all the central characteristic features of such studies, was that carried out by Stanley Milgram on the issue of 'obedience to authority' (Milgram, 1974).

In Milgram's core experiment (he carried out fifteen related studies in all, some with procedural modifications) volunteer adult subjects answering an advertisement were asked to be 'the teacher' in a task which purported to measure the effects of punishment on learning. The experimenter led each teacher to a large box of electronic equipment containing thirty switches marked in fifteen-volt intervals going up to a maximum of 450 volts. Above the switches were descriptions of the intensity of the shock each would deliver; these ranged from statements such as SLIGHT SHOCK to those warning DANGER – SEVERE SHOCK.

The teacher was instructed to read a series of questions, one at a time, to another subject (who, unknown to the teacher, was actually working in collusion with Milgram's experimental team) who was designated 'the learner' in the study. Each time the learner gave the wrong answer to the teacher's question, or, alternatively, failed to give any verbal response, he was to be punished with an electric shock by the teacher. The intensity of the shock was increased for any subsequent mistake by moving along the line of switches and continuing until the final (450 volt) shock was to be administered.

The teacher saw the learner being strapped into place and having various electrodes connected to parts of his body. Then he was led to his seat behind the shock switches and the experiment began. The experimenter stood beside the teacher throughout the experimental run; if the teacher refused to continue, he would remind the teacher what his instructions were and tell him to go on with the experiment.

Of the forty subjects tested in the first study, wherein the learner was in another room and remained unseen and unheard (save his pounding on walls as protest at the 300 volt level) twenty-six subjects (65 per cent) obeyed instructions until the completion of the run. In a second experiment where forty subjects heard vocal protests from the learner, twenty-five (62.5 per cent) obeyed instructions until the completion of the run. In a third study where forty subjects remained in the same room and only a few feet away from the learner who gave obvious verbal and bodily cues to his increasing distress, sixteen subjects (40 per cent) obeyed instructions until the completion of the run. In a fourth variation, where subjects were ordered physically to place the learner's hand on a shock plate, twelve out of forty subjects (30 per cent) obeyed instructions until the completion of the run. In a fifth study, where the learner began to express his concern over his heart condition and made loud, anguished, verbal protests, twenty-six out of forty subjects (65 per cent) obeyed instructions until the completion of the run. (Interestingly, only seven of these subjects expressed their willingness to sample the shock that they doled out.)

Since all the subjects in the above studies had been males, a further study was carried out (following similar conditions to those of the second experiment) with female subjects; of the forty female subjects tested, twenty-six (65 per cent) obeyed instructions until the completion of the run.

Certain variations, however, provided quite different data. In one study (Experiment 7), the experimenter left the lab and monitored the study by telephone. Under this condition, only nine out of forty subjects (22.5 per cent) obeyed instructions until completion of the run and subjects tended to administer shocks of lower voltage than was required. Under another variation (Experiment 11), when subjects were free to choose their own shock level, only two out of forty (5 per cent) went beyond 150 volts. And in yet another (Experiment 12), where the learner insisted on being shocked but the experimenter forbade the action, all twenty of the subjects (100 per cent) obeyed the experimenter. In an extension of this last study (Experiment 15), when there were two experimenters present and each gave contradictory orders to the subject, all the subjects stopped giving shocks at an early point in the study and made attempts to guess which experimenter had the higher authority.

When interviewed after the completion of the experiment, subjects often attempted to justify their conduct by blaming the learner for his own stupidity, or by arguing that the learner knew the conditions of the study and therefore was responsible for the punishment, or that, commonly, they were simply obeying the experimenter's orders, and that he held ultimate responsibility. Many subjects resorted to the explanation that they simply *had to* follow orders.

As Milgram suggests, subjects saw their actions as having an external origin. 'Subjects in the experiment frequently said, "If it were up to me, I would not have administered shocks to the learner"' (Milgram, 1974: 146).

There are significant similarities in subject responses in both Zimbardo's and Milgram's studies. In both cases, the psychologically compelling situation seemed dramatic enough to alter the subjects' ordinary behaviour such that, explicitly or implicitly, it no longer fitted in with their view of their 'ordinary' selves. But if, as is generally claimed, 'the self' maintains a relatively stable and permanent core of characteristic attitudes and behaviours, how *could* individuals act in the way that they did?

The explanation given by invocation of the term 'psychologically compelling situation' leaves us with more questions than it answers. Why is a situation psychologically compelling to one individual and not to another? Why are there marked variations in the behaviour of different individuals under these conditions? Indeed, in real-life cases, it is often difficult to find anything unusual or compelling in the immediate situation that has triggered off an extreme response such as an uncontrolled killing-spree.

It is our assumption that there is a core self which leads us to search for compelling events. That these are not easy to find should be enough to have us question the validity of this assumption.

If we approach the issue from the phenomenological standpoint, we realize that since 'the self' is dependent upon intentionality-based conditions, it will be undergoing continuous change while still appearing to be stable at any given point in time. As such, the behaviour of the Zimbardo of Milgram subjects does not reveal an aberrant self, nor an unusual strand in the core self of the individual, but rather points out the behaviour of a self which emerged dependent upon the situation it found itself in – just as 'the self' does all the time – regardless of the relative 'intensity' of the situation.

Studies of psychologically compelling situations reveal obvious changes in 'the self', not because these changes are unusual, but because they are so extreme. Under everyday conditions, such changes are less discernible. In our obedience to inadequate theories about 'the self', we construct pseudo-explanations that support the theory but obscure what may well be a more adequate conclusion.

The Phenomenology of Multiple Personalities

The multiple personality refers to an avowedly pathological condition in which two or more personalities, or 'selves', appear to manifest themselves in one human being (Schreiber, 1973; Crabtree, 1985).

The 'classic' examples of multiple personalities are all relatively modern. The first such case to be publicly recorded, that of Mary Reynolds, was written up 1816 as a case of an alternating, or dual, personality thought to be related to a state of 'double consciousness' brought about by somnambulism (Crabtree, 1985).

However, it was the success of the book (and subsequent film) *The Three Faces of Eve*, which was based on an article that appeared in the *Journal of Abnormal Psychology* under the title 'A Case of Multiple Personality' written by C. H. Thigpen and H. Cleckley, that introduced most psychiatrists and lay-persons to the idea of the multiple personality (Crabtree, 1985).

Briefly, the subject, Eve White, a shy, inhibited and unhappy woman in her early twenties exhibited dramatic behavioural changes from time to time which led to the establishment of an alternative personality – Eve Black – who dressed in sexy clothes, used 'bad language' frequently, drank liberal quantities of alcohol, and behaved in a generally uninhibited manner. The doctors and nurses who examined her even noted that she appeared to be more attractive, and that her posture and mannerisms changed markedly when she believed herself to be Eve Black.

More surprising, although Eve White had no notion of the existence or thoughts of Eve Black, Eve Black retained knowledge of Eve White's thoughts and problems. Eve White suffered from 'black outs' (pun intended) whereupon she would eventually awaken with no memory of what she'd done or where she'd been but suffering from the effects of Eve Black's 'wild' behaviour. The analysts treating Eve saw their task as that of 'fusing together' the two personalities.

That they fully succeeded (with the assistance of a third personality in Eve – 'Jane') is disputable; in 1977, Eve herself published her account of the story claiming the existence of twenty-two different personalities which required further extensive therapy before being 'merged' into the far more flexible and self-accepting 'new' Eve (Sizemore and Pittillo, 1977).

More recently, the cases of Sybil (Schreiber, 1973) and of Billy Milligan (Keyes, 1981), among others, have provided even more startling accounts of multiple personalities.

There are distinct similarities in all of these reported cases, most notably the core personality's complete lack of awareness of the existence and thoughts of the others; the existence of an 'overseeing' personality who has knowledge (and some control) over all the various personalities; and the 'representational' role of each personality as the embodiment of attitudes or behaviours that are prohibited by the core personality.

The early life of people like Eve, Sybil and Billy appears to be a significant factor in the development of their multiple personalities. Such individuals tend to have been reared in particularly violent, severely punitive settings. The parents of multiple personality individuals often hold strict moral codes which they impose upon their children via forms of severe punishment. It is possible that the genesis of the multiple personality lies in the child's attempts to deal with, satisfy and defend against parental demands and behaviour which bring on intolerable anxiety and guilt (Schreiber, 1973).

Although the phenomenon of multiple personalities has been generally accepted as authentic (through the administration of standardized psychological tests and the analysis of differing EEGs of the various personalities), its explanation remains widely open to debate and interpretation. Analyses, or 'explanations', range from possession by demonic entities (Crabtree, 1985) to unconscious defence mechanisms (Schreiber, 1973; Keyes, 1981).

Although by no means a common clinical phenomenon, multiple personalities can be seen as somewhat extreme case examples of the phenomenological position with regard to 'the self'. Commonly, the patients' memories of their violent and severely punitive early up-bringing, as evoked while in therapy, contain the shared insight that a decision of sorts was made with regard to feelings and desires that were both inexplicable and anxiety-provoking. Not being able to come to terms with such, the patients attempted to 'split' them off, deny them as part of their own complex of affects, and thereby severely limit their range of 'allowable' thoughts, feelings and behaviours.

In an attempt to deal with their unacceptable desires and feelings, and yet avoid the guilt each evoked, the extreme strategy of creating alternative personalities was put into operation.

Each of these personalities allowed the expression of the forbidden thoughts or desires and, at the same time, eliminated the guilt associated with each since it was now someone else – and more, someone that the patients did not even have any awareness of – who expressed each of these desires to the point of making them his/her own and, under extreme conditions, becoming their living embodiment.

Phenomenologically, the other personalities reflected the various selves which resulted from intentionality, *but* these emergent selves did not fit the extremely limited range of 'acceptable selves' that had been set by the patients' self-image. Faced, nevertheless, with the appearance of 'unacceptable selves', the patients were led to 'create' alternative personalities which fitted these selves, and then, conveniently, blocked all memory of their existence from the emergent selves that fitted the restricted range of allowable experiences. All the other personalities were allowed to remain aware of the existence of the others since they were not restricted to the same limited range of allowable thoughts and behaviours.

It was this flexibility that allowed the various therapists to assist their patients in 'merging' various alternative personalities prior to attempting to reunite all of the personalities together. When the patient learned to accept previously forbidden thoughts or desires, and when the range of possibilities in being was allowed to be broadened, the alternative personalities were no longer required. In consciously accepting these multiple selves and allowing them expression without resorting to losses of memory, the patients became 'whole' once more.

Is this so different from ordinary experience? Is it not the case that, when forced to acknowledge thoughts or actions which run counter to our theories about our self, we typically evoke external agencies – be they human, circumstantial, chemical or demonic – which *compel* us to act in such ways? And do we not also, if necessary as a defence, claim and create memory lapses which both alleviate feelings of guilt and allow the maintenance of restricted views of our selves? The sole difference between 'ordinary' individuals and 'multiple personality' individuals seems to lie in the *frequency* of such claims.

From this phenomenological perspective, we are *all* 'multiple personalities'. We continually construct and reconstruct our selves. As long as the current constructed self falls within the range of possibilities that holds true to our self-concept, we can acknowledge ownership. But when we think or act beyond this sedimented range of possibilities, we construct meaningful – if phenomenologically absurd – explanations to make sense of the thoughts or behaviour *and* either reduce or remove the anxieties that such thoughts or behaviours generate.

The Fiction of the Self

The separate issues of variations in proprioception, psychologically compelling situations and the cases of multiple personalities all suggest that deeply ingrained Western assumptions concerning 'the self' obscure and confuse, rather than clarify, our attempts to understand its origin and basis.

Although the areas discussed above do not, by any means, provide direct evidence in favour of the phenomenological position, I hope that my discussion has demonstrated the value of pursuing a phenomenological line of enquiry with these issues. Indeed, such pursuits pave the way for novel and enlightening approaches to many other areas related to 'self' studies, such as that whole complex of 'self-related' phenomena dealing with mind-manipulation, brainwashing, conversion and possession. I hope to focus on these in a future text.

For the moment, however I hope that my discussion – however limited – has stimulated readers enough to bracket at least temporarily their assumptions about the exclusivity of a singular and permanent self.

Part of the difficulty in presenting this phenomenological view of 'the self' lies in our very language. So sedimented is our stance and conviction as to the existence of a unitary core self that any alternative to this view is difficult to express in words – to speak of 'self-creating selves' *sounds* like patent nonsense.

Nevertheless, other cultural systems have developed languages which avoid this problem. Many Eastern approaches, most notably some schools of Buddhism, support an alternative perspective which argues for the impermanent and transient nature of 'the self' (Benoit, 1955; Watts, 1957). This does not mean, of course, that phenomenology and some branches of Eastern philosophies are one and the same thing; only that they have arrived at certain similar and specific conclusions about aspects of existence. A phenomenological perspective simply seeks to point out that although 'the self', as a product of intentionality, undergoes continuous alteration throughout life, at each point of self-analysis or 'meaning production' it *appears to us* as having stability and permanence.

In considering the adoption of this phenomenologically derived view of 'the self', we confront a major dilemma. As the British philosopher Hume once wrote: 'I venture to affirm . . . that [we] are nothing but a bundle or collection of different sensations, succeeding one another with inconceivable rapidity, and in a perpetual flux and movement' (Sacks, 1985: 119). Personal identity, he argued, was a fiction. But how does such a fiction originate? The phenomenological 'I' undergoes constant reconstruction. In our reflections upon straightforward experiences, we require the 'I' to bring order and meaning to our perceived world. The constancy of the 'I' is an illusion; the 'I' that defined who I was when I began to write this book no longer exists, not because *it* has changed, but because the intentional variables which give rise to the construction of 'I' have changed.

As I argued earlier, an invariant of human perception is that process known as the figure/ground phenomenon. This invariance leads us to the recognition that, in order for an individual to assign any descriptive features to the self (the figure), some acknowledgement of, comparison with and distinction from others (the ground) is required.

Stated more phenomenologically, the 'I' defines itself through its interactions with 'not I'. As such, the process of conscious self-definition bears striking similarity to our perception of ambiguous figures. The shifting of the figure/ground in such figures produces quite different perceptual phenomena. Equally, the less sedimented we are in what we allow ourselves to perceive, the greater will be the number of valid interpretations of the ambiguous figure. The more flexible we are with our meaning-constructions, the more adequate will be our knowledge of that figure.

If we conceive of 'the self', or 'I', as yet another example of an ambiguous figure, we become readily aware of the fact that it, too, is open to a multitude of meaningful interpretations. Whatever limits may have been set on its definition are not inherent in the 'I' itself, but in the strictures of sedimentation. The more willing we are to bracket our sedimented beliefs and theories about our selves, the more adequate (if, nevertheless, still incomplete) will be our knowledge of who we are – and can be.

The Problem with Memory

In spite of the potential value to our understanding of the self that the phenomenological approach offers, we are left with one crucial issue which, at first, seems to raise major logical obstacles to the argument. That issue is, of course, the role played by **memory** in the self-concept.

A critic of the phenomenological view I've put forward might well argue that our notion of 'the self' is tied up with one's remembered past. If I have no memory of who I have been, I can say very little about who I am today. This would suggest a continuation of self over time rather than, as is being proposed, a continual reinterpretation. If so, then there must indeed be a core self which remembers, which acts upon those memories, and which defines itself through them.

This is a valid criticism, requiring a suitable response. To give this, however, I must make a brief excursion into the problematic area of memory.

The study of memory, one of the earliest and most widely studied subject areas of modern experimental psychology, has remained popular to this day. Most contemporary theorists of memory are convinced that human memory consists of three central systems: sensory, short-term and long-term memory. Such theorists typically adopt an information-processing approach to the topic, and focus their studies on the encoding of information, its storage into the memory system, and its recall or retrieval (Gregory, 1981).

It is generally agreed by such theorists that although the brain's capacity to store memory is very large, the duration of most memories is very brief; it has been suggested, for instance, that memory can start to decay after only one-tenth of a second, and can completely disappear after one second (Crider et al., 1986). The basis for such conclusions rests on the substantial amount of data obtained in a wide variety of experimental studies which typically measure subjects' ability to recall stimuli such as rows of letters (Sperling, 1960) or, more classically, nonsense syllables (Ebbinghaus, 1964).

Nevertheless, several critics have pointed out that the data obtained in these studies, though they certainly reveal that human memory may encounter problems when it attempts to *recall* information, need not lead us to conclude (as many researchers have) that memory *storage* is temporary. For all we can say, the storage of memory is permanent and faultless, but our ability to get at the stored data may vary.

In addition, if our ability to recall stored data should in some way correspond to its meaningfulness or significance (a not surprising correlation) then it is little wonder that typical memory experiments, based as they are on insignificant or meaningless stimuli, should provide us with the kind of data that they do obtain.

Furthermore, as one of the great researchers on memory, Sir Frederick Bartlett (1932), demonstrated, it is both false and misleading to conceive of memory as being primarily concerned with the *exact reproduction* of material. Once again, however, this is exactly what most studies on memory ask subjects to achieve. As such, the results obtained by a great number of 'recall' studies may merely be demonstrating, again and again ad nauseam, the accuracy of Bartlett's hypothesis.

An alternative to this dominant view of memory storage was suggested by Bergson (1911), among others, in the early part of this century. Bergson argued that memory storage was permanent to the extent that each of us is potentially capable of remembering all that has happened in our life, regardless of its significance. It was Bergson who first pointed out that the primary function of the brain was to filter incoming stimuli so as to protect our consciousness from being overwhelmed by a constant barrage of information. Were the brain not capable of this feat, our lives would be both chaotic and unbearable.

The brain seems to order incoming data into hierarchies of importance. Just like the phenomenological notions of straightforward and reflective experience, most data entering the brain remain at levels below our consciousness – we remain unaware of them – with only a small fraction of all the incoming data being consciously experienced. Even so, there is no necessary reason to suppose, as do many psychological theories of memory, that the remaining data go unstored and 'disappear'. Since storage capacity appears to be no problem, it makes little evolutionary (if not logical) sense to suppose that the data will be 'thrown out'.

Is there, however, any evidence in favour of this alternative position? Certainly, one could point to any number of reported psychoanalytic case studies in which, either by hypnosis or by free associations, patients have recovered long-forgotten (repressed or suppressed) memories which commonly originate from the patients' infancy and early childhood. However, it could be argued that, even if these memories are subconscious or unconscious, they are still meaningfully significant to the patients and, hence, they (as opposed to insignificant memories) have been retained in their storage system.

Is there, then, any evidence to suggest that we are capable of remembering *insignificant* memories on a long-term basis? One important experimental study which strongly suggests this possibility was carried out by Haber (1970). Haber presented a total of 2560 photographic slides showing a range of images to a group of volunteer subjects. Each individual slide remained on screen for a total of ten seconds before being replaced by the next. Each session with subjects lasted either two or four hours in all. After having seen each of the slides, the subjects were shown 280 picture-pairs, one of which had been seen in the slide show, the other being similar in nature but previously unseen. The subjects were asked to state which of the picture-pairs were familiar to them. Nearly all subjects gave the correct response nine times out of ten. In addition, the length of the slide demonstration did not produce significantly different scoring results. Even when Haber showed the familiar pictures in reverse, scores declined only slightly.

Haber's study places the adherents of short-term memory theories in a quandary. Not only were the subjects able to remember large numbers of briefly observed images over a fairly lengthy period of time, the images contained nothing of any obvious or intended personal significance to them. Even so, they were recognized accurately nearly all of the time.

In order to explain these odd results, Haber himself argued for the possibility that there is a distinction between linguistic memory and pictorial memory. Perhaps so; but recognition is not merely visual, it can be acoustic, olfactory and so on. The complexity of a system which can distinguish between all these inputs and store them and yet remain resistant to the storage of linguistic inputs seems unnecessarily burdensome and unwieldy in comparison to the system that simply stores all inputs.

Similarly, we can turn to evidence supplied by research dealing with exceptional instances of the ability to recall rote memories. Studies reported by the great Russian psychologist, A. R. Luria (1969), for instance, provide, at times mind-boggling, evidence of some individuals' almost limitless ability to demonstrate near-perfect recall.

One of Luria's subjects, for instance, could recall which suit Luria had worn at the time of his earliest experiments with him – experiments carried out some thirty years in the past! If this subject, like many others who have been studied, had memory-related problems, they had to do not with recall ability, but with forgetting. Anything which remained fixed and unchanged over time, such as word-lists and suits, could be forgotten by him only if he carried out rituals of forgetting. Interestingly, however, more ambiguous, changing items, such as people's faces, however, were difficult for him to recognize or recall.

This suggests that the subject's memory dysfunctions were related to unusual limitations in his ability to understand, or give meaning to, his memories, not to problems of storage. This dysfunction may well be the explanation for the amazing feats of memory that many so-called *idiot savants* are capable of. The ability to state accurately, for example, what day 10 February 1849 fell on relies on relatively simple levels of understanding which depend on a form of 'rote' memory rather than symbolic meanings.

Similarly, there is some suggestive evidence that eidetic imagery ('photographic memory') may be a precursor to, or early form of, human memory proper, since evidence for this ability seems strongest with subjects in the first few years of their lives but declines as the subjects become chronologically older (and, by implication, add to their intellectual abilities) (Haber, 1969).

The ordinary individual's problems with rote memory, therefore, may have nothing to do with the process of memory storage but, rather, derive from a growing reliance upon active interpretations of input rather than upon passive recall. Put in this light, the intriguing findings reported by Wilder Penfield in his book *Speech and Brain Mechanisms* (Penfield and Perot, 1963) become extremely significant.

Penfield's subjects were, in fact, patients of his who were undergoing brain surgery which, in most cases, was being carried out to eliminate the debilitating attacks, and subsequent suffering, of epilepsy. The patients' temporal lobes were electrically stimulated with micro-electrodes. Conscious throughout the operation, these patients would suddenly report that they had just experienced a multi-sensory 'flashback' of a single event from their past. All insisted that the experience was ineffable in its vividness and fullness of sensory data.

This experiential response seemed to be made up of 'a random reproduction of whatever composed the stream of consciousness during some interval of the patient's past life' (Penfield and Perot, 1963: 687). Yet, powerful as the experience of 'reliving' one's moments of past time was, the incidents recalled were rarely loaded with strong affective meaning or significance.

The localization of these memories was specific. Stimulation of a certain point of the temporal lobe always evoked exactly the same memory in a complete form; but it was only that one memory and no other. In many cases, these memories had a musical component to them: orchestras, choirs, piano pieces, even radio-show theme songs were heard over and over again, and always as exact reproductions of each other.

On the basis of these reports, Penfield concluded that 'the brain retained an almost perfect record of every lifetime's experience, that the total stream of consciousness was preserved in the brain, and, as such, could always be evoked or called forth, whether by the ordinary needs and circumstances of life, or the extraordinary circumstances of an epileptic or electrical stimulation' (Sacks, 1985: 130–1).

A recurrent criticism of Penfield's conclusions (principally by researchers committed to short-term memory, of course) has been that one can never be certain that these memories are true and not made-up fantasies. This is a valid point so long as there are no examples of instances which can be checked for their historical reliability. Close reading of Penfield's text, however, reveals a number of specific instances where patients' memories were anything but fantasy.

In one particularly disturbing example, a twelve-year-old female patient saw herself frantically running away from a man who pursued her while carrying a bag full of writhing snakes and whose intentions, she perceived, were clearly murderous. Although this might initially read like a classic example of Freudian symbolism, the experience was found to have been a precise replay of an actual event which had occurred some five years earlier (Sacks, 1985).

Further independent evidence for Penfield's conclusions is recounted by Sacks (1985), who reports the case of a male patient who had previously killed his girlfriend while under the influence of a powerful narcotic (PCP). This man had no conscious memory of this experience, nor could it be evoked through hypnosis or sodium amytal. During his trial, in fact, doctors attested that the loss of memory was not due to repression, but, rather, was the result of organic amnesia brought on by the drug. In addition, although the murder held a number of macabre details, they were left concealed from both the culprit and the general public.

Four years after he began serving his sentence in a psychiatric hospital, the man became the victim of an accident and sustained a severe injury to both his frontal lobes. Emerging from a two-week coma, he began to regain a full memory of his criminal deed, and was able to describe the murder complete with all its suppressed details. His memory now fully recovered, the guilt he experienced became so unbearable that he attempted suicide on two separate occasions.

Put together, all these disparate, if related, findings place doubt on the often attested suggestion that much of our memory is of short-term duration. Instead, they lead us to conclude that *all* experiences from our past can be permanently stored and are at least theoretically capable of being remembered, regardless of the level of significance we have assigned them.

Memory and the Phenomenology of Self

Now, what has this somewhat lengthy digression into memory to do with 'the self'? At one obvious level, our awareness of self depends on memory. Through our memories, each of us constructs a history, a narrative, of who we are. But here is a phenomenological paradox: the very method by which we come to interpret ourselves (that is, memory) is itself an interpretative construct arrived at through intentionality.

The events in our lives require explanation, meaning, interpretation. But the noematic and noetic variables which allow such are under constant flux. We typically assume that memory is static; but why should it be so? Is it not more likely that at every moment in our experience of the world, our memory is reconstructed, altered and reshaped both by the sensory experiences that we encounter and by our interpretation of them?

At any given point in time, the memory that exists allows us to construct our past and, in doing so, permits 'the self' to emerge. However, although all the sensory data that we've stored over time (that is, the noematic items of our past) remain largely unchanged and, at least potentially, consciously accessible, it is the noetic constituent that gives those incidents significance, and determines which items out of the infinity of items of the past should be allowed to filter into our consciousness. Our past undergoes continuous reassessment and reinterpretation. The 'raw matter' of memory may be finite and fixed, but what we make of that 'raw matter' is continually novel.

On reflection, the point being made should become quite obvious. If we think of incidents in our past that had great emotional significance to us, it may well be that the emotions produced when the incident took place and the emotions produced by our current memory of such an event will be radically different.

For example, imagine that at the age of fifteen you were jilted by your then boyfriend or girlfriend. You took that incident as being the most catastrophic event in your life, and experienced any number of emotions linked to that event. You may have felt a despair the likes of which you have never felt again. If you reconsider that incident now, at a later age, years gone by, the memory of that incident remains as vivid, but the emotional experience of it that you have now is unlikely to have remained the same. It might be a humorous anecdote that you now tell your children as a way of preparing them for the traumas of life; it may fill you with a great relief that that particular relationship did not continue; it may bring about a realization of the naivety of your thoughts at that time.

In each case, the raw matter of memory has remained the same, but the manner by which that memory is understood and interpreted, the significance it now has to you, the status and meaning that you bestow upon it, has altered – just as your current perspective, in all likelihood, will alter at any future point in your life at which you consider these same events.

But note: in reconstructing our past, we redefine our selves. Whereas at the age of fifteen you might have placed that incident as the centrepiece of your narrative story, now, at a later age, it may simply be a brief footnote or addendum; it may even be considered to be so unimportant as not even to assume any great significance, or, alternatively, it may have taken on such pain-filled significance that it can only be evoked in some less threatening guise. Whatever the case, a process of interpretation, constant and continuous, has taken place.

Not long after I completed my first draft of this section, I happened to have a conversation with my mother with regard to a diary she has kept over most of her life. Without any prompting on my part (a wonderful example of serendipity, in fact), she announced suddenly that when she has occasion to reread her passages, she is struck by the uncanny sensation that the person who wrote those passages and the person who reads them now must be two very different people. To be sure, she acknowledges the 'raw data' – the noematic components – contained in those passages; she remembers, through them, *what* happened. But the noetic constituent, the manner by which she reviews them, is, so often, so very different to the noetic perspective supplied by her 'earlier' self (the writer of those passages) that it might almost (if it did not seem so absurd) convince her that different people (that is, different selves) had inhabited the same body, and called themselves by the same name, at different points in time.

This conclusion, though simply stated, is the essence of the phenomenological stance on 'the self'. That such a conclusion might seem to be fanciful or even absurd to us at first is, I believe, the result of cultural sedimentation. We remain unaware of the process during the daily run of events, and so conclude that no such process exists. It is only when we distance ourselves from this assumption, when we examine the changes in our lives, in our selves, in a more detached, more neutral manner, that we become aware of the fluidity of being. We are beings with an infinity of pasts, at each moment believing there to be only one past.

The phenomenology of 'the self' suggests that, just as our development allows us to move from an egocentric view of the world to one which acknowledges alternative views which are ascribed to 'others', so too is it possible to come to regard 'the self', or 'I', that defines itself, to be a temporary construct, just one of an infinity of possibilities. As Richard Wollheim has recently stated: 'A person lives his life at a crossroads: at a point where a past that has affected him and a future that lies open meet in the present' (1984: 31).

6
Existential Phenomenology

How does it feel
To be on your own
With no direction home
Like a complete unknown . . .

Bob Dylan

As I originally noted in the first chapter of this text, phenomenology is generally divided into two distinct, though interrelated branches, generally referred to as transcendental phenomenology and existential phenomenology or, as this latter branch is more popularly known, existentialism. Of the two, transcendental phenomenology has been largely influenced by, and derived from, the writings and ideas of Edmund Husserl; a number of its central ideas have served as the basis for the previous chapters on the perception of objects, others and 'the self'.

While it would be false to argue that Husserlian thought has played no role in the development of existential phenomenology, it is the case (as I hope will become increasingly evident throughout this discussion) that this second branch places different emphases on issues of subjective experience.

For existential phenomenologists, the key concern for investigation is 'existence as experienced by man as an individual' (Misiak and Sexton, 1973: 71). Whereas transcendental phenomenologists, from Husserl onwards, have focused on the issues of essence (that is, 'that which makes things what they are' (Misiak and Sexton, 1973: 72)), existentialists, on the other hand, have tended to argue that existence *precedes* essence in that 'Man does not possess existence . . . he is his existence' (Misiak and Sexton, 1973: 72).

In making this claim, existentialists have sought to emphasize the fluidity of human existence – that is, those aspects which allow all members of our species continually to develop, change and 'become'. This emphasis is in keeping with the etymological basis of the Latin verb *existere*, namely: 'to stand out, or to become, to emerge' (Misiak and Sexton, 1973: 72). Although it is far from being a unified system, or school, within philosophy, existential phenomenology characteristically employs or extends the phenomenological method in its analyses of existence.

Obviously, such a complex realm of discourse as 'existence' demands some degree of subdivision in order for methodological investigation to be carried out. As such, existential phenomenology can also be characterized by its emphasis on several key 'themes' of human existence, namely: freedom, responsibility, nothingness or death, aloneness or isolation and meaning/meaninglessness.

As we shall see, each of these themes has a major psychological impact on the way we elect to live out our lives. As such, there is some justification to the claims made by a number of its adherents that existential phenomenology is, first and foremost, a practical philosophy with clear-cut political and social implications. Indeed, it is probably due to the powerful works of fiction created by existential writers such as Samuel Beckett, Albert Camus, Simone de Beauvoir and, of course, Jean-Paul Sartre that existentialist thought gained (and retains) a fair degree of popularity.

For instance, both the 'beat' and 'angry young man' influences on the drama, literature, poetry and music of the West during the middle years of this century owe a great deal to existential notions (whether misunderstood or not!) just as, more currently, here in the UK an 'existential style' has resurfaced in the somewhat fragmented music and fashion industries.

As a philosophy, however, existential phenomenology initially made little impact outside Continental Europe. Both North American and British philosophers tended to dismiss key works as 'unreadable' and from a tradition in philosophy which was alien (and, implicitly, inferior) to the schools of logical positivism and linguistic analysis which were then dominant. Even Bertrand Russell, in his otherwise masterly *History of Western Philosophy* (1946), failed to so much as mention, much less discuss, Heidegger's ideas.

The current situation has changed somewhat. There are clear signs that North American philosophy is now more willing both to read and to analyse existential thought; indeed, there appears to be a sudden flowering of Heidegger-inspired writing. UK philosophers remain more reticent on the whole, although the dominance of logical positivism is on the wane.

As we shall see, the influence of existential phenomenology on psychology has grown steadily and is generally conceded to have had impact on theories of personality, abnormal psychology and psychotherapy. Most significantly, perhaps, as I will discuss in Chapter 8, the somewhat undefinable 'third force' in psychology – humanistic psychology – is heavily dependent upon existential notions.

The Roots of Existential Phenomenology

As is now generally acknowledged (Barrett, 1958; Warnock, 1970; Grossmann, 1984), the seeds of existential phenomenology are to be found in the writings of two major nineteenth-century philosophers: Sören Kierkegaard and Friedrich Nietzsche. Both writers invoked an anti-rationalist stance and, in a sense, sought to 'convert' their readers to their ideas via a combination of emotional appeal, provocation and, perhaps most of all, through profoundly moving, unique and insightful writing styles which succeeded in turning their texts into major works of literature as well as of philosophy.

Interested readers are referred, in particular, to Mary Warnock's invaluable and highly readable introductory text, *Existentialism* (1970), for a detailed summary of the influences of these two philosophers on the development of existentialism.

Briefly, what both authors attempt to demonstrate is that each of us possesses a far greater degree of freedom of thought and belief (and, by implication, of behaviour) than many of us think possible. Such freedom, when acknowledged, may be truly liberating, but it also forces man into a recognition of subjective responsibility. While Kierkegaard explores the anxiety and isolation that this recognition forces upon our thoughts, Nietzsche marvels at the power it provides us with. Both authors rail against the collective, socially imposed morality in Western culture and invoke a utopian vision of man as conscious self-generator of his beliefs and morality; for each, it is less important *what* we believe than *the manner* in which we believe. These arguments play central roles in the ideas of existential phenomenology.

Martin Heidegger and the Development of Existential Phenomenology

The development of existential phenomenology proper took place between the two World Wars in Continental Europe. More specifically, we can say that a series of important writings by the German philosopher Martin Heidegger (1889–1976) make up the formal origins of existential thought. Although never claiming to be an existentialist, Heidegger's contributions are pivotal in their examination of key existential notions and are acknowledged major sources in the development and rise of existential thought in France, most notable in the writings of Jean-Paul Sartre (1943, 1948) and Maurice Merleau-Ponty (1962, 1964).

Though never a pupil of Husserl's, Heidegger worked as his principal assistant at the University of Freiburg during the early 1920s and eventually went on to succeed him as Professor of Philosophy, where he remained until the end of the Second World War. Following the war, he isolated himself in the Black Forest region of Germany in order to continue his writings undisturbed by the administrative demands of a professorship and, possibly, as has been suggested, to avoid further criticism of his ambiguous relationship with National Socialism.

Although now generally acknowledged to be a brilliant and original thinker, his writings (though widely available) remain difficult to read in English translation both because of the unwieldiness of their terminology and because of their stylistic uniqueness. As an associate of mine once put it: 'with Heidegger, you're forced to always have to literally read between the lines; it's there, in that "nothingness" of white space, that Heidegger's message comes across' (Rosen, 1984).

Such a stance may well be somewhat extreme, but it remains the case that the divergence of opinion among Heidegger's many interpreters leads one to wonder whether the injunction holds some truth. At any rate, what follows is yet another 'between the lines' interpretation of some of Heidegger's ideas.

Being-in-the-World (Dasein)
Heidegger's principle 'existentialist' text is *Sein und Zeit* (1927, translated into English in 1962 as *Being and Time*). Here, Heidegger argues that 'Human existence ... is tied inseparably to the world' (Misiak and Sexton, 1973: 75).

For Heidegger, a human being is a *Dasein* which, literally translated, means 'being there', but which has been more commonly translated into English as being-in-the-world. This position holds that, not only are we unique (as far as we know today) in our ability to be aware of our existence, but this awareness reveals an inseparable relationship between existence and the world. Our awareness is not solely subjective, but rather, intersubjective.

This (complex) view forced Heidegger to pose a central question: what does it mean to be? Unfortunately, having posed it, Heidegger failed even to attempt to provide an answer for us. *Being and Time* was to be the first of a two-part investigation; the second part has never appeared and may well have never been written. Nevertheless, one key theme that *is* explored by Heidegger is the notion of authentic versus inauthentic existence, which I will now attempt to clarify.

Authentic versus Inauthentic Existence
Following on from Kierkegaard, Heidegger suggests that in finding ourselves thrown into an incomprehensible, uncertain and threaten-

ing existence which eventually, incontrovertibly, leads to our death, we, as a species, give way to the experience of dread and overwhelming anxiety. In order to defend against this dread, we convince ourselves (that is, we lie to ourselves) that this is not so, that it cannot be the case, that existence is meaningful and rule-bound and open to convention. Via this defensive action our existence becomes **inauthentic**. The relative security of inauthentic existence has a price, however, and it is a heavy one: it is the very 'deadening' of our existence through self-imposed limitations on our potentials as beings-in-the-world.

Let me pursue this point by first of all clarifying the differences between authentic and inauthentic states of being. I must, however, introduce a cautionary note. There is a degree of naivety and misrepresentation through generalization in any theory which attempts to subdivide human beings into two broadly defined characteristic 'types' or 'attitudinal beings'. Although Heidegger's view initially suggests that he has imposed yet another of such minimally useful dualities, this seems to me to be a serious misunderstanding of his argument. I would, instead, suggest that Heidegger's principal point is that each of us, depending upon interpreted circumstance, adopts, at different points in time, either an 'authentic' or 'inauthentic' mode of being. Heidegger's duality exists *within* individuals rather than *between* them.

As **authentic** beings, we recognize our individuality. Further, we recognize that this individuality is not a static quality but is, rather, a set of (possibly infinite) potentialities. As such, while in the authentic mode, we maintain an independence of thought and action, and subsequently feel 'in charge' of the way our life is experienced. Rather than reacting as victims to the vicissitudes of being, we, as authentic beings, acknowledge our role in determining our actions, thoughts and beliefs, and thereby experience a stronger and fuller sense of integration, acceptance, 'openness' and 'aliveness' to the potentialities of being-in-the-world.

In contrast, our thoughts and behaviour as inauthentic beings are marked by conventionality and conformity to the prevailing attitudes and morality of the culture that we reside in. As inauthentic beings, we respond to the experiences of life from a passive, reactive and ultimately unresponsible/irresponsible stance. According to Warnock, the inauthentic being:

> ignores the reality of his own relation to the world. There is an ambiguity in his dealings with reality. He partly knows what things are, but partly does not, because he is so entirely caught up in the way other people see them, the labels attached to them by the world at large. He cannot straightfor-

wardly form any opinion, and his statements are partly his own, partly those of people in general. If he seems to be interested in something, this is less because he is in pursuit of genuine understanding, than because of curiosity, a superficial and inconclusive motive. The conversation of the man who is inauthentic is said to be *Gerede* (prattle) as opposed to *Rede* (discourse). (1970: 57)

Our relationship with self and others varies significantly depending on the mode of being we have adopted.

When adopting an inauthentic stance, our actions are directed by competitive notions of success fed by grandiose fantasies of our self-importance and strivings for superiority over others. Our inauthentic stance leads us to view the self as possessing fixed characteristics which must be applied for the purposes of achieving success. The self that is experienced under such circumstances is both fragmented and passive, viewing others as the primary means of defining one's status. Sought after for applause, the final judges of right and wrong, fellow game-players and opponents in the struggle for status, others become 'playthings' or possessions, both valued and disdained. As inauthentic beings, we interpret ourselves as reactive victims of experience.

In marked contrast, while in the authentic mode, our experience of ourselves and others is characterized by openness, flexibility, co-operation and responsibility. Ultimately, our authentic stance acknowledges both an *equality* of importance and status between self and others and the active interpretative role that each of us has in our experience of being.

Put in this way, it would seem perverse for us to opt for a 'style' of being which is primarily in the inauthentic mode. And yet, this remains the common tendency. Why should this be so? What values may there be in adopting inauthenticity as our principal mode of being?

Freedom of Choice and its Limitations

In order to begin to understand this perplexing tendency, we must first recall the existentialist insistence that human beings are in a unique position. As far as we know, we are the only animals capable of consciously choosing the way in which we give meaning to our experience. It is in this way that we possess an extensive, if rarely fully recognized, capacity for freedom.

Uniquely, humans have the ability to override many of the biological constraints that other animals are tied to. Our behaviour is nowhere near as dependent upon hormonal change, or other biochemical alterations that take place in us, as compared to similar substantive changes occurring in other species.

Drive-reduction theory, for example, may well be a useful means of understanding the behaviour of other living things, but it is woefully inadequate and misleading when applied to human activity. Our most recently evolved brains, the cerebral hemispheres, can often reduce, realign or even reject demands originating from older centres (Crider et al., 1986).

One obvious example of this can be seen in our sexual behaviour. Other than some preliminary evidence relating to certain species of dolphins, it would appear that we are the only animal that isn't entirely dependent upon biological factors which determine cyclical periods for arousal and mating, nor is it the case (once again, unlike virtually all other animals) that we engage in sexual activity solely (or even primarily) for the purposes of reproduction. Indeed, ensuring the *avoidance* of reproduction is a much more characteristic concern of human sexuality! Although it would be wrong to conclude that we are completely free from biological restraints upon our behaviour, it would still be fair to argue that we do have a very great capacity for choosing our behaviour in any given situation.

We must be clear, however: our freedom does *not* lie in our ability to control or determine the stimuli or events that impinge themselves upon us. If I cross the road and get hit by a passing car, I'd be mistaken if I were to believe that I, in some way, *chose* this particular stimulus to appear when it did! However, the significance and meaning I give to the stimulus, the interpretation I might make of the event, ultimately, the way I experience the stimulus, is a matter of choice. Such a view, of course, is a direct extension and application of Husserlian intentionality. Existentialists, however, emphasize its implications on being since it is this basic acceptance of the freedom to choose our experience that is an integral aspect of all beings-in-the-world.

Existentialists also acknowledge the very real limitations to freedom that exist for all human beings. Obviously, we are all limited by the temporality of our existence. Similarly, we are limited by bio-physical determinants which impose any number of experiential restraints upon us. We are also limited by the codes and laws of the society we inhabit so long as we wish to remain members in good standing within it. Ultimately, as I stated above, we are limited by our lack of control over the appearance of the various 'stimuli' which impinge themselves upon us.

Nevertheless, the freedom which existentialists stress, and which is ours to act upon, is the experiential freedom to *interpret* the stimulus-events in our lives as we choose to (within the boundaries first set by the innate bio-physical invariants of our species). Herein lies the basis for our freedom to choose. Though it is by no means a freedom in any ultimate or complete sense, it *is* a far greater degree of freedom than that which we, as inauthentic beings, convince ourselves is at our disposal.

Meaninglessness

Authenticity requires us to acknowledge this freedom of choice in our experience of the world. But if we do so we are led, inevitably, to a number of initially unsuspected and disagreeable conclusions.

If we are free to interpret our experience of the world, then we can no longer presuppose any definitive or ultimate interpretation; we can no longer be *certain*. As we have already seen, phenomenologists argue that our interpretation of any event at any given point in time is dependent upon a number of experiential factors which imbue our interpretations with impermanence and fluidity rather than 'fix' them in time and meaning. If we accept this stance, we are immediately confronted with the meaninglessness (that is, the interpretative openness) of our experience of the world.

This very meaninglessness prevents us from asserting any indisputable finality, absolute truth or 'correctness' of one interpretation over any other. All sedimented beliefs, attitudes, rules, certainties must be forsaken in favour of disquieting uncertainty. This does not mean, of course, that we must give up our beliefs; rather we must acknowledge them as being just that – beliefs, or suppositions, that we might choose to live our lives by.

But, we might well ask, are there *no* truths at all? Is there nothing that we can say with any certainty about our existence? Existential phenomenologists argue that there are certainly two truths which are common to all of our experiences of life: at some point, each of us was thrown into the world (that is, each of us was born), and, at some later point in time, each of us will experience death.

These two experiences stand outside all beliefs, theories or rules that we might make about our experience of the world. None of us had any choice in determining our birth and, equally, none of us has any choice in determining the moment of our death. Even if we were to opt for suicide, the actual moment that we cease to be is outside our control or choice.

Other than these two certainties of existence however, existentialists argue that nothing else can be counted upon with absolute conviction. If we have faith in an after life or reincarnation or, alternatively, if we are convinced of the inconceivability of either, we must accept the uncertainty of such faiths; we simply do not know in any complete or final sense, nor are we ever likely to know while we live.

Many of us assume a purpose or meaning to life; it worries us when we feel we have lost it and will search for it in philosophical texts, religious pronouncements of faith, and so forth. Existential phenomenologists argue that this is the path to inauthenticity. To be authentic, we must concede that all our being-related knowledge is, and will remain, incomplete and uncertain; whatever meaning life may seem to have for us is our construction and that, hence, in an ultimate sense, our existence is meaningless.

Isolation
As if meaninglessness were not enough, each of us is also presented with the realization that not only are the meanings we give to existence uncertain, they are also, ultimately, unsharable with anyone else. Just as our perceptions of objects, others, even our selves, are unique and not fully communicable to others, so is it also the case that what meanings about existence we may construct for ourselves are our own and cannot be anyone else's.

A shared language, for example, might initially lead us to suppose that if we agree in labelling objects in the same way, then we can conclude that we perceive the same object. But, as I have argued in previous chapters, this is simply not so. You and I might point to the same object and declare it to be, for example, a geranium. We might even go on to give it the same Latinized generic title and agree to provide it with certain defining characteristics such as the colour of its flower, the shape of its leaves, and so forth. But my experience of that geranium still remains unique and not fully sharable, as does yours. The moment that each of us ceases to be, so, too, does the unique world we inhabit, and the unique meanings we bring to it, also cease to be.

Ultimately, we are led to the recognition of our aloneness or isolation. Just as in the end each of us must die alone, so too will that uniquely experienced world that is inseparably tied to us also cease to exist. We can do nothing about this; no record, no testament, no artefact, nothing can prevent the end not only of our being but of that world that both defines and is defined by our being. Like the figure/ ground relationship, each complementary element requires the other for its definition; remove one and the other also ceases to be.

Nothingness
Not surprisingly, existential theories argue that the realization of the meaninglessness of our experience and our isolation in the world fills us with dread. According to Heidegger, such knowledge leads us to the experience of nothingness.

Actually, Heidegger gives two distinct, though interrelated interpretations of nothingness. First, nothingness is the recognition of the fact that each of us exists only temporarily, and that at some point sooner or later each of us will cease to be. The second interpretation of nothingness refers to the growing realization that our life leads to nothing possessing any absolute certainty other than death. We each come into being out of unchosen and uncontrollable chance which hurls us into the world; equally, death will touch each of us at an unpredictable moment in time. All is arbitrary, a seemingly random occurrence.

Angst

The acceptance of our freedom of choice, our meaninglessness, our isolation and our nothingness leads us towards an authentic mode of being. However, this is no easy step to take. Under such conditions, existence is likely to seem to be all too unbearable, frightening, anxiety-provoking. This basic, raw, existential anxiety, or angst, as it is typically called in the literature of existential phenomenology, is the key to our rejection of authenticity and our subsequent accept-ance of inauthenticity.

Authenticity provokes continual insecurity, a lack of certitude in our lives. If there is no discernible ultimate purpose, or final and complete meaning to life, if we are all alone, then why do anything, why bother to act, why seek to communicate, knowing that those communications cannot be fully communicated?

Such questions fill us with ineradicable – if variable – angst. Under certain circumstances, such fears may actually seem minimal. Many practitioners of contemplative or meditative techniques, for exam-ple, claim to experience 'altered states' during which authentic uncer-tainty becomes acceptable and is the means to 'spiritual enlighten-ment'. Similarly, altered states brought about by drugs, sex, religious ecstasy and so forth may also induce temporary experiences of authentic acceptance. Most often, however, uncertainty seems frigh-tening, unacceptable, ultimately 'wrong'. In opting for inauthenti-city, we succeed in defending against, even temporarily denying, our experience of angst – but at a heavy cost to our potentials as beings-in-the-world.

Responsibility

If we reject the implications of authenticity and argue, instead, that life *must* be meaningful and purposeful, we are forced to conclude that such is the case because something outside ourselves makes it so. But, if this is the case, we are also forced to accept that we are not in control of our existence, that, in any number of ways, we must be passive pawns in the purposeful plans of something else – be it supernatural or physical – that is the ultimate source of all purpose and meaning; all our actions, all our thoughts, all our 'choices' are not of our own making. We are as puppets in the hands of an unknown, incomprehensible puppeteer.

True, this stance allows us to negate any responsibility for our thoughts and behaviours, but it also forces us to deny what freedom we have in our experience of the world. And yet here is the quandary: it is in those moments when freedom is acknowledged that we feel most alive. We yearn for such experiences, bemoan their elusivity, turn to agents of change such as drugs or psychotherapy when we feel we have lost the means to recapturing or re-experiencing such moments.

In this way, we vary our modes of being: when it suits us, we declare ourselves to be free, responsible, authentic agents in our experience of the world; but, equally, when that responsibility of the choices to be made, or the acts to be acknowledged, or the wider implications of such, is painful, frightening, tension-provoking, we seek the safety of denied responsibility, lack of choice, inauthenticity.

A particularly striking experimental example of the denial of responsibility and its consequent effects can be seen in the research on obedience to authority carried out by Stanley Milgram (1974). Recall that, when confronted with the question why they had continued to carry out instructions that were clearly causing major distress and threatened severe physical injury to the 'learners' in the study, many subjects claims that they had had no choice.

The major significance of this claim, I would argue, was that it reduced the levels of anxiety in the subjects, since, in the adoption of this claim, they could deny responsibility for the choice each had made to administer the electric shocks. And yet I suspect that if the studies had been so constructed that the 'learners' did not claim injury and the results indicated the positive effects on learning ability from such a procedure, those same subjects would have claimed that their decisions to carry through the actions had been self-generated, and they would have experienced some degree of (pleasurable) responsibility for the results. Equally, I would doubt that any of the subjects who denied responsibility for their choice would then go on to agree that they were not, under ordinary circumstances, free, choosing agents.

It is this very inconsistency in our beliefs about our freedom of choice and its consequent responsibility that is the source, as existentialists argue, of many of the experienced anxieties of life. To paraphrase a line from Woody Allen's film *Manhattan*, 'we're just too easy on ourselves.' In maintaining both positions, we provoke a 'split' in our experience of existence. We become fragmented beings.

Like the hysterical patients discussed in Freud and Breuer's *Studies on Hysteria* (1955), as inauthentic beings we suffer from repressed memories, and, again like those patients, through our symptomatic behaviours and 'neurotic' thought processes our yearning to reveal such memories to ourselves remains ever-present. To pursue the analogy a littler further, for existential phenomenologists the core repressed 'memory' is that we are free – free to choose the meanings in our lives, free to construct our interpretations of experience, free to reassess and alter them if we choose to. Our freedom *is* limited – we have, for instance, no control over the stimuli of life – but it is more than we typically acknowledge.

Authenticity and Self-Actualization
The notion of authenticity bears striking similarity to Maslow's ideas concerning self-actualization (1968). There is no end-point (other than death) to authenticity just as there is no end-point to self-actualization; nor is there a purposive element to either which is in any sense akin to need or drive reduction. Each simply is because it is; it is inseparable to being-in-the-world.

Authentic/self-actualizing beings value their aliveness, acknowledge the choices they make and the responsibility that comes with them, show greater autonomy and resistance to enculturation, are more integrated, creative and tolerant or accepting of others, place more emphasis on the 'here and now' than on future rewards, recognition or redemption, are more 'means' oriented than 'ends' oriented (Maslow, 1968, 1971). There is no 'special' or 'secret' learning or ritual which leads us to this mode of being. Indeed, it is highly likely that each of us experiences it at various points in our lives. The variability of its incidence is not due to biology or environmental circumstances; it is the result of choice.

Sartre's Extensions of Heideggerian Thought
If Heidegger introduced the basic concerns of existentialism, Jean-Paul Sartre (1905–80) placed them at the centre of his vision of humanity. Like no other philosopher before or after him, Sartre approached the issues of existence head on with characteristic vehemence and absolute conviction of their practical importance to day-to-day living.

Sartre, as philosopher, does not make easy reading. On the other hand, Sartre, as playwright and novelist, is a pleasurable, if disturbing revelation. The three novels that make up his *Roads to Freedom* trilogy and plays such as *Huis Clos*, and *The Flies* are acknowledged masterpieces of twentieth-century literature. The recent publication of his (rejected) scenario (1984) for John Huston's biographical film on Freud reveals penetrating critical insight on the development of psychoanalysis and, if flawed as a screenplay, my belief is that it would still have led to a far more interesting and exciting film than the one that was eventually screened. His award of a Nobel Prize for Literature in 1964 (which he refused for both moral and political reasons) confirms his literary genius. As an introduction to his 'brand' of existentialism, Sartre's fictional works are a perfect starting point and I would urge interested readers to begin with them.

Like Heidegger, Sartre did not maintain the same philosophical position throughout the substantial output of his writings. Many of his works refer explicitly to 'phenomenology' (*Being and Nothingness*, for example, is subtitled *An Outline of Phenomenological Ontology*) but deal with issues which lie outside the focus of this text.

Additionally, Sartre is considered by many to be primarily a moral philosopher who, as both existentialist and marxist, sought to unify both systems into a political ideology of freedom which gained him much notoriety during the 1960s but seems to have had little, if any, influence upon current political theory; these issues, too, must remain outside our realm of discourse.

Lastly, even a great deal of proper Sartrean existential writing requires so much background explanation that it is impossible (for me, at least) to do it justice in a brief summary.

As such, I've been highly selective in my discussion of Sartre; what follows, then, is not by any means a detailed analysis of Sartrean thought, but, rather, 'selected highlights' dealing with topics that I think bear most relevance on what has been argued previously and what is to follow.

Sartre's Phenomenology

For Sartre, the world is a chaotic void full of absurdity which humanity is thrown into and attempts to cope with more or less adequately through its degree of recognition of the vast amount of freedom it has at its disposal.

Sartre argued that human beings do not *possess* freedom, they *are* freedom; like it or not, we are condemned to choose our mode of existence. Any attempted escape from this knowledge only leads to anxiety and despair. One of Sartre's most famous epigrams accurately encapsulates his position 'Man is a useless passion' (Misiak and Sexton, 1973: 76).

Although Sartre emphasizes his great debt to Husserl's writings, he is unwilling to assume, as Husserl originally did, that in following the steps of the phenomenological method our attempts to 'bracket' the various assumptions we have about the world will get us to 'the thing itself' as it actually is. In pursuing Husserl's arguments, Sartre is led to conclude that no amount of bracketing will ever be complete. In this, Sartre echoes contemporary phenomenological thought: ultimate reality is unknowable.

Bad Faith

For Sartre, inauthentic beings live in a state which he terms **bad faith**. Bad faith allows us to deny the freedom of responsibility and choice in our actions and strengthens the belief that we are passive reactors to externally predetermined influences. In the state of bad faith, an individual becomes nothing other than a 'thing', an object that has no control over its actions. These actions, when analysed, are seen as highly ritualistic and limited by the individual's beliefs about what can and cannot be done.

Such beliefs dominate our being, encase it in a 'must/should' moral order that achieves both a fragmentation in being and automaton-like behaviour. Individuals in the state of bad faith deny a vast range of potentials, claiming them to be impossible as a result of the strictures imposed by society and biology. Class, culture, gender, parental upbringing, religious ideology – anything external to the individuals themselves – become worthy originating factors and excuses for their actions.

Without labouring the point, Sartre's notion of bad faith has many similarities to that of Heideggerian inauthenticity. But the power of Sartre's term rests with the brilliance of the examples he employs to demonstrate the state. Here, Sartre the playwright and novelist comes to the fore and presents us with illuminating, brutal, finely observed vignettes of individuals (often in the setting of Parisian café society) who are living exponents of beings in the state of bad faith. For instance, consider the following example:

A girl who is taken to a restaurant by a man, and who, in order to preserve the excitement of the occasion, and to put off the moment when she must face making a definite decision, saying either 'yes' or 'no' to him, pretends to herself that she does not notice his intentions towards her. There finally comes a moment when he takes her hand; and the moment of decision would be upon her, only at this very moment she becomes totally absorbed in intellectual conversation, and leaves her hand to be taken by him, without noticing it, as if he has just picked up some 'thing' any thing, off the table. She has dissociated herself from her hand, for the time being, and is pretending that it is nothing whatever to do with her. Her hand just rests in his hand, inert and thing-like. If she had removed it, or deliberately left it where it was, she would in either case have manifestly come to some decision. But by simply not taking responsibility for her hand and what happened to it, she avoided the need to decide; and this is Bad Faith. (Warnock, 1970: 102–3)

Or, alternatively, consider the following portrait of an all-too familiar waiter:

> All the movements and gestures of the waiter are slightly over-done. His behaviour is essentially ritualistic. He bends forward in a manner which is too deeply expressive of concern and deference for the diners; he balances his tray in a manner which is just a little too precarious. His movements are all of them like the movements in a mime or game. The game which he is playing is the game of 'being a waiter'. (Warnock, 1970: 103)

As Warnock is right to point out, the power of such examples lies not in the fact that each of us can recognize others who act in these ways, but that, if we are honest enough with ourselves, we are forced to confess: 'there am I' (Warnock, 1970: 103).

As well as having close affinity with Heidegger's inauthenticity, bad faith reminds us of Freud's notion of repression in that each is based on self-deceit: our unwillingness to allow into our consciousness certain desires, to acknowledge them regardless of how we might feel about them leads us to repress them.

Nausea
There are also some parallels between Heidegger's notion of angst and Sartre's term **nausea**. If one of Heidegger's principal questions is to ask what is it like to exist, Sartre's reply is unequivocal – it is nauseating.

Recall that angst is said to arise out of authenticity; only authentic beings consciously experience the existential anxiety of meaningless, isolated being-in-the-world. Similarly, should we stop living in the state of bad faith, all the defences that we have built up around ourselves in order to be provided with the illusion of a meaningful, ordered and limited existence would be recognized as illusions. What would we be faced with then?

First, argues Sartre, we would be confronted with a realization of our weakness, how difficult we find it to avoid being in bad faith, how easily we can each slip back into it. Secondly, we are confronted with the knowledge of the deception we have carried out both upon ourselves and upon others, we are forced to hold ourselves responsible for the lies told, the abuses we chose to enact, the myriad of ways in which we both trivialized and limited both our own being and that of others. At this point, Sartre argues, we are overwhelmed by an almost literal gut-wrenching nausea; if this is existence, it is sickening, revolting. The very knowledge of it induces a state of nausea in us.

Where Heidegger posits angst arising out of authenticity, Sartre conjures up the notion of nausea; in either case, it is our avoidance of each that keeps us in states of inauthenticity and bad faith.

The Three 'States' of Being

So far, I've tried to focus on Sartre as reinterpreter of some of Heidegger's ideas. But Sartre was able to see that, at this level, existentialism opened itself too easily to criticisms of solipsistic pursuit and abuse. It was not enough to merely explore existence, the moral implications of our interpretations of existence required analysis. Primary among these was the relationship of beings to each other.

One of Sartre's central themes is his distinction of three states, or manners, of being. These have been translated as being-in-itself, being-for-itself, and being-for-others.

A **being-in-itself** is any unconscious object or 'unconscious physical reality' (Sprigge, 1984: 128) in general. As such, any 'thing', like a tree, a table, which has a physical reality, is a being-in-itself.

In contrast, a **being-for-itself** is conscious of both itself and others. The major feature of a being-for-itself is its ability to 'consider the world' (Warnock, 1970: 93) in which it finds itself and to think of itself as separate from other beings. Human beings are beings-for-themselves and, indeed, may well be the only beings in this category.

Much has been made among philosophers about the distinction between these two being 'states'. For one thing, this somewhat unique dualism of being allows Sartre to give a new centrality to the notion of nothingness. Nothingness, now, is seen as being the gap or space which divides a being-in-itself from a being-for-itself since it is only through being able to consider the world that the experience of nothingness can emerge. Somewhat paradoxically, if not circularly, however, Sartre subsequently argues that it is also nothingness which 'makes it possible for a Being-in-itself to both perceive the world and also to act in it' (Warnock, 1970: 94) – that is, to become a being-for-itself.

For Sartre, then, the notion of nothingness is inseparable from being-for-itself. Like the noematic and noetic foci of intentionality, being-for-itself and nothingness are equal 'shapers' to the interpretations we make of our existence.

It is, however, Sartre's third manner of being – **being-for-others** – which is of greatest interest to us. Unfortunately, it is far from clear what exactly Sartre meant by this term. Although Sartre suggests that a being-for-others is not a distinct object or entity from a being-for-itself, the *manner* in which a being-for-others goes about interpreting its world is markedly different from that of a being-for-itself.

If I am correct in my understanding of the distinction, a being-for-others is required to be in an authentic state or, alternatively, in a state of good faith in order to arrive at its position vis-à-vis others. Once again, it seems to be nothingness (though, this time, in a more Heideggerian sense) which allows this manner of being.

Recall that phenomenology argues that others, as experienced by each of us, are firstly a construct, based upon any number of interpretational factors related to our experience of the world. This argument further implies that others are necessary to our ability to give a definition and meaning to our *selves*.

But this suggests a seemingly insoluble problem: others are required if we are to give sense, identity, meaning to each individual self, and yet our experience of others is principally a construct which is dependent upon the being who interprets others, who, in a very important sense, constructs their existence.

Sartre, I think, attempts to resolve the paradox by arguing that we must consider others as independent beings having reality. Although this might at first sound like a solution which is antagonistic to that derived from phenomenological investigation, I would suggest that it is not.

Just as others are constructs, largely the product of our own unique experience, so too, are we ourselves, the individuals that we believe ourselves to be, equally constructs. Self and others, 'I' and 'Not-I', are both constructs; what each actually is, or may be, is equally unknown, and unknowable in any complete sense. Each self is conscious (is a being-for-itself) but its consciousness of itself is dependent upon its consciousness of others since the only means by which it can be-for-itself lies in its contrasts with and distinctions from others.

Now, here, I believe, is the crux of Sartre's argument: the realization that the being-for-itself is or exists (in a phenomenal sense) only as a result of others, that it is quite literally nothing without others, forces each being-for-itself to concede an existence of equal status to others; each is no more or less significant or important than the other.

A being-for-others, rather than interpreting others as antagonists, or competitors, or whatever other rival defining construct it selects, recognizes instead that others form an integral and essential component of self; self and others are inextricably bound to each other. As such, a being-for-others views its relationship with others not as a competitive 'you *or* me' relationship but as a co-operative 'you *and* me' one. By implication, what this perspective leads to is the understanding that a being-for-others cannot attach greater (or less) importance or significance to itself in relation to others (or vice versa). As such, any action taken or construct definition made by a being-for-others must take into account the effects it may have upon others.

In this way, Sartre was able to eliminate the element of solipsism that might conceivably be implied in the phenomenological stance. A being-for-others can no longer justify a stance of superiority or inferiority with regard to others; each demands equal status in the world, each has an equal 'right' to be. Any steps taken to limit, diminish or deny this equal status lead the being who takes such steps into the state of bad faith.

The moral implications of this are, I think, fairly obvious: any action each of us takes must now be considered from the stand-point of the recipient of the action – be it self or other. If the act is designed physically or mentally to injure self or other, if its purpose is to limit or diminish the status of either self or other, it is morally unjustified.

The political and social implications of this position are, of course, dramatic. Just as individual beings-for-others shift their perspective from competitive superiority/inferiority to that of co-operation and 'equal rights' for all beings to be to their fullest potential, so, too, must it be the case that the social, cultural, political and religious ideologies shared by beings-for-others also reflect this perspective. If the actions of one nation/ideology/religion imperil the potentialities of being either of its own citizens/followers/believers or of the citizens/followers/believers of an alternative nation/ideology/religion, those actions are in bad faith and will ultimately imperil the potentialities of being of the nation/ideology/religion that enacts them.

I think it is unnecessary for me to provide examples to demonstrate the accuracy of this conclusion; unfortunately, we are faced with over-abundance of such on a daily basis.

Although Sartre was a committed atheist, and particularly antagonistic to the Christian religion, it is interesting to note the similarity between his position and one of the two fundamental laws of Christianity, that is, 'to love others as one loves oneself'. When considered, does not this law urge followers to place their being on the same level as that of others, and to not make one or the other more or less important in relation to the other? In other words, is this not a command to be-for-others?

The division that we construct between self and others is phenomenal as opposed to real in any ultimate sense. Perhaps, there is an ultimate unity of self/others that each of us might 'catch glimpses of', even work towards, but which, typically, remains unknown and unknowable. Still, if we are obliged to place our faith, our beliefs, in anything, being-for-others, and its implications, seem eminently worthy of our consideration.

Existential Phenomenology: a Summary

As brief and selective as this overview of existential phenomenology has been, it seems both useful and necessary to present a brief summary of the points considered.

Existential phenomenology stands in direct opposition to rationalist, idealist and materialist philosophies. It takes as its central focus of attention issues which revolve around the notion of existence, that is, issues concerning an individual's being and that individual's relation to the world and to others. Shaffer (1978) has deftly outlined the four main themes of existential phenomenology which have been the basis for my discussion. These are:

> (1) a person's unavoidable uncertainty when confronted on the one hand by a universe devoid of any clear-cut or easily fixed meaning, and on the other hand by the inevitability of his own eventual nothingness, or death; (2) his or her inherent freedom to choose the attitudes and actions that he or she takes in the face of this potentially meaningless situation; (3) the omnipresent constraints, or limits, that the person's situation places upon his or her freedom; and (4) the impossibility of successfully evading responsibility for whatever choices he or she makes. (Shaffer, 1978: 19)

Existential phenomenology argues that, if we are to face up to our potential for being, we must accept our freedom to give meaning to our experience and that whatever meanings we do come up with are not the result and responsibility of outside, predetermined, perhaps even unknowable sources, but are products of our choice. As such, we are responsible for whatever we make meaningful about our unique and specific existence, that of the world, and that of others.

Faced with the unavoidable anxiety (angst) we experience when faced with this knowledge and its subsequent implications concerning our nothingness, meaninglessness and isolation, we defend against this anxiety by placing a number of limitations (varying in extremity) which, while relieving our anxiety to a more or less bearable degree, lead us to impose limits on our potentials for being such that we become beings who are characterized by their degree of inauthenticity or bad faith. The only way out of this position is for each of us to cease denying our freedom and to face up to the necessary anxiety that being generates.

Interestingly, although many of his ideas were strongly attacked by existentialists such as Sartre, Freud, too, arrived at a highly similar conclusion: for him, the aims of psychoanalysis were not necessarily, or even primarily, curative; rather they sought to make analysands more truthful and honest with themselves so that, if not necessarily emerging as 'happier' people at the end of analysis, they were certainly more capable of facing the vicissitudes of life (Gay, 1988).

Existentialist Influences on Psychology

Mention of Freud brings us to the consideration of the impact and influence that existential thought has had on Western psychology.

Misiak and Sexton have referred to existentially oriented psychology as a 'movement which focuses its inquiry on man as an individual person as being-in-the-world' (1973: 84) and whose principal aim is to provide existent schools of psychology with new approaches, insights, themes and methods with which to reassess, revise and make more adequate their views and conclusions regarding the understanding of human thought and behaviour.

A number of prominent and influential psychologists have written on general issues raised by an existential approach to psychology (principally, Binswanger, 1968; May, 1958, 1983; Van Kaam, 1966; and Giorgi, 1970). Others, such as Maslow (1968), Allport (1955) and Rogers (1961) and Rogers and Stevens (1967) have more or less aligned their own approaches to it. And still others (notably Fromm, 1956), while remaining allied to an established school in psychology, nevertheless readily admit the influence that existential thought has had upon their ideas and writings. Even so, these writers clearly pursue differing emphases and implications of existential thought and present interpretations which may not be readily agreed upon by other writers.

In spite of this lack of cohesion, the broad themes of existential phenomenology, that is, freedom, responsibility, isolation, anxiety, and death/nothingness, form the nucleus of issues raised by existentially oriented psychologists.

Similarly, these writers stand united in their common interest in and pursuit of clearer theories of the various facets of human consciousness and take variants of the phenomenological method as their starting points to such investigation.

Lastly, existentially oriented psychologists take as a basic presupposition that human beings cannot be adequately understood or explained by a psychology which is modelled solely upon the natural or biological sciences. Rather it is through the remaking of psychology into a fully *human* science which, while not rejecting empirical data and investigation, nevertheless is required to develop new paradigms for investigation, that we gain an increasingly adequate understanding of ourselves.

Giorgi's influential book, *Psychology as a Human Science* (1970), for instance, presents a compelling case against the reductionist tendencies in contemporary psychology and offers initial steps towards the development of a more human-based approach which takes into account the unique features and problems that must be recognized when taking human beings as subject matter.

In many ways, just as existential phenomenology can be seen as a 'branch' of phenomenology, so too, I would suggest, is existential psychology a branch, or sub-set, of phenomenological psychology in that, within the broad number of topics open to consideration to a phenomenologically oriented psychologist, those issues broadly concerned with theories of personality and motivation clearly benefit from existentially derived analyses.

Not surprisingly, existentialism's greatest psychological impact has been in the field of psychotherapy and counselling – as we shall see in the next chapter.

7
Phenomenological Psychotherapy

I suppose I'm one of the symptoms of the times.

R.D. Laing

What influence phenomenology – and existential phenomenology in particular – has had and, increasingly, still has on general psychology is most apparent in the applied fields of psychotherapy and psychodiagnostics.

This chapter will first of all consider phenomenological approaches to therapy in general and then go on to focus on two highly influential theoreticians, R.D. Laing and Carl Rogers in order to demonstrate how each of these authors has incorporated and extended phenomenological ideas into his style of therapy.

Unlike most other writers, I've preferred to employ the term 'phenomenological therapy' instead of the more commonly used 'existential therapy' in this discussion. This is not meant as a sign of dismissal or disrespect for both theoreticians and practitioners of existential psychotherapy. Rather, I have adopted this stance in order that I may introduce arguments and points of discussion which are more obviously derived from phenomenological insights originating from the transcendental branch of phenomenology. In addition, as I hope has become clear to the reader, I have stressed the position that both the transcendental and existential approaches are best understood as 'branches', or sub-sets of the more general approach known as phenomenology. For such reasons, and for the added purpose of clarity and consistency, I have given this chapter the more general title of 'Phenomenological Psychotherapy'. Those readers who, in spite of my clarification, remain incensed by this decision, have my permission to re-title the chapter 'Existential Psychotherapy'.

I must emphasize, however, that, rather than being a particular technique or method of therapy, the phenomenological approach to psychotherapy provides therapists with a set of principles which serve as guidelines in any broad or general interpretation of clinical material (Ruitenbeek, 1962).

Similarly, rather than stress a standard technique, representatives of this approach hold that any over-emphasis on technique is one of the main obstacles to understanding the patient and, thus, to any truly long-lasting outcome of therapy. It is the basic view of phenomenological therapists that 'it is not the understanding that follows technique, but the technique that follows understanding' (Misiak and Sexton, 1973: 87).

General Emphases in Phenomenological Therapy

The Aims of Phenomenological Therapy

As, I hope, will become apparent, if there is an ultimate aim to phenomenological therapy, it is to offer the means for individuals to examine, confront, clarify and reassess their understanding of life, the problems encountered throughout their life, and the limits imposed upon the possibilities inherent in being-in-the-world.

Therapists de-emphasize any 'curative' aims and place little value on any specific manipulative or re-educational techniques which seek to modify current behaviour. For phenomenological therapists, what other models have labelled as neurotic or psychotic defence mechanisms must be understood as imposed blocks against authentic living brought on by the individual's desire to deny and avoid the necessary angst that authentic living demands.

In order to emphasize that the role of the phenomenological therapist is not a medical/curative one, but, rather, that of stimulus to exploration, phenomenological therapists refer to their patients as 'clients'. All this is not to say that clients might not emerge from therapy 'cured' of any number of symptoms or having learned how to modify their behaviour for their own 'betterment' – obviously this occurs in phenomenological therapy just as it does in most other therapeutic approaches – but this is not its primary aim or concern. Rather, phenomenological therapists strive to assist their clients in regaining greater control and mastery over their lives in order that they may experience a more authentic being-in-the-world. As van Deurzen-Smith has put it:

> The existential approach to counselling centres on an exploration of someone's particular way of seeing life, the world and herself. The goal is to help her to establish what it is that matters to her, so that she can begin to feel more in tune with herself and therefore more real and alive. Before the person can rearrange her lifestyle in accordance with her priorities she has to examine her own preconceptions and assumptions which stand in the way of her personal development. Much of what has always been taken for granted is therefore re-examined in the light of a search for truth about life. (1988: 27)

The Exploration of Inner Experience

Common to the various 'attitudes' within phenomenological psychotherapy is the acknowledged emphasis placed upon the exploration of clients' consciousness and experience of being-in-the-world. In this way, clients' various choices or assumptions about being-in-the-world can be exposed, examined, questioned and evaluated in relation to the problems encountered throughout their lives, and the limits imposed upon the possibilities inherent in being-in-the-world.

In keeping with this stance, it follows that an equally distinct feature of the phenomenological approach to psychotherapy is the central effort on the part of the therapist to enter into the client's inner world in order best to clarify and expose the client's **world-views** and reflectively mirror them back for consideration.

The Dimensions of World-Views

How can phenomenological therapists assist clients in clarifying their world-views? One highly influential therapist, Ludwig Binswanger (1968), argued that an individual's world-view can be seen to consist of three dimensions: the Umwelt, the Mitwelt, and the Eigenwelt.

The **Umwelt** can best be described as the 'natural world with its physical, biological dimension' (van Deurzen-Smith, 1988: 69). Although each of us is limited by innate, biological invariants, we still provide unique meanings and interpretations of the physical world we inhabit. We might experience this physical dimension as being essentially harmonious, secure and pleasurable, or it may fill us with anxiety due to perceived dangers, doubts, injustices and so forth. Our attitudes to a wide range of variables within the physical dimension – our bodies, the weather, ecological variables and so on – rather than being seen as insignificant when mentioned in therapy, are duly examined and considered as valuable means to clarifying clients' meanings and concerns.

The **Mitwelt** dimension focuses on the everyday, public relations each of us has with others. The inferences each of us draws about our race, social class, gender, language, culture, the rules and codes of our society (and those who enforce those rules), our general work environments – all may lead us to develop a wide range of differing attitudes and values. We might feel empowered or invalidated by our public-world interactions, they may engender feelings of acceptance or rejection, dominance or submission, conformity or rebellion. The public world might be perceived as loving and respectful, or petty, spiteful and dangerous to the point where it must be avoided whenever possible. Once again, clients' stated perceptions of their dealings with the public world demand attention and investigation.

The **Eigenwelt** deals with the private and intimate relations each of us has with both ourselves and the significant others in our lives. How we view ourselves, the degree of self-confidence, self-acceptance and individuality we define for ourselves is an obvious area of concern as is the way we interpret our interactions with our family, friends, sexual partners – those 'intimate' beings in our lives upon whom we place so much significance and importance, and who seem to have the power to make our lives seem meaningful or meaningless, rich or arid, full or empty, secure or wracked with anxiety.

In addition to these three dimensions, a fourth – the **Überwelt** – has been suggested recently by van Deurzen-Smith (1988). This dimension 'refers to a person's connection to the abstract and absolute aspect of living' (van Deurzen-Smith, 1988: 97) and incorporates our ideological outlook on life, the beliefs we hold about life, death, existence – those beliefs which underpin or are a basis for all subsequent beliefs and interpretations. In voicing such attitudes and beliefs, clients are invited to examine and assess them more carefully, more honestly, in order that they might either 'own' them (perhaps for the first time in their lives) or come to realize that they can do so no longer and are in a position to consider and confront what beliefs they *do* hold.

All the above dimensions are open to investigation and clarification; in doing so, clients confront the attitudes, assumptions and values they place upon each and, as a result, are more likely to make sense of the problematic 'symptoms' in their lives as extensions of, or defensive reactions to, any of these dimensions.

The Phenomenological Method Applied to Therapy

In keeping with the phenomenological method, while they are with their clients, phenomenological therapists bracket, as far as is possible, their beliefs, theories and assumptions concerning any hypothesized dynamics that might underlie the client's symptomatology so that these have minimal effect on their attempts to see and experience their client as clearly and accurately as they can and, thereby, provide as undistorted a reflection as possible for the client to assess and examine.

I emphasize that bracketing is attempted 'as far as is possible' for three principal reasons: first, in order to make it quite clear that this is the central task of the phenomenological therapist; secondly, to acknowledge that, in keeping with phenomenological theory, the task cannot ever be fully achieved but, rather, is an ongoing process of clarification (much like life itself); and, thirdly, that, like any other system, phenomenological therapy, too, has a number of basic underlying assumptions which must be acknowledged.

The Client as Autonomous Being

The first of these assumptions is concerned with the phenomenological view that all individuals are autonomous beings. The phenomenologically oriented therapist will be primarily interested in maximizing the autonomous-being aspects of the client. As such, the therapy places strong emphasis on the immediate, here-and-now experience of both the client and the therapist. This demands a great deal of effort not only on the part of the client, but on that of the therapist as well, who must, in a very real sense, learn to enhance the client's freedom by literally 'letting the client be', or, to put it another way, to accept clients just as they are, fully acknowledging their right to hold on to their thoughts and behaviour, and to resist all efforts at therapy.

Phenomenological therapists argue that no comments and interventions made by the therapist can alter, affect or improve the clients' mental state *unless* the clients themselves freely choose to open themselves to the therapist's influence and, thereby, take their own steps towards change in their experience of being-in-the-world.

What is being stressed here is the idea that therapy is not something that one has done to oneself by another who has quasi-magical ways of 'making you better'. Rather, therapy is the opportunity to look at oneself more accurately and realistically in order to explore, reconsider and possibly choose to alter the various meaningful conclusions arrived at in the past and better to understand how such conclusions may have limited one's potentialities for being and, hence, be the 'source' of current unhappiness or disturbance.

The Therapist's Empathy and Neutrality

In order to assist clients in their investigation of their world-views as optimally as possible, it is necessary for phenomenological therapists to maintain both empathy with and personal neutrality towards their clients' life experiences. Through empathy, they are able to enter the clients' internal experience of the world as far as is possible in order to reflect it back as accurately as they are able.

Equally, through neutrality, they are more able to bracket their own meanings and interpretations of the world so as not to make it their task to value, judge or criticize their clients' experience, nor to instruct their clients as to how to live out their lives in ways which imitate and have the approval of their therapist.

Phenomenological therapists must maintain this awareness of the wide range of existential possibilities available to their clients and have the inner integrity (not to say humility) to allow their clients to arrive at their own decisions and make their own choices about how to live their lives. This, in turn, requires therapists to have a substantial degree of self-knowledge so that they are more aware of the biases and assumptions in their own lives in order to be better able to bracket them.

Similarly, phenomenological therapists attempt to bracket any personal feelings or attitudes towards their clients other than those which acknowledge an unconditional respect towards all clients' existential autonomy and integrity. They do not seek to become 'friends' with their clients, nor do they view them as 'inferior beings', nor do they open themselves to clients' demands which are above and beyond the specific contractual conditions set down and agreed upon in their first session together.

A common example of such unacceptable demands is time. As has often been noted, a wealth of 'important' insights tend to occur to clients during the last few minutes of a session, making it 'reasonable' for clients to demand extra time in order to explore them. Various approaches have hypothesized the hidden or unconscious significance of this phenomenon. While not being categorical as to its true meaning, phenomenological therapists are in agreement with most other therapeutic approaches in their typical (though not totally inflexible) refusal to allow such time-extensions.

The Emphasis on Descriptive Questioning
In the pursuance of the broad aims of the phenomenological approach to therapy, and in keeping with its underlying assumptions, questions posed to their clients by phenomenological therapists will rarely begin with *why*, since attempts to answer such questions inevitably lead to theories and speculation on the clients' (and therapists') part, concerning hypothetical originating past 'causes'.

Rather, in focusing on questions having to do with the *what and how* of experience (that is, the noematic and noetic foci of intentionality), phenomenological therapists seek to assist their clients in striving to focus on their current, or *here-and-now*, conscious experience of being-in-the-world. In this way, it is argued, clients can more easily reflect upon their experience *as it is occurring in the present* rather than be generating unprovable hypotheses as to how they might have dealt with or understood their experience at various points in the past or would like to some time in the future.

This emphasis on the present situation allows for more adequate and honest conclusions to emerge and increases the likelihood that clients will recognize the elastic nature of their experience and, thereby, reacknowledge their role as active interpreters of, rather than passive reactors to, the 'givens' of life.

The Therapist as 'Attendant'

The shift of perspective from passive, 'sick' patient requiring a
medical cure to that of a client as co-operator in exploration leads
phenomenological therapists to a position where it becomes essential
to cease, or at least minimize, any tendencies to approach their
clients as further examples of symptomatology, potential 'subjects'
upon whom they can test out their theories or hypotheses, possible
case studies, or, in general, 'objects' that can be analysed and mani-
pulated from an objective, impersonal, 'scientific' standpoint. As
R.D. Laing has noted, the term 'therapist' is originally derived from a
Greek word meaning 'attendant' (Evans, 1976: xlix) and, as such, a
therapist should be a specialist in attentiveness and awareness.

Phenomenological therapists explicitly remind their clients that,
ultimately, the task remains up to them – the clients – to find their
own meanings and truths, and, hence, to realize their role and
responsibility in the choices they have made and will continue to
make throughout their lives.

Unfortunately, one of the greatest obstacles encountered by the
phenomenological therapist is that the vast majority of clients wish
neither to hear nor to accept this argument. Most individuals who
seek therapy have convinced themselves that someone else (the
therapist) knows better than they how to live out their lives. Feeling
powerless, often expressing a deep self-hatred and loathing, such
individuals want to be told what to do, who to be, how to change for
the better, what technique they need to be taught in order to improve
a particular aspect of their lives (for example, sexual dysfunctions,
phobias, self-assertion and so on) or their lives in general so that they
will somehow, magically, emerge 'cured'.

No therapist who adopts a phenomenological orientation can claim
to provide such results solely and directly; what *can* be achieved
through phenomenological therapy, however, is the realization that
such demands are impossible to satisfy and, more importantly, both
limit and impair the client's experience of being-in-the-world. It is to
this, by no means easy, task that phenomenological therapists
address themselves.

The Emphasis on Existential Anxiety

Phenomenological therapists take the experience of anxiety to be a
fundamental 'given' of being-in-the-world. The defences that individuals raise up in order to minimize, deny or repress anxiety are, in
themselves, central factors in subsequent experiences of fragmentation, confusion, learned helplessness, denial of freedom and so
forth. In other words, the great variety of unwanted and unpleasantly

experienced 'symptoms' that clients want to be cured of are themselves defences against the acceptance of the various existential anxieties of being-in-the-world: nothingness, meaninglessness, isolation and so forth.

As such, it is not the 'treatment' of these symptoms that is central but, rather, it is the reconsideration of one's defensive, limiting beliefs that is the focus of phenomenological therapy. As Yalom has stated: 'Existential psychotherapy is a dynamic approach to therapy which focuses on concerns that are rooted in the individual's existence' (1980: 5). The phenomenological focus does not exclude the influences of unconscious forces; nor does it dispute that an individual's fears, denials and anxieties are likely to be operating at different levels of awareness. Nevertheless, its primary interest lies in the exploration and clarification of current conscious experience and the perceived conflicts inferred from this experience.

Unlike other therapeutic approaches, the phenomenological stance argues that the sources of conflict in an individual's life are not due to instinctual demands which are not being sufficiently met or which are in conflict with opposing demands, nor are they directly due to conflicts with significant others, or to misunderstood, incomplete or improper learning experiences, but, rather, they lie with the 'givens' of human existence: death, freedom, isolation and meaninglessness, and the degree to which each individual sets up defences either to minimize or to deny the anxiety they provoke.

In his valuable text, *Existential Psychotherapy* (1980), Irvin Yalom explores at length the various defences that might arise in response to the anxiety provoked by each of the existential 'givens'. Interested readers are strongly urged to refer to this text for its detailed analyses of these defences.

Let me just outline the types of symptoms that Yalom argues might arise from an individual's death anxiety. Yalom posits that there are essentially two modes of defending against this most basic of anxieties. One way is to convince oneself of one's 'specialness and personal inviolability' (Yalom, 1980: 115). That is to say, we might logically accept that, like everyone else, we will die at some point, but this rational understanding may be met with a more powerful, opposite belief that, whereas others may be doomed to die, we are somehow different, more important, 'special', and, as such, will be spared this fate. In order to convince themselves of their unique status, some individuals will enact all manner of 'death-defying' symptoms. For instance, the compulsive heroism characteristic of a writer such as Hemingway reveals the recurring need in such individuals to 'prove' this conclusion to themselves by testing themselves in more and more dangerous situations.

Equally, the workaholic, as well as being motivated by desires of 'getting on top of things', is convinced that no one else is capable of doing the work as successfully, or knowledgeably as he or she can. If no one else can match these set standards, the workaholic individual becomes more convinced of his or her indispensability – the world could not possibly survive their death.

Like the compulsive hero and the workaholic, the narcissist, the autocratic controller, the aggressor, all place their desires and abilities to control, determine, manipulate their world at centre stage. The power they convince themselves they have acts as a means to a deeper conviction: the more 'god-like' they appear to be to others and to themselves, then, like 'god', the more they can view themselves as immortal.

The other defensive road taken against death anxiety is characterized by Yalom as being that of 'The Ultimate Rescuer' (Yalom, 1980: 129–41). This ultimate rescuer may be perceived as a supernatural entity or force which guides, watches over and protects us at all times, which is omnipresent, and which often bestows 'ultimate' reward or punishment upon us. Most importantly, this version of the ultimate rescuer minimizes the power of death, reducing its finality to a mere turning point, or step, into another realm of experience. Alternatively, the ultimate rescuer need not be a supernatural entity, but another, albeit superior, human being. Religious and political leaders, charismatic personalities, the very personifiers of a cause or movement, may all be perceived as ultimate rescuers.

In either case, the ultimate rescuer fulfils the function of rule-maker, law-giver and meaning-constructor. If we believe in the words and deeds of the ultimate rescuer, if we follow the ultimate rescuer's ordinances, we gain an existential security: the world becomes an easy place to understand, all questions have their answers, our life is placed under the control of the ultimate rescuer whom we seek to emulate and serve and demonstrate unswerving allegiance to – even to the point of giving up our own life in his service.

If death has meaning and purpose, if it offers the promise of something better or finer, then it becomes more acceptable, less anxiety-provoking; it is the thought that death has no meaning, leads to nothing, that is unbearable and which the ultimate rescuer allows us to deny.

The price we pay for our beliefs in an ultimate rescuer is, of course, the loss of a great deal of what freedom we possess. Not allowed to think certain thoughts, to hold certain desires or to enact certain behaviours because they are contrary to the dictates of the ultimate rescuer, we lay ourselves open to a wide range of symptoms: masochism and depression, hysteria and fanaticism, obsession and ritual, may all follow from this defensive act.

Beliefs in our 'specialness' and beliefs in an ultimate rescuer often intermingle. While we can separate these beliefs for the purposes of discussion and analysis in a textbook, in real life it is not uncommon to note both influencing the behaviour of the same individual. We commonly tend, or gravitate, more or less to one defensive stance rather than towards the other, but both can and do coexist – after all, they share the same function and purpose.

The Anti-Medical Stance in Phenomenological Therapy

In keeping with their view that the symptoms of mental disturbance are expressions of an individual's attempts to defend against central existential anxieties, phenomenological therapists argue that the problems of mental disturbances are principally rooted in **socio-ethical bases** rather than in medical ones; that medical forms of intervention and treatment at best provide only temporary alleviation from anxiety and, at worst, may induce an even greater psychic breakdown in the sufferer; and that, rather than being random, meaningless confusion, the behaviour of the disturbed individual is meaningful and revelatory of the anxieties that are being defended against.

This stance is perhaps the most far-reaching and controversial arrived at by phenomenological therapy since it contradicts the more generally advocated view that all symptoms are the direct outcome of physical illness and are to be treated as one would treat any other medical problem.

While some practitioners might be willing to concede that many 'neurotic' symptoms may be tied to defences against the various 'problems of living' dealt with by phenomenological therapists and, as such, a neurotic might benefit from such therapy, they are likely to baulk at the notion that more severe forms of mental disturbance – the various 'psychoses', including schizophrenia, of course – may also have their origins in these same anxieties and, like most neurotic symptoms, serve as meaningful defences against these anxieties.

Phenomenological therapists have reacted strongly against the 'physical disease' model of the mind and the reliance upon physical methods of treatments such as surgical, electrical and drug therapies which have become the norm in most Western hospitals. Similarly, phenomenological therapists downplay the overwhelming importance that their physicalist colleagues ascribe to bio-genetic factors in mental disturbance. Instead, they argue that while there may be *correlates* between certain mental disturbances and the bio-genetic make-up of the individual, such factors are not in themselves directly *causative* of the wide-ranging variety and strength of individual responses to such stimuli. Phenomenological therapists argue that, rather than being problems open to medical treatment, mental disturbances reveal primarily ontological (that is, 'being'-related) issues. I will have more to say on this view in the following section.

On the basis of his theoretical insights and the impact of his ideas concerning the genesis and treatment of extreme mental disturbances, I would suggest that the leading contemporary proponent of the phenomenological viewpoint in psychiatry is R.D. Laing. What follows is an attempt to summarize a number of his phenomenologically derived contributions to our understanding and treatment of the mentally fragmented individual.

R.D. Laing and Phenomenological Psychotherapy

During the 1960s and 1970s, R.D. Laing's highly original and forceful writings increasingly identified him as a particularly insightful and innovative spokesperson for a growing number of British psychiatrists who, in their adoption of a phenomenological approach to their profession, became vociferous opponents of the prevailing ethos of physical methods of treatment of severe mental disturbances.

Like others such as Thomas Szasz (1970, 1974), Laing rejected the disease model of mental illness and expressed open hostility to exclusively bio-chemical or genetic explanations of these disturbances. Laing criticized these forms of treatment on the principal grounds that, on the whole, they ignored the social context under which the various disturbing symptoms arose and so failed to give due consideration to their underlying meanings.

When reconsidered phenomenologically, these symptoms can be seen to be defensive reactions to basic existential anxieties. In this light, the often seemingly absurd and random statements and behaviours of severely mentally disturbed individuals take on new and clarificatory significance. Moreover, when considered in a wider social context, the symptoms reveal as much about the structure and demands of the society that the disturbed individuals grow up and live in as they do about the individuals themselves. Loose colloquialisms such as 'sick' or 'mad', or psychiatric terms such as 'paranoid schizophrenia' and 'manic-depression', make plain society's denial of shared responsibility in the production of the symptoms which these labels are assumed to define.

So long as a society holds on to medical models of mental illness, no examination and criticism of that society need be considered since the origins of the problem are considered to be primarily biological or genetic in nature, thereby minimizing – and exculpating – any socio-environmental factors.

An analogous, if extreme, example of the potential dangers in denying or minimizing environmental factors when considering social or mental disturbance can be seen in the Soviet Union's treatment of critics and dissidents during the late 1970s and early 1980s when it became an acceptable practice to place political prisoners of conscience inside mental institutions. It was argued, that, if it is the case that Soviet society is the most politically advanced in the world, anyone claiming otherwise and who advances the cause of more regressive societies *must* be insane and, as such – progressive as the leaders of the Soviet Union claimed their society to be – their psychiatrists were urged to 'cure', rather than punish, internal dissidents.

Laing's interactions with individuals who had been labelled 'schizophrenic' led him to conclude that their inner experience and symptomatic behaviour could be understood as a defensive strategy that had been adopted in order to cope with 'close-to-impossible, existentially precarious situations' (Shaffer, 1978: 49).

'Normality' in Western society, for Laing, rather than proving a 'measuring stick' to determine the relative mental health of an individual, as is often assumed, instead reveals an adaptability to bad faith or inauthenticity. Schizophrenics might be abnormal, but not necessarily existentially unhealthier than 'normal' individuals.

'Who is more dangerous,' Laing asked in a now famous example, 'the seventeen-year-old girl who claims that an atom bomb sits within her, or the nuclear strategist who helps the Pentagon find efficient means of destroying, within minutes, one hundred million people. The girl is diagnosed as schizophrenic and is institutionalized, whereas the Pentagon consultant is wined, dined, fawned over, and paid extremely handsome fees.' (Shaffer, 1978: 55)

The Schizoid Split

In *The Divided Self* (1960), Laing concluded that the basic anxiety that his patients defended against could best be understood in terms of **ontological insecurity**, that is, an insecurity about one's very being. Ontologically insecure individuals experience a major *split* in their relationship with the world. This split extends into two main relational dimensions.

At one level, the split being experienced reflects an internal fragmentation, that is, a split within oneself such that a rent is experienced between aspects of self that have been accepted and other aspects which appear to be alien and open to attempts at denial. At another level, the individual experiences a split between self and others who are perceived as being dangerous and destructive agents to self-autonomy.

The case of multiple personalities can be seen as an extreme example of ontological insecurity which the individual attempts to cope with by literally creating multiple personalities to deal with this experience of internal fragmentation.

Similarly, the person who experiences a strong sense of alienation from the rest of society, who feels little or no contact with others, or who experiences what contact there is as being frightening, unpleasant and full of danger, will seek to maintain a distance from the world in order to avoid becoming in some way contaminated by it. The case of Howard Hughes (Drosnin, 1985) can be seen as a famous example of this split. Hughes constructed an ornate hierarchical system which allowed him to run his empire while at the same time avoiding any form of physical contact with virtually all of his employees. No one was allowed to be near him, no one could breathe the same air that he breathed, or touch the same objects that he touched. Any form of physical contact with others exposed Hughes to their 'killer germs'. 'Others', for Hughes, literally became dangerous to his life and health.

The existential split that the ontologically insecure person experiences has been referred to as the *schizoid condition*. In the same way that Freud employed the term 'neurotic' to include everyday psychopathological symptoms rather than restricting it to specifically clinical cases, so too did Laing make it plain that the term 'schizoid' was not to be restricted only to extreme forms of psychotic or schizophrenic 'splitness' since most (if not all) individuals experience some degree of schizoid splitness in their lives. The symptomatic, defensive behaviour of ordinary individuals differs only in degree – not in kind – from that of the 'abnormal' individual.

Like existential phenomenologists who focus on authenticity and inauthenticity, or on good faith and bad faith, as aspects of being-in-the-world, Laing presents an analysis of mental disturbances focusing on the degree of ontological security/insecurity in an individual's experience of life.

Laing did not, of course, argue that those individuals who come to be labelled 'schizophrenic' or 'psychotic' did not exhibit uniquely different, not to say bizarre, forms of behaviour; it was the assumed chaotic meaninglessness behind these behaviours that he disputed. Rather than being manifestations of medical disease, these symptoms could be better understood as expressions of, and defensive reactions to, ontological 'dis-ease' or insecurity.

When explored phenomenologically, these seemingly meaningless acts revealed attempts to deal with – even communicate – the frighteningly precarious existential condition that such individuals found themselves in. For the individual who feels this level of insecurity, the experiences of life become 'a matter not so much of gratifying oneself as of preserving oneself' (Shaffer, 1978: 52).

Ontological Insecurity and Being-in-the-World

Rather than accept, and to some extent take for granted, one's very status of being-in-the-world, the ontologically insecure individual *questions* it on three distinct levels: the level of existence (that is, *that* one is), the level of essence (that is, *what* one is), and the level of identity (that is, *who* one is).

Faced with such insecurities, any interpersonal or intrapersonal interactions may easily be interpreted as highly threatening and, hence, to be avoided as much as possible for the sake of preserving what there is of one's being. Under these circumstances, symptoms of withdrawal such as anti-social behaviour, extreme timidity and aloofness become more comprehensible. Even the extreme claims made by many schizophrenics that they are 'robots', 'unreal', 'someone else' or even 'dead' take on a sudden clarity.

The Fears of the Ontologically Insecure Individual

But what *are* the central fears of the ontologically insecure? Laing presents three specific conditions of fear as experienced by the ontologically insecure person, which, although ultimately linked in that they reflect anxieties about living, contain differing emphases in their expression.

The first fear, that of **engulfment**, focuses on anxieties related to feelings of being swallowed up, stifled, or being taken over by some alien external force. The fear of being controlled by some superior being whose powers force you to enact its wishes can be seen as an example of engulfment.

The second fear, **implosion**, shares certain similarities with engulfment in that it, too, is a fear of being taken over. In this case, however, the possessing agent resides *within* the individual and, little by little, takes control of its victim's thoughts and deeds. Here, the experience is one of being filled with something alien and dangerous. The individual who claims that there is some poison in his bloodstream or who is convinced that he has begun to emit disgusting odours, or who must wash away imaginary 'dirt' from his body expresses fears of implosion.

The third fear, **petrification**, focuses on fears of being turned into something lifeless, being somehow dead yet retaining the knowledge of once having been alive. Petrification is not 'death anxiety' in the sense that Heidegger used the phrase, but a fear of somehow being turned into inert matter which is no longer either truly alive or dead. The individual who claims 'I'm dead' reveals that this 'death' is psychological, even if the expression of this fear may well be via somatic symptomatology, such as the onset of partial or complete catalepsy.

It is in the schizoid's attempts at self-defence, Laing argues, that we see the origins of much of the strange behaviour that characterizes the psychotic or schizophrenic individual. Motivated by desires to defend against these fears, they act in remarkable, yet meaningful ways. Among their problems, unfortunately, is that very few of those who claim to seek to 'help' them find anything at all 'meaningful' in their behaviours. Interpreting ontologically based fears as signs of illness or madness, they succeed in further alienating the ontologically insecure individual from the world.

As I was preparing my notes for the above discussion, it occurred to me that these three fears are highly reminiscent of the archetypal themes of fictional and cinematic tales of horror. Being possessed by the devil, a demon or a mad hypnotist reveals the terrors of engulfment. A recent representative example of implosion can be seen in the latest cinematic version of *The Fly*, wherein the principal character's own genetic make-up begins to alter his thoughts and appearance. Equally, once the 'poison' in Dr Jekyll's formula has been imbibed by him several times, it begins to 'fight' him until he can no longer control his alterations into Mr Hyde. As for petrification, simply consider vampires (often referred to as 'the undead'), zombies ('the living dead'), even the mythological monster Medusa (whose looks do worse than kill – they turn you into stone!). Might it not be that our continuing fascination with themes of horror is fuelled by the fact that they provide vivid, if safe, means to give expression to those very fears that, to some degree, we might all share? Whatever, for the schizoid individual, life may well be seen as a series of vignettes from a horror story.

The Phenomenological Method and Laingian Therapy

In contrast to his more clinically oriented colleagues, Laing saw his task as that of decyphering the hidden meanings behind the behaviour of the mentally disturbed individual. Rather than intervene, dispute the individual's claims or numb the fears with medication, Laing observed and provided his presence, empathy and reassurance so that he could eventually reconstruct the individual's situation and understand the fears being defended against.

In contrast to what might at first seem to be the more natural, more curative, step of preventing an individual from enacting bizarre, regressive or potentially injurious behaviour as soon as that behaviour is noted, Laing argued that the first task of the therapist is not to intervene, but to attempt to discern its meaning and defensive significance.

For example, imagine that in the middle of your conversation with someone who has been diagnosed as schizophrenic you note that he has begun to tug at his hair and that, over the next minute or so, the tugging increases to the point where it seems to you that if it is allowed to continue he will do himself serious injury.

If you adopted a medical approach you would conclude that this was behaviour symptomatic of his illness and you would, in all likelihood, attempt to stop it through some form of intervention. You might, perhaps, take hold of his hand and prevent him from continuing his action. This might succeed; on the other hand, it might anger him to the point of threatened violence. At this point, you might well decide that he required a sedative and called an orderly to assist you in keeping him still long enough for you to give him an injection or force-feed a pill down his throat – actions which are highly likely to make him even more angry and violent.

Laing's position urges an alternative approach: rather than intervene at the symptomatic level, you should be initially attempting to discern the meaning behind the symptom and its significance as a defence against the fears brought on by ontological insecurity.

Just as a child might respond to a perceived shadow-like 'presence' of danger or evil, the ontologically insecure individual devises a magical, ritualistic action which wards off the presence. The child who is frightened that there might be a monster under her bed enacts a specific ritual to make the monster disappear or become harmless. She might open the doors to her cupboard three times while reciting a made-up incantation, or she might skip around her room with her eyes tight shut, or she might require the counter-active, soothing presence of a teddy bear or some other favourite object which has the power – invested by the child – to conquer the monster or bring it to a standstill. Whatever the case, a specific ritual *must* be enacted in order to rid her of her fear.

Anyone's attempts to prevent the child from carrying out such rituals lead her to become increasingly more agitated and angry, possibly even violent. Similarly, any attempts at rational argument which seeks to deny the child's experience will not assuage the child. Even acts of punishment, though possibly temporarily successful in controlling her unacceptable behaviour, will not eradicate the child's fears – rather, punishment will increase them since, now, the child has reason to fear not only the monster under her bed but also the adult 'monster' who, in denying her experience, might actually convince her that the two monsters are in league with each other, or that they are one and the same.

The adult who is concerned that a child's rituals may lead to possible injury needs first to convince her that her behaviour is accepted as being meaningful, purposive and successful in warding off the perceived dangers. Presented with acceptance rather than denial, the child is likely to be more willing to explore and reconsider the dangerous presence, treat the adult as an ally, perhaps even begin to give expression to underlying fears in a more concrete rather than symbolic manner.

At the very least, the creative adult might even present the child with alternative social rituals for her to consider and attempt so that, even if her fears are not resolved, the rituals are no longer potentially physically harmful, nor are they likely to single her out as being aberrant or 'odd' in the eyes of others. So long as the child enacts rituals which are tolerated or even valued by adult society, both the rituals and the child will be no cause for concern; indeed the child's behaviour is more likely to be viewed as 'cute', rather than as symptomatic of mental imbalance.

In acknowledging the sense behind the ritual, the adult has at least opened the way for the child to express fears more openly; more significantly, in the long run, the adult, as representative 'other', shows the child that 'others' need not be further sources of fear but, rather, can be 'stimuli' for experiences of love and ontological security.

The person who has been labelled 'schizophrenic' might fear 'poison in the bloodstream' rather than 'a monster under the bed', but his fear is of the same shadowy presences as those imagined by the child. And, like the child, he has learned to defend against those fears by enacting rituals – such as 'tugging at his hair'.

If you decide to take interventionist measures like those of the adult above, you may succeed in stopping the behaviour temporarily through manipulative treatment (which is experienced as 'punishment' by the person being treated), but, inadvertently, you will also increase his fear and, worse, convince him that you, too, are dangerous and a threat to his being.

In essence, Laing's approach asks the therapist to acknowledge each individual's experience; to provide a neutral, yet empathic stance that invites description, exploration and assessment of the fears being experienced and their underlying issues of insecurity; and, rather than 'infantalize' individuals further by taking action over their lives, to assume their right to autonomous action.

In following this procedure, the therapist disconfirms many of the fears and insecurities concerning others that fragmented individuals are likely to be experiencing, and allows the breaking down of any number of the defensive symptomatic reactions to others that they have felt a need to employ for self-protection. As a result of breaching these defences, individuals are more likely to regain a growing sense of integration and ontological security.

With regard to my example of the hair-tugging schizophrenic, by asking what he's doing, or by pointing out his action to him, or even by imitating it yourself, you might be told, for example, that through this sensory experience he is able to reassure himself that he still exists and that, hence, the greater his doubt, the more forceful the activity of hair-tugging needs to be.

Knowing such, it becomes evident that any preventative measures you might take would increase his doubts (and his fear-wrought insecurities) rather than allay them. It is only in your acceptance of his act, in your willingness to attempt to discern its meaning rather than treat it – and, by implication, the individual carrying it out – as 'sick' or 'mad', that its significance might become clearer to you.

Ultimately, your stance requires your respect for the individual before you – a respect that makes a basic assumption that his actions, no matter how meaningless and confused they might appear to you, are his means of coping with terrifying fears, frightening insecurities. Destructive and physically harmful as his actions may seem to be, their aim is to *preserve* what he experiences is left of his being; misguided as they may be, his acts are attempts at self-survival rather than self-destruction, and, as such, though possibly ineffectual, they are by no means meaningless or 'crazy'.

The Schizoid Individual as Critic of Society

Some critics of Laing have accused him of 'glorifying' severe disturbances such as schizophrenia and of elevating the often bleak and pain-filled behaviours of these individuals into acts of bravery or mystical insight (Evans, 1976). This, I think, is a serious misreading of Laing possibly resulting from his public statements to the general media in order to 'stir things up' in medical circles.

While not glorifying mental disturbances, Laing does argue against dismissal of the statements and actions of the mentally disturbed on the grounds that they are meaningless. Instead, he suggests that those who experience the world from an extreme schizoid condition might actually be capable of more clearly pointing out and clarifying the absurd and life-endangering acts of inauthenticity that characterize 'normal' living in industrial society. The extremely schizoid are not here being viewed as in some way 'superior to' or 'more heroic' than normal individuals; rather, all that is being stated is that, because of their deep fragmentation, unlike normal people they are less able to deny or defend against the shared anxieties of being-in-the-world. It is in this sense, and this sense alone, that the schizoid individual might be considered to be a 'seer' of some clarity.

The Aetiology of the Schizoid Split

Laing's theory (1960, 1961, 1967, 1982; Laing and Esterson, 1964) posits that the schizoid split originates in our earliest interactions with others; it is the very structure of the family that nurtures both the normal and extreme variants of ontological insecurity.

Through our earliest interactions with the family we learn that certain of our behaviours are deemed to be good and others are judged as being bad. Good acts are valued and positively reinforced, bad acts are either negatively reinforced or, more commonly, punished by the family. For Laing, the term 'good' primarily equates with compliance to the family's wishes or codes of behaviour, where-as the term 'bad' refers to acts which defy or rebel against the family's code of conduct.

Laing's criticism is not that it is wrong for the family, or any other social institution for that matter, to seek to impose rules of conduct (for whatever reasons). Obviously, any social institution requires codes of behaviour. The problem which is of central concern to Laing arises when a social structure such as the family fails to make a distinction between one's actions and one's being. This distinction, Laing suggests (I think correctly), is rarely considered or made explicit.

Although the distinction between the statements 'what you are doing is bad' and 'you are bad for doing that' may seem superficial at first, their existential implications vary considerably, since, once one's being is directly linked to one's actions, any attempts to prevent, punish or deny them are equated to threats to one's being. Under the terms of this equation, schizoid fragmentation becomes inevitable.

If the child is told, for instance, that because he's acted badly, 'daddy doesn't love him', what the child is likely to understand is that he (or at least a part of him) has no right to exist in the physical world, and that, in order to maintain his very physical existence, the child must adopt a variety of fragmentatory defences. Equally, the child learns that others – even significant others – will either value or threaten his existence on the basis of what he does.

The issue is further exacerbated when we recall that the young child makes little, if any, distinction between mental and physical acts (Ginsburg and Opper, 1969). Even 'bad thoughts' become threats to one's existence and must be defended against.

As a result of the family's injunctions and rewards, we learn to define who we are and whether we have a right to be. The family, then, becomes not only the source of our 'good' or positive definitions of self, it also serves the function of defining those 'bad' or negative aspects of self which must not be allowed to be expressed (mentally or behaviourally) because to express them threatens not only our relations with the family (and others in general) but also our internal relations, that is, our very being.

Our attempts to deny the 'bad' self lead to fragmentation. Further, faced with the 'bad' self's inevitable appearance, we can only explain its presence on the basis of external or alien internal agencies. At worst unable to explain or control them, we might see no recourse other than to completely 'shut off' our capacity to experience. Here, then, lies the origin of the three schizoid fears discussed earlier.

Laing further argues that, however threatening the appearance of the 'bad' self may seem, our attempts to deal with the conflicts its presence generates lead to the development of an adult, autonomous identity. In other words, the conflicts of identity which, for most of us, arise during our adolescence can be seen as our attempts to come to terms with the 'bad' self. The degree of our success in this task is reflected in the development of a relatively independent – if also relatively schizoid – adult.

Laing became convinced that the basis for severely schizoid individuals' symptomatology lay in their lack of any lasting development of an autonomous adult identity. The extremely schizoid have an arrested development since, in their failure to incorporate the 'bad' self into their identity to some degree, they cannot achieve a sufficient level of autonomy. In perceiving the appearance of the 'bad' self as being overwhelmingly threatening to their existence, they strive to be 'good' all the time and seek the approval and love of their family.

If the power to decide that one is 'good' lies entirely in the hands of the family and the family's love is removed when one is 'bad', then the solution is obvious: one must simply never be 'bad'. Yet such a position is impossible to maintain; the 'bad' self asserts its existence in verbal and/or behavioural outbursts that the 'good' self can neither explain nor 'own'. This erratic and incomprehensible appearance of the 'bad' self is interpreted by the family as a symptom of 'madness'.

Laing's studies of the family structure of 'mad' individuals revealed a particular intolerance of 'bad' behaviour in their children, an intolerance expressed in any number of ways which threatened the schizoid's sense of being. In response, the family might act as if the individual simply did not exist when the 'bad' self emerged (as in the case of Peter in *The Divided Self* (Laing, 1960)), or, in their (claimed) inability to make sense of the 'bad' behaviour, insist that its genesis must be due to constitutional 'madness'.

In the film *A Family Life*, which presented these aspects of Laing's theory in a dramatized form, the 'mad' heroine's parents claim that their daughter used to be 'good' (that is, 'obedient'), turned 'bad' as a result of the rebellious, anti-social individuals she'd met, and who has now been driven 'mad'. Overwhelmed by existential anxiety, too frightened to assert any autonomy because of the threat to her sense of being it produces, incapable of explaining her 'bad' thoughts and behaviours as being self-generated, their daughter can only collude with their conclusions – she *must* be 'mad' to behave as she does.

Laing's analysis of the schizoid split points out the existential dimensions which, though so often neglected in modern psychiatric theories which focus on exclusively organic variables, seem so central to the onset of 'mental illness' and to medical science's attempts to understand and treat it.

Laing's critics have argued that he minimizes the organic variables to the point of dismissal, thereby sidestepping the dramatic advances being made in the medical treatment of such extreme forms of mental disease as schizophrenia, senile and alcoholic psychosis, depression and so forth. Laing's response is that, whereas he acknowledges the organic factor as one among several, he sees no reason to assume that this factor is, in itself, any more *significant* than any other. More importantly, the insistence on the part of medical science that this factor is the originating or causal factor is a 'sedimented bias' which hinders a more adequate contextual analysis of the problem.

> If I am disturbed, I may be disturbed spiritually, intellectually, emotionally, and physically. Many neurologists, once they find something, as they say 'organic', they think that's it . . . Until chemists and geneticists see the focus within the *context*, and realize there is an interplay between chemistry and social interaction, we can't develop the theoretical speculation at a pure science level we must have. (Laing in Evans, 1976: 18–22)

The following example should clarify Laing's argument. A group of people are given the same dosage of LSD. For the sake of argument, assume that their physical constitutions are roughly the same so that their bio-chemical responses to the drug will not vary significantly. Each individual's experience of, and response to, the drug's effects will, nevertheless, be different. One individual may experience overwhelming fear; another may experience profound ecstasy. Yet another may find it impossible to control sudden feelings of joy and express them through unrestrained laughter, while still another may be flooded with feelings of abject misery and begin to cry like a baby. There may also be an individual whose behaviour shows no demonstrable change whatsoever, and so forth.

Even when the observed behaviour of one of these individuals shares a variety of features with that of others, the perceptions and memories which act as stimuli to the evocation of such behaviours will remain *unique* to each individual. In other words, each individual will *interpret* the chemical changes being experienced in a unique manner.

To argue that the drug alone directly caused all these reactions is both simplistic and misleading. The drug may have caused chemical changes to take place in the nervous systems of the individuals, but these changes had to be interpreted by each individual so that they could be acted upon in the way that they were. Similarly, providing an individual with an antidote that may counteract the drug's effects does not guarantee that other stimuli (be they chemical or otherwise), at some future point in time, might provoke similar changes in an individual's behaviour.

In the same way, it is, at best, naive to suggest that an imbalance in the bio-chemistry of an individual, or some unusual combination of genetic factors is the sole or primary cause of an observed mental disturbance. Rather than being a direct cause–effect relationship, it is the interpretation given to the stimulus that will determine an individual's subsequent response. For all we know, there may be any number of individuals with the same bio-chemical imbalances or genetic combinations who never exhibit any signs of 'mental illness'.

Laing's view does not dismiss or deny possible bio-chemical or genetic factors in any mental disturbance. But it does argue against any tendency to view these factors as the sole or direct causes of that disturbance. Instead, Laing insists that the primary concern of the therapist should be the interpretations given by the disturbed individual to these, and any other, factors. By exploring the created meaning of the experience, testing out alternative explanations, and exposing the existential anxieties which provide the context for the disturbance, the 'mad' behaviour may well be better understood, alleviated, and possibly even extinguished.

·l Rogers and Phenomenological Therapy

Very similar insights on the phenomenological basis of mental disturbances characterize the work of another highly influential therapist,
Carl Rogers (1902–88).

Rogers, the founder of **client-centred therapy** has had an enormous
influence in the fields of counselling, psychotherapy and education
(Rogers, 1942, 1951, 1964; Rogers and Stevens, 1967). Although
most textbook accounts of Rogers's client-centred therapy fail to
reveal his obvious indebtedness to the phenomenological method,
Rogers himself made explicit reference to phenomenology as the
primary basis for his approach (Wann, 1964; Evans, 1975). It is this
central aspect of Rogers's contribution to psychotherapy that I wish
to examine.

The Rogerian Self-Concept
The concept of the self and the individual's subjective conclusions
about 'self' are central themes running through all of Rogers's writings. Adopting an unequivocally optimistic view of human nature, he
argues that all human beings strive for **self-actualization**, that is, 'the
urge . . . to expand, extend, become autonomous, develop, mature –
the tendency to express and activate all the capacities of the organism
. . .' (Rogers, 1961: 35).

Rogers hypothesizes that this urge might become less apparent,
'contaminated', by self-imposed defences arising out of inauthentic
interactions with significant others – principally, one's family – which
lead to the subjective experience of fragmentation and restrict
growth and development. Like Laing, Rogers sees the therapeutic
process as an opportunity for clients to explore their subjective
experience of the world, expose fragmentatory defences, and begin
to liberate and reintegrate their various potentials for being, thereby
regaining a sense of their autonomy and allowing a more direct
expression to their actualizing tendency.

Client-Centred Therapy
Decrying the medical orientation to therapy for much the same
reasons as do Laing, Szasz and others, Rogers takes his criticisms one
step further by insisting that the therapist's dependence upon, and
therapeutic preoccupations with, *theory*, while engaged in therapy,
result in a defensive and distancing intellectualization on the part of
the therapist which itself hinders the client's steps towards
reintegration.

Therapists cannot attend to both client and theory at the same
time. Any attempts to do so will succeed only in distancing them from

the special relationship required of successful therapy. Instead, for Rogers, the therapist's attitude and aim should be to enter the client's subjective world in order to experience it and to reflect it back to the client as accurately and concretely as possible.

This client-centred approach emphasizes an extreme reluctance to ask questions of clients and, in particular, to avoid asking those questions which, rather than seeking clarification of the client's current experience, involve hypotheses and ruminations concerning the client's remembered past experience. Further, the client-centred approach urges therapists not to make interpretative comments, offer advice or argue with the client's conclusions since these, too, hinder the therapist's ability to 'mirror the client's phenomenology as faithfully as possible' (Shaffer, 1978: 82).

Although Rogers takes an extremist stance on the issue of asking questions, it is evident that it is both a derivation and an extension of the phenomenological attitude which avoids asking questions related to assumed direct causality (that is, questions beginning with 'why') and focusing on questions designed to describe an individual's noematic and noetic experience (that is, questions beginning with 'what' or 'how').

Rogers's Three Necessary and Sufficient Attitudes

The client-centred approach insists that the therapeutic relationship must include three necessary attitudes or qualities on the part of the therapist which will allow the development of a unique and unthreatening relationship, opening the way for clients to expose, reconsider, and evaluate their subjective experiences of themselves and the world (Rogers, 1951, 1964).

The first of these attitudes is usually referred to as **unconditional positive regard**. Rogers identified the features of this attitude in the following manner:

> I hypothesize that growth and change are more likely to occur the more that the counsellor is experiencing a warm, positive, acceptant attitude towards what *is* in the client. It means that he prizes his client, as a person, with somewhat the same quality of feeling that a parent feels for his child, prizing him as a person regardless of his particular behavior at the moment. It means that he cares for his client in a non-possessive way, as a person with potentialities .... It means a kind of love for the client as he is, providing we understand the word love as equivalent to the theologian's term *agape* and not in its usual romantic and possessive meanings. What I am describing is a feeling which is not paternalistic, nor sentimental, nor superficially social and agreeable. It respects the other person as a separate individual and does not possess him. It is a kind of liking which has

strength, and which is not demanding. We have termed it positive regard.
(Rogers and Stevens, 1967: 94)

This attitude of positive regard is said to be 'unconditional' in the
sense that client-centred therapists strive never implicitly or explicitly
to threaten to take away their positive regard from their clients
regardless of what they think or feel about the clients' behaviour.

Client-centred therapists must be clear on the point that while what
the client *does* is open to judgement (be it positive or negative), *who
the client is* (that is, the client's being or 'personhood') must be
accepted under all and any conditions (that is, unconditionally). This
distinction, so often misunderstood even by those claiming to be
client-centred therapists, is, initially, as difficult to understand as it is
to accept.

As I discussed in my previous section on Laing's ideas, from our
earliest interactions with others – and especially with significant
others like our parents – most of us learn that their positive regard for
us is **conditional** upon our behaviour.

If no distinction is made between 'being' and 'doing', an obvious
lesson is learned: in order to be loved, one must be/do certain things
and avoid being/doing others. This lesson leads directly to self-
imposed limitation and fragmentation – certain potentialities of
being *must* be avoided, rejected, denied or repressed because if
they're not, one's being is threatened.

But how can a therapist, even a client-centred therapist, avoid
giving only *conditional* positive regard?

Although Rogers does not provide a specific prescription for the
giving of unconditional positive regard, a clue can be ascertained
from phenomenological theory. Recall that phenomenology argues
that every experience contains both a noematic and a noetic component. Put simply (if not simplistically), every experience is made up of
a 'story' (that is, *what* happened) and the affective components
linked to the 'story' (that is, *how* what happened is interpreted and
'felt' by the experiencing being). If the therapist focuses primary
attention upon the affective components rather than upon the 'story'
elements of an experience, the giving of unconditional positive
regard becomes far more likely to occur.

For example, a number of years ago I had a female client who had
great difficulty in resolving a major issue in her life. In spite of her
academic abilities and her parents' wishes for her to take up a grant
she'd been offered to attend a prestigious university, her great desire
was to enter the armed forces. As a consequence of the conflict she
experienced, her anxiety had risen to such levels that she'd attempted
suicide.

As my personal attitude to the armed forces is more than tinged with negativity, had I focused my attention on the noematic or 'story' element of her situation, I would have found it difficult to avoid judging her conflict as being somewhat ludicrous and might have been tempted to minimize the significance of her problem, and perhaps even 'side' with her parents. My client's noematic focus of experience was alien to me; her problem would never have arisen in my own life. On the basis of her 'story', her experience was difficult for me to empathize with.

Luckily, however, I focused my attention on the noetic focus of her experience and was able at least partially to enter her feeling-world of confusion, anguish, guilt, incompatible desire and so forth. Consequently, I had no difficulty in either sympathizing or empathizing with the feelings underlying her experience. In the end, having explored and partially resolved the various anxieties which created her conflicts, she elected to join the navy.

Our differing 'stories' demand judgements which can either unite or separate us. But the affects that are linked to each are shared by all members of our species. In focusing on these unifying affects, both story-teller and listener acknowledge their humanity, recognize each other's being and are at least more likely to accept it *unconditionally*.

So long as we relate to and define individuals solely in terms of their behaviours and fail to consider the affective elements linked to them, we perpetrate the type of society that places its emphasis on conditional positive regard. In doing so, we foster schizoid defences that, in themselves, may act as primary influences towards the engendering of those very acts which we wish to eradicate.

The second necessary condition in client-centred therapy is that of **accurate empathy**. Here, the Rogerian therapist is interested in grasping and adhering to the client's frame of reference as closely as possible in order to reflect back or (to use Rogers's term) to 'mirror' the client's experience as accurately and effectively as possible. To do so, the therapist refrains as far as possible from imposing personal and theoretical values and biases, since to do so would only lead to unwanted interpretation, judgement and prescription, each of which places obstacles in the way of the development of the desired relationship. Rather than engage in these divisive activities, the client-centred therapist *attends* to the client's statements and their underlying affects at a neutral and descriptive level so that the client may clarify and explore subjective experiences. This practice, sometimes referred to as active listening, promotes accurate empathy.

The third necessary condition of client-centred therapy is **congruence**, and, in Rogers's view, is perhaps the most important of the three variables. Congruence refers to the therapist's ability to be present and without façade, that is, to be a living embodiment of integration. The congruent therapist acts as role model for authentic being. Once again, it is not so much what the therapist does as the therapist's willingness to be as real, as transparent, as free of defences, as possible that, Rogers argues, provides clients with the necessary strength and willingness to engage in honest and accurate self-exploration and revelation.

As well as being necessary, Rogers argues that the three attitudes or, as they are sometimes called, therapeutic conditions discussed above are also *sufficient* in themselves for successful therapy to occur. No other specialized skills or knowledge are required of the therapist; indeed, as I've pointed out above, these might actually impede rather than support the development of the therapeutic relationship.

At first, this stance might seem naive or even dangerous to some. But, as Rogers has pointed out, this reaction reveals a view of therapy which emphasizes 'doing' skills as opposed to 'being' skills, and, as I have tried to demonstrate, Rogers sees the symptomatology of mental disturbance as originating from a fragmentation in one's self-concept which imposes unnecessary limitations on one's being-in-the-world. It is the degree of unity, or integration, in an individual's experiences of the world that either impedes or promotes self-actualization. The more capable individuals are in examining, accepting and integrating their subjective experiences, the more often they are likely to experience themselves as real, or authentic, beings-in-the-world.

Client-Centred Therapy as a Restatement of the Phenomenological Method

In theory, client-centred therapy seems to be simplicity itself. As Rogers himself once said of his approach:

> I can state the overall hypothesis in one sentence, as follows. If I can provide a certain type of relationship, the other person will discover within himself the capacity to use that relationship for growth and change and personal development will occur. (1961: 33)

However, in practice, client-centred therapy is perhaps among the most difficult to adhere to.

First, both clients and therapists must overcome what biases they hold concerning their roles and attitudes. Clients typically want to maintain the role of defenceless victim that they have placed themselves in and assume that the therapist will take over their lives (like an idealized parent) and, in so doing, resolve their problems, make decisions for them, provide them with the truth.

Equally, therapists, having learned a wide number of theoretical approaches to and skills-based techniques for therapy, find it difficult not to offer to supply what the client wants and, in so doing, enter an unequal and experientially limited relationship with them.

Thirdly, and perhaps the source of greatest resistance, what client-centred therapy asks, initially of the therapist, but ultimately of both therapist and client, is that they engage in a relationship which almost certainly runs counter to any that has been sanctioned by society. Having learned to build up any number of defences which now seem essential to survival, the client is urged to examine and reconsider these defences not via the therapist's argumentative or manipulative skills but through the therapist's own willingness to *be* defenceless.

In many ways, these difficulties are highly similar to those encountered when attempting to practise the phenomenological method. Indeed, I would argue that client-centred therapy is a restatement of the essentials of the phenomenological method. The client-centred therapist, like the practitioner of the phenomenological method, attempts to bracket prior assumptions, biases and sedimented assumptions (the rule of epoché); focuses upon and describes (rather than seeks to interpret or explain) immediate experience (the rule of description); and avoids making hierarchical distinctions or judgements with regard to the value of one experience over another (the rule of horizontalization).

Such similarities are not superficial; both methods point to an attitude towards the investigation of a problem which demands an adherence to neutrality, accuracy, honesty and recognition of subjective involvement. Further, just as the phenomenologist admits the investigation to be an ongoing process, so, too, does the client-centred therapist accept that there is no end-point (except death) to the process of self-actualization. Finally, and perhaps most importantly, both focus on issues of 'being' rather than 'doing'.

More generally, both accept as given the infinite varieties of interpretations that a situation might provoke, both take for granted the initial validity of all interpretations, and both, in their openness to 'being', make possible the experience of startling and potentially valuable insights.

Phenomenological Therapy: a Summary

The phenomenological approach to therapy is primarily concerned with the emphasis on and exploration of mental fragmentation. Rather than being primarily concerned with the alleviation or removal of symptoms (that is, 'cures'), phenomenological therapists place the focus of concern upon their clients' interpretations of themselves and their relationship to others or the world in general.

Phenomenological therapists guide their clients towards a confrontation with the anxieties of being that have been encountered and defended against at the cost of existential fragmentation. In developing a relationship with their clients that encourages a more honest and accurate, and less defensive, self-examination, the therapeutic aim of regaining autonomy and leading an authentic existence becomes more of a possibility. If not any happier, life will become at least more bearable and more directly 'felt' than before.

R.D. Laing is generally acknowledged to be one of the central contemporary figures among practitioners of phenomenological therapy. On the other hand, some readers may have been surprised to find a summary of client-centred therapy in this chapter since both it and its founder, Carl Rogers, are most commonly linked with the humanistic approach to psychology. Though he acknowledged his phenomenological grounding, Rogers did, nevertheless, strongly associate himself with humanistic psychology and is often recognized, along with Abraham Maslow, as a founding father of the movement. Rogers's 'dual allegiance' encapsulates a more general problematic issue: the distinction between phenomenological psychology and humanistic psychology is far from clear to most psychology students (or to psychologists in general).

The next chapter will consider this problem and, in pointing out the similarities and differences of these two psychological systems, will offer an initial attempt at its resolution.

8

Phenomenological and Humanistic Psychologies: Similarities and Contrasts

If it feels good, do it.

Anonymous slogan of the 'Me' generation

Over a decade ago, when I first began to teach psychology courses, the vast majority of introductory texts made reference to humanistic psychology as the **third force** or orientation in contemporary psychology (the first and second orientations being those of behaviourism and psychoanalysis). Very little mention, if any at all, was made of phenomenological approaches to psychology. A cursory glance at current introductory texts will reveal that the situation has reversed itself; it now seems that phenomenological psychology has become the 'third force' in contemporary psychology and far less reference is made to humanistic approaches.

What makes this situation all the more interesting (and amusing), however, is that, although the section headings in these textbooks have undergone a change of name, a comparison of the text summary of these approaches reveals only slight, if any, revision. (An example of this tendency can be seen when one compares the résumé of humanistic psychology given in the sixth edition of Hilgard, Atkinson and Atkinson's *Introduction to Psychology* (1975) to that provided for phenomenological psychology in the ninth edition (1987) of the same text.) Clearly the authors of such texts are assuming that the distinctions between one approach and the other are minimal, or that both humanistic psychology and phenomenological psychology refer to the same approach.

But are these assumptions correct?

The Origins and Development of Contemporary Humanistic Psychology

The earliest indications of the humanistic approach to psychology can be seen to have emerged contemporaneously with both the behaviourist and psychoanalytic approaches. The writings of Wilhelm Dilthey (Hodges, 1944) and Eduard Spranger (1928) during the first decade of this century protested against the tendency to link psychology to the natural sciences. Rather than pursue this reductionist tendency, these authors argued for the development of an **understanding** psychology which 'emphasized the dynamic nature and unique growth of each individual' (Misiak and Sexton, 1973: 108).

Parallel to this position, Gestalt psychology, while maintaining an experimental approach, emphasized its **holistic** stance and implicit dependence upon the phenomenological method as an essential means to psychological investigation (Kohler, 1929; Koffka, 1935).

It is also clear that major figures in the early development of psychology, individuals such as William James (1890) and G. Stanley Hall (1904), were strongly influenced by these movements in that their concerns lay with the investigation of subjective experience as a means of developing a scientific model of psychology that avoided mechanistic reductionism and preserved the distinctly 'human' qualities of its subject area. This argument continued to be advocated during the 1930s and 1940s by Gordon Allport (1955), Carl Rogers (1942) and Abraham Maslow (1968), among others.

It was only in the 1950s, however, that their views coalesced into a formal movement of North American and European psychologists strongly critical of the dominant trends in the psychology of their time. Primary among their dissatisfactions was the limited and one-sided view of humanity that dominated psychology and which tended to base its 'explanations' on bio-physical models which either dismissed or minimized conscious experience and thereby 'dehumanized' and reduced human beings to relatively simple reactive mechanisms.

Instead, humanistic psychologists argued, psychology should focus on the **primary, 'human' dimensions** of our species, dimensions which emphasized the human being's liberation from the bio-physical restraints that control and determine the behaviour of the 'lower' species. Human creativity, decision-making, interpretation of stimuli, moral development – all these issues and more had been sorely neglected by the dominant trends, or else insufficiently 'explained away' via reductive models. Humanistic psychologists were intent on redressing the balance. The British psychologist, John Cohen, effectively summarized this stance in his influential text *Humanistic Psychology* (1958):

> the subject matter of psychology is distinctly human; it is not the 'mere lining of physiology.' Our first step should therefore be to study what is characteristic of man, the blossom rather than the root. (Cohen, 1958; quoted in Misiak and Sexton, 1973: 111)

However, humanistic psychology, as it now tends to be understood, only truly came to the fore during the 1960s, principally as a result of three separate, though related factors significant to both psychology and Western culture in general.

The first of these was the growing disenchantment with both the behaviourist and the psychoanalytic models adopted by psychologists. For different reasons, each approach was beginning to be recognized as having seemingly in-built limitations which prevented a more complete understanding of human behaviour. In particular, the deficiencies in each model with regard to conscious mental processing had become increasingly apparent. Subsequent attempts to deal with this problem led to the so-called **cognitive revolution** within experimental psychology, the growing influence of **object relations theory** and **ego psychology** within psychodynamic approaches, and, not least, the rise of humanistic psychology.

At about the same time, the **human encounter movement** with its focus on self-discovery and the development of more 'liberating' ways to interact and communicate with oneself and others gained sudden popularity and massive media interest (particularly in North America). Loosely based on Lewin's **T-groups** (Rowan, 1976), encounter groups attracted an ever-increasing clientèle who demonstrated an unflagging willingness to indulge in a seemingly never-ending variety of techniques aimed at the exploration of one's potentials for being. By the end of the decade, this loose conglomerate of growth techniques became known as the **human potential movement**.

The third, and perhaps most significant, factor in the emergence of humanistic psychology was the rise of the youth-dominated **counter-culture**. Emphasizing its allegiance to 'new left' politics, its rejection of 'role-appropriate', 'establishment' thinking and behaviour, and its insistence on both freeing and expanding one's self-awareness via drugs, political, social and sexual 'consciousness raising', alternative lifestyles and so forth, it found its unity and strength in its protest against the war in Vietnam and adulation of rock-and-roll music.

The key feature in all three of these factors was a disenchantment with the norm, and a desire to develop more satisfactory, more relevant alternatives. Under such conditions, traditional approaches to psychology (as with everything else) became open to challenge; it is hardly surprising that a 'humanistic' psychology offering 'freedom, authenticity, and openness to experience' (Shaffer, 1978: 8) seemed worth serious investigation.

The Central Tenets of Humanistic Psychology

In his important text, *Humanistic Psychology* (1978), John Shaffer outlines five basic principles, or emphases, which distinguish humanistic psychology from the other contemporary approaches. In summary, they are as follows:

1. Conscious experience is seen as the source of primary data. The recognition of the uniqueness of subjective experience allows for a greater sense of freedom and openness to one's potentials.

2. Rather than separating being and experience into various dichotomies, components, typologies, traits or functions, humanistic psychology retains a holistic and integrated view of human beings.

3. In spite of the bio-physical limitations placed upon them, human beings are essentially autonomous and experientially free.

4. Humanistic psychology insists on the genuineness of conscious experience and avoids taking a reductionist stance.

5. No complete, final, all-encompassing theory of human behaviour and experience is possible.

Phenomenological Psychology versus Humanistic Psychology

It should be evident that, on consideration, these five characteristic emphases are as applicable to a phenomenological standpoint as they are to the humanistic. However, on closer analysis, divergences begin to emerge.

First, the primary orientation through which humanistic psychology is typically identified today emerged primarily as a result of the massive cultural and political unrest of the 1960s. Although this upheaval was world-wide, the focus and concerns of humanistic psychology have a peculiarly North American slant. As such, humanistic psychology's greatest impact has been on North American psychology. Various attempts to introduce it to Europe have been met with some significant resistance such that what *has* developed in Europe remains very much on the fringes of academic respectability, and what ground it does seem to have gained is principally oriented in the therapeutic community in general and in the counselling movement in particular. In other words, much of humanistic psychology appears to be largely culture-bound to the North American experience.

On closer reflection, it is the emphases given to humanistic psychology as a result of these cultural limitations that clarify the differences between it and the phenomenological approach. Put crudely, much of humanistic psychology reflects a North American attitude which, in its emphasis on technique, can be summarized as: 'If it works, do it.' Phenomenological psychology, on the other hand, firmly rooted in Continental European philosophy, takes a much more guarded stance which de-emphasizes technique and explores the wider implications of its ideology.

Yalom, for example, aware of this divergence, has labelled humanistic psychology as existential psychology's 'flashy American cousin' (1980: 17–21). More significantly, he has noted that whereas humanistic psychology has focused almost exclusively on individual freedom, choice and liberation, European existentialism, while acknowledging those features as requiring proper consideration, has also stressed the inherent limitations and 'tragic dimensions of existence' (1980: 19).

Echoing this view, van Deurzen-Smith has decried humanistic psychology's assumption that human beings are 'basically positive creatures who develop constructively, given the right conditions' (1988: 56). Instead, she reminds us, the existential attitude is 'that people may evolve in any direction, good or bad, and that only reflection on what constitutes good and bad makes it possible to exercise one's choice in the matter' (1988: 56–7). Both writers suggest a 'skewedness' in the humanistic approach; where phenomenology stresses a balanced consideration of both the unexplored potentials and inherent limits to freedom, humanistic psychology speaks:

> less of limits and contingency than of development of potential, less of acceptance than of awareness, less of anxiety than of peak experiences and oceanic oneness, less of life meaning than of self-realization, less of apartness and isolation than of I–Thou and encounter. (Yalom, 1980: 19)

It is this imbalance, for example, that marks out Carl Rogers's stance. Whereas, as I've tried to show, his approach to therapy has its basis in the phenomenological method, his unwavering optimism as to the basic 'goodness' of human beings runs counter to the more guarded phenomenological stance as expressed by Yalom and van Deurzen-Smith, and, as a result, places him as firmly in the broad humanist camp as it does within the phenomenological orientation.

More generally, although phenomenology provides the primary

considerations and philosophical bases to the wide (even confusing) variety of contemporary humanistic techniques, many of the developers and practitioners of these techniques have failed, on the whole, to examine these bases fully and, as a result, have 'tainted' humanistic psychology with unnecessary, misguided, even potentially dangerous, overly optimistic tendencies.

The solipsistic excesses of the 'Me' decade of the 1970s can be seen as direct results of this unbalanced perspective. Emphasizing only self-growth, self-development and self-interest without paying due consideration to the effects of such on others, most of the North American engendered techniques employed by humanistic psychologists clearly fail to acknowledge and duly consider phenomenology's conclusions with regard to the indivisible definitional nature of the self/other (or 'I'/ 'not I') relationship.

As a result, rather than promote co-operation, humility and shared responsibility, the great majority of humanistic techniques (if unwillingly) have fostered competition, self-aggrandizement and disdain for others' subjective experiences. In their failure to give equal weight to a number of central phenomenological conclusions in their writings, teachings and techniques, many humanistic psychologists broke away from the very method (that is, the phenomenological method) that they claimed to follow or to have been influenced by.

One effect of this, I would argue, has been the very slow progress and development of humanistic psychology since its heyday a generation ago; more tellingly, it has retained its alternative status within psychology, taking on a role very similar to that of the agreeable, though somewhat dotty, member of the family whom everyone speaks of with some concern and means to get around to doing something about, but somehow never does.

Lest my contention might sound unduly harsh to humanistically oriented readers, I wish to make it clear that my points are not meant to dismiss nor diminish humanistic psychology's contributions to the field. I have myself referred to several important and well-argued texts which bear great relevance to both phenomenological psychology and psychology in general that have been written by psychologists who would wish to be closely identified with the humanistic orientation.

At the same time, my suspicion is that such authors have adopted the term 'humanistic psychology' in order to designate their allegiance to movements in psychology which place the study of the conscious experience of human beings at their centre rather than out of their wish to be identified with any particular technique or 'complex' of techniques whose principal (if not sole) aim is to provide the means for 'better' or 'more fulfilling' ways of being.

Obviously, the possibility of enriching one's life is not to be scorned or dismissed, but it is equally important to be aware of the very real physical, social and political obstacles limiting the life experiences of a great many individuals. Such obstacles do not simply 'disappear' as a result, say, of acknowledging one's responsibility for one's subjective experience of the world. The recognition of responsibility may well change our perspectives of ourselves as beings-in-the-world, but such change does not necessarily promise (as do a great many humanistic techniques) increased happiness or 'betterment'.

Perhaps, on balance, the ideology espoused by humanistic psychology can be most accurately viewed as an offshoot of that which is at the core of phenomenological psychology. Admittedly, their dividing lines are hazy and vary from one humanistic technique to another. In order to demonstrate the difficulty of applying strict criteria of distinction between the two approaches, I want briefly to consider two highly influential humanistic techniques representative of both humanistic psychology proper and its more extremist tendencies as advocated by the human potential movement.

Gestalt Therapy and Phenomenology

One of the more established and respectable approaches within humanistic psychology is that of Gestalt therapy (Perls, 1969; Perls et al., 1973).

Not to be confused with Gestalt psychology, whose main, experimentally-based contributions have been in the area of perception, Gestalt therapy, principally derived from the writings and therapeutic technique developed by Frederick ('Fritz') Perls (1893–1970), is, as Shaffer has put it, 'supremely experiential, in that it encourages the patient to focus intensively and specifically on what *is*, and not what was, will be, should be, or could have been' (1978: 87).

The Gestalt therapist, in focusing on the client's current experience, urges the deeper exploration of this experience by verbal questioning designed to clarify and define the experience more concretely (often by asking 'what' and 'how' questions) or by pointing to the (often subconscious) body language which accompanies the client's verbal statements and instructing the client to exaggerate or dramatize these movements in order that the affects linked to these actions may be exposed. Alternatively, the Gestalt therapist might invite the client to explore experience through a series of 'games' or 'exercises' designed to facilitate often powerful, even cathartic, affective discharge.

While this may seem to be a far more directive technique than that associated with phenomenologically derived approaches, the aims of Gestalt therapy – the encouragement of acknowledging responsibility for one's subjective experience, self-acceptance and reintegration – are essentially the same as those of phenomenological therapies. However, its optimistic stance on human nature, its emphasis on liberation, and the high degree of active intervention on the part of the therapist remain major (if implicit) sources of division between the two approaches. Interested readers are urged to refer to other texts (Rowan, 1976: Kovel, 1976; Graham, 1986), as well as to Perls himself (Perls, 1969) for further accounts of the Gestalt approach to therapy.

est and Phenomenology

My second example is the now defunct, if still widely discussed, technique known as est (Rhinehart, 1976; Tipton, 1982).

est (meaning 'it is' in Latin, and not, as often assumed, an acronym for 'Erhard seminar training') made its first appearances in the early 1970s. Devised by Werner Erhard, the est training took place over two consecutive intensive weekends with each daily session lasting anywhere between twelve and sixteen hours.

Uniquely, and controversially, as many as three hundred clients ('trainees') under the supervision of one or two 'trainers' participated in the sessions at any one time. Though never advertising its existence or dates and locations of its seminars through the media, est attracted an estimated 300,000 trainees from major cities all over the world (though, predominantly, in North America). Disclaiming any status as a therapeutic system, est stressed an *educative* function. This is a somewhat moot point, however, since, in its own words:

> The purpose of the est training is to transform your ability to experience living, so that the situations you have been trying to change, or have been putting up with, will clear up just in the process of life itself. (est training memorandum, 1979)

In order to achieve this admittedly diffuse aim, trainees carried out a variety of techniques ('processes') designed to induce the experience of 'getting it' – a catchphrase loosely analogous to 'enlightenment' or 'transformation'. Three distinct categories of processes were enacted.

First, trainer monologues, often scabrously humorous and laced with emotionally loaded terminology ('asshole', for example, being an oft-repeated title bestowed upon trainees), were used to confront the trainees' assumptions or sedimented beliefs about various subjective experiences such as the nature of the mind, choice, responsibility, reality and so forth.

Secondly, dialogues were carried out between the trainer and a volunteer trainee who wished to 'share' an experience. *Always and only* between that trainee and the trainer, these often led to sudden, dramatic, even at times abreactive, insight on the part of the trainee.

Thirdly, the trainer presented a variety of exercises such as fantasy games, role-reversals and self-confrontational techniques, which trainees were invited to attempt, and which often resulted in the release of guilt, anxiety or fears related to experiences of living.

On analysis, the various processes point to the est training's dependence on, and use of, phenomenology – even if the term 'phenomenology' was never explicitly referred to. For instance, est trainers argued that what is truly known is ineffable, thereby rephrasing the phenomenological conclusion that experience is initially straightforward (that is, ineffable) and only subsequently becomes reflective (that is, open to description and statement). Similarly, in another exercise known as the 'truth process' trainees were taught to confront and examine various issues in their lives by means of description rather than via interpretative analysis.

If there was a common theme underlying all the processes, it was that of choosing one's experience. Trainees were reminded, harangued, ultimately (if but temporarily) convinced that they were the cause of their experience, and that their actions were products of interpretative choice rather than passive reactions to external manipulation. This conclusion, the trainer argued, was not based on the acceptance of a new belief system but, rather, was the product of observation based on direct conscious experience. It was this acknowledgement of experiential responsibility (or, as an est trainer might put it: 'Listen, asshole, you're the sole creator of your experience!') that produced the 'getting it' experience.

In some ways, with its usage and coinage of simple, emotive terminology, and its emphasis on action rather than thoughtful contemplation and logical analysis, the est training succeeded, at least partially, in presenting often difficult, linguistically obscure phenomenological notions at a highly accessible, 'mass-market' level; if for no other reason, it merits the attention and consideration of phenomenologically oriented therapists.

This is not to say that there are no serious psychological criticisms to be made of the est training. (Several significant social and organizational criticisms have also been levelled (Tipton, 1982).) Yalom (1980), for instance, by no means an unsympathetic critic, questions the authoritarian nature of the est organization and of the training itself. In a similar vein, though far more antagonistically, Tipton

(1982) points out the psychologically regressive features in the processes employed during the training. Unfortunately, most critics have focused on rather naive charges of mass-brainwashing, or hypnotic suggestion (Rosen, 1984), in order to account for the overwhelmingly favourable reactions to the training by its 'graduates', their continuing involvement with the organization either by attending 'graduate workshops' dealing with specific topics (for example, 'On Sex', 'About Money', 'What's So' and so forth), or by acting as unpaid volunteers who carried out often menial jobs within the various city centres, and their enthusiastic and insistent attempts to convince family, friends and strangers to take the training. Putting aside the possibility that these behaviours stemmed from genuine appreciation of the training and, subsequently, a not surprising desire to share it with others, better explanations than those resorting to brainwashing can be presented.

For instance, Wooler (1981) has argued that, like many other therapies, est set up a powerful 'transference relationship' between each trainee and the trainer. However, unlike other approaches, est often failed to terminate this transference relationship by the end of the training. To make matters more complicated, trainees were explicitly told several times during the course of the training that the trainer was not just a representative of Werner Erhard but was, rather, a *channel* between Erhard and each trainee. For some trainees, the established transference thereby became focused upon est's founder and the totality of the organization that was the embodiment of his thoughts. In maintaining the transference, some graduates could not extinguish the link between themselves and the organization and, subsequently, were prepared to do almost anything to ensure its continuation. In this way, they became 'enslaved' to est (that is, they became 'esties') and exhibited behaviour much more in keeping with that of followers of certain cult movements than that of the liberated, enlightened beings they claimed themselves to be.

My own principal criticism of the est training is that it generally failed to put across one major phenomenological conclusion – that of 'being-for-others'. Many est graduates that I've talked to emerged from the training convinced that they were now free to act as they wanted to, regardless of the effects that their behaviour might have on others since others' interpretative subjective experience of these acts was their (that is, the others') responsibility. This view, of course, leads to a potentially dangerous form of misguided solipsism and seriously weakens est's claims to have produced 'enlightened' beings.

This last criticism, as I have mentioned elsewhere in this chapter, can be applied to the great majority of humanistic techniques. Similarly, Wooler's point concerning unbroken transference is equally applicable – especially so to those techniques which fall under the broad canvas of the human potential movement where the 'cult of personality', as focused on a particular technique's founder, seems at times to run rampant.

Further summary of other humanistic approaches would be redundant, since several well-written texts which fulfil this aim already exist (Rowan, 1976; Shaffer, 1978), as well as repetitive in its argument that a distinction between phenomenological and humanistic psychology does exist even if there is much in common between the two approaches.

Many humanistic psychologists have an inadequate knowledge of the philosophical bases to their approach. But it is these very bases that link humanistic theory to phenomenology. It is, I think, this weakness which accounts for the ever-increasing number of techniques, and the great reliance and status placed upon them, which dogs humanistic psychology and which has weakened its impact on other schools of psychology.

Unfortunately, due to the current confusion as to the distinction between phenomenological and humanistic psychology, many criticisms which are specific to particular aspects of humanistic psychology have been misguidedly presented as critiques of phenomenological psychology. This has often led to a naive dismissal of phenomenological psychology by adherents of the remaining systems of contemporary psychology.

This is a particularly unwelcome development, not only because it rests upon false assumptions concerning phenomenological psychology, but, more significantly, because phenomenology's stated aim is not to deny the accomplishments of other approaches but, rather, to increase the adequacy of their investigations and theoretical models.

That there may be – perhaps insurmountable – theoretical and methodological disagreements between phenomenological psychology and the remaining systems in contemporary psychology does not deny the value of a phenomenological input to psychological thought. This issue forms the central concern of the following chapter.

9

Phenomenology and the Major Systems in Psychology

Though adjoining states are within sight of one another, and the sound of dogs barking and cocks crowing in one state can be heard in the other, yet the people in one state will grow old and die without having had any dealings with those of the other.

Lao Tsu

Husserl originally proposed the view that all the sciences could and should be constructed along phenomenological lines (Ihde, 1977). In recent years, various attempts to examine the benefits of this suggestion have provided a variety of intriguing results: the rise and development of modern-day ethnomethodology, as presented by Harold Garfinkel (Ihde, 1977), is clearly indebted to phenomenological theory, as is Berger and Luckmann's highly influential text, *The Social Construction of Reality* (1966). The authors of this latter text, for example, make this indebtedness explicit when they explain that the method they consider to be the best suited to allow the clarification of a scientific understanding of the process of ascribing meaning to everyday life is that of phenomenological analysis.

Similarly, Filmer, Phillipson, Silverman and Walsh, in their important text *New Directions in Sociological Theory* (1972) assess (positively) the potential impact of the phenomenological alternative to sociological theories and research.

What unifies these authors is a criticism of their sciences as being exclusively *noematic* in their orientation, and, thereby, able to arrive at only limited and insufficient conclusions; since noetic considerations are also clearly required, phenomenology offers a useful and rewarding starting point for future research.

As this text has argued, phenomenological investigation allowed the development of a unique and systematic approach to psychology. In addition, as this chapter will attempt to demonstrate, phenomenological psychology seeks neither to dismiss nor to diminish the contributions of other contemporary psychological systems. Rather, wherever possible, it attempts to reconsider and reassess their assumptions, both to point out their weaknesses and to incorporate significant findings obtained from phenomenological enquiry.

A case can be made that much of phenomenological psychology's language is somewhat esoteric and unwieldy. This may be so; nevertheless, it is its *ideas* that demand major consideration. As Erdelyi (1985) has recently shown, for instance, once the highly specific terminologies of psychoanalysis and cognitive psychology have been 'deconstructed', numerous important similarities and areas of agreement emerge and make inter-system communication and (at least partial) rapprochement more likely and potentially highly rewarding. There is no reason to suppose that similar benefits would not arise as a result of increasingly regular dialogue between phenomenological psychology and the remaining approaches.

Often, the conclusions arrived at by phenomenological psychologists challenge those held by other psychological systems. This is not because phenomenological psychologists judge the findings of the other schools as being 'incorrect' (a term which, like the notion of 'correctness', is avoided by phenomenology due to its implication of the ultimate knowability of 'truth' or 'reality'), but, rather, because their findings are often both limited and limiting.

In general, phenomenological psychology's criticism is primarily concerned with other systems' minimization or exclusion of conscious experience from their studies. This lacuna, phenomenologists argue, has harmed psychology, and limited its practical applications. As Rollo May once wrote: 'We need a form of psychology that does not dwell on behaviour to the exclusion of experience, or experience without regard for behaviour, but centres on the relation between experience and behaviour' (1969a: 27). An early attempt to explore the possible phenomenological contributions to psychology took place in the form of a symposium held at Rice University in 1963 and later published as *Behaviorism and Phenomenology* (Wann, 1964). I urge interested readers to refer to this important selection of papers, in particular R.B. MacLeod's contribution (Wann, 1964: 47–74) for its clarification of the centrality of meaningful constructions of experience to phenomenological investigation.

In what I hope is in keeping with the spirit of this symposium, I now wish to consider some areas of potentially useful dialogue between phenomenological psychology and the remaining major systems in contemporary psychology.

Phenomenological Psychology and Psychoanalysis

With its emphasis on internal subjective states, phenomenological psychology at first appears to be closer in its interests and applications to the various current psychoanalytic theories than to any others within contemporary psychology. In general, both approaches can be seen to consider the limits and potentials of human growth and change, and to take the view that people are active interpreters of their environment.

On the other hand, a traditional psychoanalyst steeped in the ideas of Freud and his immediate followers would point to a number of important differences and divergences between the two approaches. Traditional psychoanalytic theories stress the role of the unconscious of our earliest infantile experiences, of the instinctual forces of eros and thanatos, and of the psychic conflict between id–ego–superego as prime determinants of conscious thought and behaviour. Equally, traditional psychoanalysts argue that unresolved sexual and aggressive wishes lie at the heart of human motivation. As one of the most complete systems within contemporary psychology, psychoanalysis provides a coherent – if highly controversial – theory of mind. How might its views be reconcilable with phenomenology?

Let me first consider the psychoanalytic unconscious. As Grossman has argued, 'an unconscious desire is a desire which a person *experiences*, but which the person does not recognize for what it is' (1984: 56). In other words, the psychoanalytic unconscious refers to a *misidentification* of experience for the purpose of temporarily reducing or removing the guilt-laden anxiety that would be generated from the correct identification of experience. Put in this way, the divide between psychoanalysis and phenomenological psychology becomes far less intractable since the issue now can be seen to revolve around patterns of meaning construction.

Similarly, the psychoanalyst's emphases on sexual and aggressive conflicts, rather than being disputed by phenomenological psychology, are placed within the broader (and more deep-rooted) set of conflicts arising out of the individual's being-in-the-world; one's sanctioned social interactions and concepts of self will, of necessity, impose limitations on being in general and, most commonly, upon the expression of sexual and aggressive urges.

Phenomenological psychologists would argue that it is not these urges *in themselves* that produce feelings of guilt and anxiety, but rather, it is the perceived threat to the individual's sense of being as manifested by these urges that leads to the various defensive mechanisms deduced by psychoanalytic theory.

Equally, while phenomenological psychologists would certainly agree that past experience plays a major, even central role in the individual's current psychic life, they would also take the view that the past is a far more flexible, more plastic shaper of current experience since its noetic aspect undergoes continual reassessment and reinterpretation. The *significance* of past events is by no means fixed, though it may seem to be to someone who, through self-construed defences, refuses to engage in honest and open examination of current experience.

Whereas the psychoanalyst might seek to lead the analysand to an *acceptance of the past*, the phenomenological psychologist focuses on the description and examination of current experience as a means of liberating oneself from sedimented defensive beliefs and behaviours which prevent one's *acceptance of present experience*. In both cases, one's past is exposed to examination, but whereas the psychoanalyst seeks to establish causal links between past and present experience, the phenomenological psychologist eschews both the necessity for and, more importantly, the very possibility of such links, and instead seeks to expose the interpreted significance of past events in the light of current experience. This reorientation, if adopted by psychoanalysis, would free it from its somewhat out-moded mechanistic orientation without doing serious damage to its central emphases.

In terms of its psychotherapeutic applications, the central technique of psychoanalysis – *free association* – can be seen as similar in many ways to the phenomenological method. Analysands are instructed to allow their mind to flow freely, to speak of whatever comes into their thoughts no matter how trivial or absurd it may seem. The phenomenological method directs us to bracket our beliefs and assumptions, to describe experience as accurately as possible, to avoid placing any immediate hierarchies of significance on our descriptions. The similarities are, I think, obvious.

Equally, though the aims of these two processes might at first seem entirely dissimilar, it can be argued that in a broad sense, both seek to allow individuals to be more honest and accurate in their perceptions of their experience.

Another central process of psychoanalytic therapy, the development of the *transference relationship* between analyst and analysand, requires some degree of reinterpretation. Considered from a phenomenological perspective, the analysand's directing of deeply felt positive and negative emotions on to the therapist is not only, or necessarily, a regressive act through which the therapist becomes a temporary substitute for the analysand's past significant others. It is also (and perhaps more importantly) a demonstration of the analysand's growing respect for and trust in the therapist and of the analysand's acceptance that no revelation will threaten the analytic relationship and, by implication, the analysand's sense of being.

Further, during the transference relationship, analysands manifest behaviours which suggest either their growing affection and 'love' for their analyst – **positive transference** – or, alternatively, their growing aggression or 'hatred' towards their analyst – **negative transference**. It may well be the case that, as psychoanalysts suggest, the analysand's positive and negative transferences are aspects of regression and allow the analysand to re-enact past wishes and fears in a symbolic manner.

But this may be just one aspect of the transference relationship. It might be just as likely that the analysands are also 'testing' their analysts' claimed open-minded neutrality in their opinions of their patients (that is, their unconditional regard) in order to ensure the truth of such claims (negative transference), and also under other circumstances, are expressing their desire to continue to explore and maintain this unique, unusual and highly desirable relationship via whatever means the analysand has learned to employ when dealing with others who provide only conditional regard (positive transference).

Once again, phenomenological psychologists take issue not with the necessity and strength of what has been termed 'transference' but with the *limited interpretation* that has been given to it by psychoanalysts.

With regard to the traditional psychoanalytic 'metapsychology' and its notions concerning instinctual forces and existing conflicts between the hypothesized 'structures' of the mind, not to speak of the many theoretical concepts that make up the psychoanalytic view of man (for example, concepts such as the Oedipus complex, castration anxiety and penis envy), it is first of all important to note that psychoanalysts themselves are by no means united in their acceptance of these concepts or on the relative importance of the role of each in the development of the human psyche.

Freud, much to his credit, continually revised his theories when both theoretical inconsistencies and analytical data seemed to demand both major and minor revisions in thought, and was willing to accept some degree of divided opinion among his followers (Gay, 1988).

Phenomenological psychologists might well view many psychoanalytic conclusions as open hypotheses which, though neither proven nor disproven, might act as useful metaphorical ways of considering the workings of the mind. Nevertheless, they would also avoid considering such theories as 'invariants' of human experience until such a time as there was sufficient evidence for such an assumption.

If there is a major division between psychoanalysis and phenomenological psychology, it lies in the former system's pronounced tendency to rely on interpretations and theoretical formulations and of the equal, though opposite, tendency on the part of phenomenological psychology to avoid them in favour of description and open-ended reflection in order to bracket biases and sedimented beliefs as far as possible.

True, phenomenological psychology has its own assumptions and, to some extent, a number of these might hold similarities to those of psychoanalysis. The psychoanalytic notion of 'thanatos', for example, bears some (if initially seemingly superficial) resemblances to the existential notion of 'nothingness' and both concepts might find some gain in being considered and contrasted in relation to one another. However, though no easier to 'prove' or 'disprove' than are psychoanalytic assumptions, there is, to me at least, a simplicity and experiential clarity within such assumptions that convince me of their greater adequacy. It takes little effort, for example, to experience at least some of the angst that the realization of one's eventual death brings forth. Similar attempts to experience, let us say, the Oedipus complex, are as likely to provoke disbelief as they are to induce guilt.

Of course, one might argue that the Oedipus complex is so deeply entrenched in our unconscious that we defend much more strenuously against its conscious acceptance. Perhaps so, but is not the anxiety which accompanies Oedipal desires an anxiety related to one's sense of being and 'wholeness'? The male child's fear of castration and the female child's sense of incompleteness as a result of not possessing an adequate penis could be interpreted as symbolic expressions of fragmentation rather than as aspects of a universal complex.

Without denying the power of psychoanalytic insights, the phenomenological psychologist argues that their adequacy might be limited in that, through their failure to apply the phenomenological method, they arrive at possibly misleading and biased interpretational conclusions. For instance, Freud's letters to his friend Wilhelm Fliess (Masson, 1985) reveal his tendency to generalize his own experience into a theory of universal validity. It is a measure of Freud's genius that so many of his conclusions *are* open to generalization. But, equally, it is also the apparent personal biases in his insights that have opened psychoanalysis to continuing controversy.

There have been various important attempts over the years to converge or reconcile psychoanalytic theory with phenomenology. Psychoanalytically oriented therapists such as Rank (Lieberman, 1985), Binswanger (1968) and Frankl (1963, 1967) among others, stressed the importance of subjective meaning and existential anxieties. More recently, Ricoeur (1970) has attempted an admirable synthesis of phenomenology and psychoanalysis, and Yalom (1980) has argued that there is much more agreement than had previously been suspected between Freudian and Sartrean psychology. Equally, the growing influence of psychoanalytic **ego psychology**, which emphasizes internal forces that promote autonomy and wholeness, can be seen as an attempt to reconcile some aspects of the two approaches. Steele (1982) has argued the case for considering psychoanalysis as a hermeneutic science, that is, a science of 'meaning' thereby opening the way for more phenomenologically derived analyses.

Most significant of all, I believe, has been the rise of **object relations theory** (Greenberg and Mitchell, 1983) within psychoanalysis. Though revolutionary in its re-evaluation of psychoanalytic theory, it has become a major movement within psychoanalysis and has led the way towards useful dialogue with cognitively oriented psychologists. Object relations theorists either disavow or diminish the importance of instinctual urges, preferring instead to focus upon the series of significant interactions that individuals engage in in order to form various interpreted relations with others, themselves and the world. Here, quite obviously, there is much scope for an illuminating dialogue between psychoanalysis and phenomenological psychology.

Phenomenological Psychology and Behaviourism

While it is relatively easy to consider similarities and possible areas of some degree of rapprochement between phenomenological and psychoanalytic theory, it would seem, at first, to be far more difficult to see what possible benefit there might be in any dialogue between phenomenological psychology and behaviourism.

After all, behaviourism arose in direct reaction to psychological schools which stressed the centrality of conscious experience. Declaiming the possibility that consciousness could be examined scientifically (that is, via experimental procedures derived from physical science), behaviourism both minimized and, in its most radical stance, rejected the role of consciousness in human behaviour. Instead, it focused its attention – for many years highly successfully – on both the observation and the manipulation of *external* or *overt* behaviour, and based it conclusions on data obtained from controlled studies. Perhaps most importantly, a key element of behaviourist theory is the notion that we are, by and large, passive reactors to natural and culturally derived environmental stimuli which mould and shape our behaviour through conditioning and reinforcement.

Presented with such stances, what could phenomenological psychologists and behaviourists find of value from each other's approach?

First, it is important to recall that both approaches share a similar reluctance to provide theoretically based interpretations which invoke hypothetical structures or mechanisms. Instead, both (initially, at least) focus upon observation and description. In theory, behaviourists should have no qualms about the phenomenological method since its emphases follow closely the broad aims of behavioural research.

Both phenomenological psychology and behaviourism stress the importance of environmental stimuli as catalysts to action. Where there is disagreement, of course, is in behaviourism's claims that we are but passive reactors to directly experienced stimuli. Phenomenological psychology's stance, on the other hand, is to argue that we are active interpreters of the stimuli in that our response to them is intentionally determined through both innate invariants and individual experience.

In this disagreement, there exists much experimental data to support the phenomenological position. Of particular interest is the argument presented by Albert Bandura suggesting the basis for a 'reciprocal determinism' between environment and behaviour, thereby strongly contradicting behaviourism's uni-directional assumption (Yalom, 1980). Yalom points out that there exists a substantial amount of empirical research to support Bandura's contention (1980: 271).

Such a position, of course, bears substantial similarity to that advocated by phenomenological psychologists who dispute the view that stimuli are directly observable. Instead, they argue, the stimuli themselves remain unknown and unknowable; rather it is the constructed meaning we add to stimuli, in order to make sense of our behaviour, that remains of importance.

It can also be pointed out that behaviourists are naive in their assumptions as to what constitutes 'objectivity'. Their views reveal an adherence to a now outmoded stance derived from nineteenth-century theoretical physics. Current theories place doubt upon the traditional distinction between observer and observed. Even in a controlled experiment, the experimenter's assumptions, biases and expectations will, to some degree, determine the kinds of measurements made and even, as Rosenthal and his colleagues have demonstrated in several controlled studies (Rosenthal, 1966), significantly influence the experimental results. In one famous study (and its two subsequent confirmatory replications), for example, it was shown that 'those experimenters expecting success ratings obtained them to a significantly greater degree than did those experimenters who anticipated ratings of failure' (Shaffer, 1978: 173).

Though behaviourists implicitly appear to suggest that we are 'slaves' to our environment, their actual attitude to this position reveals a major inconsistency.

What would a behavioural therapist do, for example, with a patient who claimed that she 'had no control' and was the passive victim of outside forces? I sincerely doubt that the patient would be congratulated for having seen the truth! Obviously, behaviourists hold some sort of sedimented (if unstated) beliefs concerning the experience of autonomy and (relative) freedom of choice. On the other hand, the phenomenological outlook, while acknowledging the uncontrollable limits to freedom, points out, nevertheless, its largely untapped and unacknowledged potentials.

Upon consideration, the most extreme behaviourist position on this issue (that is, Skinner's, as expressed in *Beyond Freedom and Dignity* (1971)) is, in a nutshell, that freedom is an illusion. Yet this conclusion requires clarification in that Skinner's critique is in reference to a definition of freedom which does not recognize *any* limits to or constraints on one's behaviour. As I hope I've already made clear, the phenomenological perspective, in its admission of the limits to freedom, falls outside Skinner's line of attack since it, too, criticizes optimistically naive notions of freedom. Interestingly, as Kvale and Grenness have argued, close comparison of the Skinnerian and phenomenological positions reveals (previously unseen) significant correspondences (1967).

The major source of dispute between the two approaches lies, of course, in behaviourism's dismissal of subjective experience since, its followers claim, any direct investigation of such experience threatens its objective, experimental stance. However, as Shaffer (1978) has pointed out, the distinction that behaviourism makes between private/subjective and public/objective events reveals a 'conceptual sleight of hand'. Shaffer argues (quite correctly, I think) that behaviourists 'must assume, however implicitly, some degree of correspondence between the research participant's verbal report and his actual perception' (1978: 175).

In spite of their dismissal of subjective experience, behaviourists depend on some degree of accurate correspondence between private experience and public report in order to provide validity and significance for their experimental data. Furthermore, as Koestenbaum (1973) has pointed out, all public statements begin as first-hand subjective experience; as such,

> to claim 'public verification' of my private experience is legitimate only to the degree to which all of us, as philosophers of science and students of human behaviour, agree on a fundamental philosophical assumption – namely that if each of our private experiences indicates a particular event

to have occurred, we can then conclude that the event has actually taken place. (Shaffer, 1978: 176)

Rather than rely upon *direct* verification, behaviourists actually depend upon indirect constructs or assumptions.

Most telling of all, I believe, critics of behaviourism have pointed to the paucity of *qualitative* data obtained from behavioural research; though vast in quantity, the great majority of behavioural findings tell us little of worth about ourselves. In a sense, having denied the importance of subjective data, their findings appear limited, alien, even 'soul-less'. In earlier chapters of this text I've tried to show how often-confusing empirical evidence can benefit from phenomenological investigation. At the very least, the phenomenological method helps to expose experimenters' implicit, even hidden, assumptions, thereby allowing them to arrive at more adequate and descriptively accurate analyses and conclusions.

If, in the end, the major differences between behaviourism and phenomenological psychology remain irreconcilable, there still exists much scope for constructive dialogue. Phenomenological psychologists, at least, can make great use of the data obtained by behavioural research – even if they must also dispute behaviourism's assumptions and conclusions.

Phenomenological Psychology and Cognitive Psychology

If behaviourism were still the dominant approach within academic psychology, the possibility of any substantial rapprochement with phenomenology would remain highly unlikely. However, behaviourism itself has undergone substantial revolution over the past three decades such that the principal trend within contemporary psychology has fallen to a somewhat loosely bound 'conglomerate' generally labelled the cognitive school.

Although still arguably a branch of behaviourism in that it adheres to the latter's principal methods for its own accumulation of data, cognitive psychology, in general, is far more open to the consideration of subjective experience and, more significantly, it stresses the importance of the interpretational elements that mediate between stimulus input and behavioural response.

A great deal of what phenomenological psychology has concluded *Similarities* about perception, for instance, would find little dispute among cognitive psychologists. Similarly, the long-standing phenomenological conclusion that there is a major distinction to be made between the unknown real world and the humanly interpreted object world has recently become an increasingly important hypothesis among a number of AI (artificial intelligence) theoreticians (Sortie, 1988). Along the same lines, cognitive theoreticians concerned with issues relating to memory would probably find that the phenomenological arguments in this area add valuable contributions to their research findings and, perhaps more importantly, clarify some of the confusion regarding the status of short-term memory recall and recognition. It would seem in fact that, for once, the difficulties of conjecturing potential areas of shared interest and possible mutual benefit are relatively minimal.

However, one of the central problems of positing areas of contact between phenomenological and cognitive psychologists lies in the lack of any truly unified approach or agreement concerning the realms of discourse that form the subject matter of cognitive psychology. More accurately, there exist *several* 'cognitive psychologies'. Although these share a common concern in the examination of cognitive processes (for example, perception, memory, concept formation), their assumptions and methodologies reveal significant disagreements and divergences of thought (Neisser, 1967, 1976; Eysenck, 1984).

Medcof and Roth have summarized three major weaknesses or 'unsolved problems' which cognitive psychology must contend with. In brief, these are: (a) the current lack of any coherent, integrated theory which links the various sub-theories united by their emphases on mediational processes; (b) its over-reliance on information-processing metaphors which, though partially useful, remain incapable of providing models of human behaviour that accurately represent human (as opposed to machine) information-processing; and (c) its failure to give proper consideration to the *emotional* content underlying human decision-making (Medcof and Roth, 1979).

There also exists, throughout the various cognitive approaches, a differing emphasis between those psychologists who are primarily interested in the study of the various cognitive processes *themselves* and those whose principal focus lies in the analysis of cognitive *processing*. Current circumstances suggest that a colloquium between phenomenological and cognitive psychology would be more beneficial with those cognitive approaches whose primary focus of interest lies in the study of 'the processes that come between stimulus and response' (Medcof and Roth, 1979: 182).

One fairly obvious example of just such an area of co-operative exploration might well be that of emotion. There have already been several interesting, if by no means conclusive, experimental studies on cognitive factors in emotion and the modification of arousal via the alteration of cognition (Hilgard, Atkinson and Atkinson, 1987) whose results might best be interpreted and clarified from a pheno-menological perspective.

Schachter's cognitive–physiological theory of emotions (1964; Schachter and Singer, 1962) for instance, emphasizes the centrality of interpersonal variables in determining how we come to label, or conclude the presence of, a particular emotion. Feedback to the brain from physiological activity, argues Schachter, is insufficient in itself to allow for any clear identification of an emotion. Instead, individuals also require information gained from *past experience* in order to be able to give a particular interpretation, or meaning, to their current emotion. This view demonstrates striking parallels with conclusions derived from phenomenological investigation.

Although the study of cognitive processes and processing has become the dominant trend within contemporary psychology, the various cognitive approaches reveal a one-sided reliance upon, and interest in, noematic data and are somewhat disinclined to give proper consideration to the noetic variables within mediative pro-cesses. This weakness may have originated as a result of cognitive psychology's historical development as an extension of behaviourism and has persisted because noetic variables do not easily fit into the behaviourist-based experimental approach which much of cognitive psychology continues to advocate.

It is here, I think, that a phenomenological 'input', which stresses the co-presence and indivisibility of noematic and noetic foci in all intentional acts, might prove to be of the greatest benefit to cognitive research in general. In particular, it would seem to be especially useful to those orientations within cognitive psychology which focus on issues dealing with the various processing systems rather than upon their physiological bases and analogous hypothesized electronic parallels.

Towards a Unified Psychology

Psychology, as a whole, has recently initiated its own period of *glasnost*. Throughout psychology, there are serious attempts being made to find areas of unity among the various disparate approaches. Since the beginning of this decade, for example, there have been several important texts published which seek some convergence between two or more schools of thought (Erdelyi, 1985; Kegan, 1982; Stern, 1985).

Though by no means an unbiased observer, it would seem to me that phenomenological psychology stands in the vanguard of this movement. Although it retains distinctive features which provide clear contrasts with other contemporary approaches in psychology, phenomenological psychology remains an 'open' system which is both capable and willing to incorporate relevant data obtained by other systems.

Piaget has argued that every interaction with the world involves the complementary processes of assimilation (that is, dealing with the stimuli of the world through one's currently available structures) and accommodation (that is, changing one's structures in response to the varying stimuli of the world). Through such processes, we increase the adequacy of our adaptive responses (Ginsburg and Opper, 1969). In much the same way, phenomenological psychology, in its ability both to assimilate and to accommodate to the 'stimuli' of the other psychological systems, increases not only the adequacy of its own assumptions and conclusions, but also (potentially) those of the other systems.

It is, I believe, this very 'adaptive' openness that allows phenomenological psychology to provide pivotal contributions to increased communication and substantial rapprochement between all the contemporary systems in psychology.

10
A Critical Overview of Phenomenological Psychology

As far as we can discern, the sole purpose of human existence is to kindle a light of meaning in the darkness of mere being.

C.G. Jung

A Summary of the Phenomenological Orientation

The founder of the philosophical movement known as phenomenology was Edmund Husserl. Strongly influenced by a number of ideas concerning conscious experience proposed by his teacher, Franz Brentano, Husserl set about developing a philosophical system which sought to clarify both the nature of consciousness and its relation to reality.

Husserl's central argument was that we do not experience the physical world as it actually is in its 'pure', or 'real', state, but that the world we experience is an *interpreted* world that has been shaped both by in-built biological invariants and by the experience-based psychological beliefs and biases that we continuously generate. The 'real' world, though it exists independent of our consciousness of it, remains obscure and is, ultimately, unknowable.

While the world as it is acts as stimulus to all our experience, our *awareness* of experience is the result of interpretation. Between any stimulus and our reaction to it lies a whole series of 'mediations' which serve to bring unique meaning to the stimulus and 'set us' into a specific and unique response. We may not be the creators of experience itself (that is, straightforward experience), but we do create the experience we are aware of (that is, reflective experience).

The phenomenological notion of intentionality provides the key mechanism through which the raw stimuli of the world become consciously interpreted and acted upon. Every intentional act contains both a noematic and a noetic focus. While clearly allowing for the development of (partially) shared constituents in the interpretations of the world arrived at by individuals who have built up similar culturally and linguistically derived schemata, nevertheless, each individual's experiential focus also contains unshared variables (such as those derived from that individual's past experience). As such, our interpretations of the world, rather than being fully shared, or sharable, remain unique.

Husserl developed a method – since known as the phenomenological method – which seeks to bracket, or set aside, immediate biases and 'sedimented beliefs'; to describe the immediate items, or 'givens', of conscious experience; and to avoid imposing an initial hierarchy on these described items in order that any subsequent interpretations may become increasingly adequate, or offer a closer (if still incomplete) approximation of the world as it actually is. As such, the goal of the phenomenological method is not to expose and explore what is truly real – since that remains an impossibility – but, rather to clarify both the variables and invariants of phenomenal reality.

This method led Husserl to place primary focus on phenomenology as an investigative science which has since become concerned with issues both of essence (transcendental phenomenology) and of existence (existential phenomenology).

Phenomenological Psychology

Since the study of subjective experience is a central defining characteristic of phenomenology, it is obvious that many of its concerns bear a direct relevance to psychology. Phenomenological psychology (which, like phenomenology proper, stresses both transcendental and existential orientations or areas of interest) applies the phenomenological method in order to pursue a more adequate understanding of the central concerns of psychology. As a separate and specific system within contemporary psychology, phenomenological psychology stresses a holistic or integrative approach and, equally, is marked by a strong reluctance to impose hypothetico-reductive models on the study of human beings. Its one central assumption lies in its view of human beings as active interpreters of their experience of the world rather than as passive reactors to both bio-physical and environmental forces.

Phenomenological psychology, thus far, has had its greatest impact on the field of psychotherapy and psychiatry. Major theorists such as R.D. Laing and Carl Rogers have applied both the phenomenological method and key existential notions to psychotherapeutic intervention, thereby deriving non-medical models for therapy which focus on reintegration rather than upon interventionist 'cures'.

Phenomenological psychology neither dismisses nor denies the contributions of other psychological systems. Instead, in its critical analyses of these systems' separate biases and assumptions, phenomenological psychology clarifies possible areas of convergence and of mutually beneficial exploration. As I have argued in the previous chapter, phenomenological psychology is likely to be of pivotal value to current trends in psychology which seek to bring greater cohesion and unity to its realms of discourse.

Nevertheless, I would be misleading the reader if I failed to give due consideration to the many criticisms that have been levelled at phenomenology in general and, in particular, at its psychological extensions. It is to the most significant of these that we must now turn our attention.

Philosophical Criticisms dealing with Possible Logical Inconsistencies within Phenomenology

As my academic background has suffered from scant philosophical training, I am particularly indebted to Reinhardt Grossmann's text *Phenomenology and Existentialism* (1984), which both clearly states and rebuts the principal logico-philosophical critiques of phenomenology. I wholeheartedly encourage those readers interested in exploring the philosophical ramifications of phenomenology to read Dr Grossmann's important text; in the meantime, I am afraid that they must remain satisfied with my summary of what he considers to be the three principal philosophical challenges to phenomenology and their rebuttals.

Are All Mental Phenomena Intentional?

This first philosophical criticism is directed more towards Brentano's definition of intentionality than it is to phenomenology proper. Brentano argued that all mental phenomena are intentional (1973). However, various philosophers have criticized this view by demonstrating that such phenomena as feelings and sensations are not intentional in that they are not directed towards an object. The *act* or awareness of feeling and sensing *is* intentional in that it is the *experience of some thing*, but the phenomena themselves need not be. As such, Brentano's thesis holds only if he limits it to the argument that all mental *acts* are intentional. This latter view is the position adopted by all branches of phenomenology and, as such, this criticism can be relatively quickly dispensed with.

The Problem of Non-existent Objects

A second philosophical argument has to do with the problem of imaginary or non-existent objects and their relation to intentionality.

Put simply, this argument suggests that if I am capable of imagining a non-existent object, let's say, 'moon cheese', how could I possibly have come up with its mental image via intentionality? If my consciousness is not directed towards an object (as intentionality insists it must be) and I am still capable of imagining 'moon cheese', then there must be something erroneous about the phenomenological notion of intentionality.

The resolution of this problem was attempted by several philosophers such as Brentano (1973) and Bertrand Russell (1946), but, according to Grossmann, the best resolution to the issue was devised by one of Brentano's students, Kasimir Twardowski. Twardowski argued:

> We must sharply distinguish between two questions. There is, firstly, the question of what a given idea represents, what its object is. There is, secondly, the quite different question of whether or not this object exists. Every idea has an object or, more generally, every mental act has an object. Thus the intentional nexus always holds. But not every object exists. Thus the intentional nexus does not always connect with an existent. (Grossmann, 1984: 49)

In other words, the rebuttal of this criticism demonstrates that the notion of intentionality accommodates all mental acts. In my example, although 'moon cheese' is an imaginary object, were I to attempt to describe its various properties and constituents I would find that those properties bore an important relationship to properties of intentionally experienced objects which would not be considered to be imaginary. That I may have found a creative way to combine various properties such that I invent a new and imaginary object out of them in no way places doubt on the phenomenological notion of intentionality.

A gryphon, to employ another example, is an imaginary creature composed of the head and wings of an eagle and the body of a lion, but I can only imagine or describe a gryphon if I have the necessary awareness of the properties or constituents from the non-imaginary objects (that is eagle, lion) that make up the creature.

The Problem of Infinite Regress

A third philosophical issue disputes the existence of mental acts by arguing that, in assuming that there *are* mental acts, we are led to assume further the implicit existence of prior mental acts (which made us aware that there were mental acts) and which, in turn, lead us further and further back until we are in a cycle of infinite regress. Therefore, this argument would tell us, to speak of mental acts assumes an infinity of mental acts, and since an infinity of mental acts doesn't occur in our experience, one single act cannot occur either. Hence, we can deny the existence of mental acts.

As Grossmann makes explicit, this argument assumes two implicit points: firstly that a mind is aware of all its mental acts *as they occur* and, secondly, that to be aware of a mental act is itself a mental act (1984: 51). If one or both of these points can be rejected, then the critics have lost the argument.

Most phenomenologists have attempted to dispute the second point and, in doing so, have developed somewhat convoluted and circuitous strategies which are not entirely satisfactory resolutions of the issue. On the other hand, argues Grossmann, the first point can be shown to be open to rejection. The mind is *not* aware of its every occurring act. The act of experiencing makes us aware of whatever there may be in our minds at any given moment, but we do not 'experience this experience itself' (Grossmann, 1984: 53). A mind, at any given moment in time, both experiences and is aware of certain consequences, or objects, of this act of experience. We can be aware of certain objects of experience at any given moment in time, but not of the act itself.

To put it another way, at any given moment in time we can be consciously aware of certain experiences, but *the act of experiencing* itself remains outside our conscious awareness. As such, we are *not* aware of our every mental act and, thus, the criticism of infinite regress can be dispensed with.

Psychological Criticisms

The most vociferous opponents of phenomenological psychology have tended to represent it as 'an anachronistic reversion to outdated doctrines, incompatible with the scientific character of psychology, and harmful to its progress' (Misiak and Sexton, 1973: 54).

Equally, behaviouristically oriented critics have argued that both the methodology and the conceptual basis of phenomenology are of little use or interest to any modern-day psychologist whose aim is to manipulate and predict behaviour from a standpoint focusing on generalizable rules which emphasize similarities in behaviour or mental processing.

Such critics have also put into question both the possible significance and effectiveness of phenomenological theory and its application by raising the issue of the subjective nature of phenomenological data and querying the validity and reliability of such data. Similarly, they have fuelled their arguments by pointing out the seeming paucity of 'appropriate methods and techniques of investigation, overdependence on verbal descriptions with their inherent limitations, ambiguity of phenomenological concepts, and sometimes the esoteric language of phenomenologists' (Misiak and Sexton, 1973: 54–5).

In their defence, phenomenological psychologists have argued that the long neglect of the issue of human experience in academic psychology has not only severely put into question the validity and reliability of psychology's own accepted views and positions, but has also restricted psychology to issues which hold little value and relevance to anyone outside the field.

In its neglect of the issue of experience, psychology has not only lost its 'soul', in a metaphorical sense, it has lost its original purpose and has focused instead on the construction, analysis and interpretation of ever more ornate and esoteric experimental studies whose far from unusual lack of replicability fuels research and fills the pages of the various (little-read) learned journals of psychology.

Phenomenologists argue that, as a science whose purported aim is the understanding of man, psychology's starting point *must* be the exploration of human experience. They do not wholly dismiss the findings and methodologies of the other approaches; more accurately, they argue that the progress of psychology requires a more fundamental investigation of the attitudes and assumptions that underlie psychological explorations.

I've already spoken in the previous chapter of the difficulties engendered by the *language* of phenomenology; I only wish to reiterate the point that these linguistic problems prove to be far less difficult to deal with in a climate where there exists a greater willingness to explore issues of common concern and interest.

Before I examine the major psychological criticisms in greater detail, I want to provide a more general rejoinder that should clarify the general thrust of a phenomenological response to these arguments.

I hope that, on the basis of the various topics discussed in this text, unbiased readers will recognize that, unlike the claims made by its critics, phenomenological psychology is neither an anachronistic reversion to outdated introspectionist doctrines, nor is its stance incompatible with a scientific approach to the understanding of human beings.

While it is true that phenomenological psychology takes subjective experience to be its primary concern, its interest lies not with subjectivity per se but with the central mechanism of intentionality and its role in determining the 'reality' that we interpret and base our actions upon. In this, phenomenological investigations lead to the discovery of a number of 'invariants of experience' that are universally shared by our species and, just as importantly, exposes the many 'sedimented beliefs' that both cultural and individual biases impose and which serve to distort and diminish our understanding of ourselves and our world.

Now, let me address the arguments with greater specificity.

Phenomenological Psychology as a Return to Introspectionism

Many critics (Wann, 1964) have assumed that phenomenological psychology is the modern-day equivalent of earlier psychological *introspectionist* approaches whose limited value to psychology was exposed long ago. This incorrect association has emerged because phenomenological psychology and introspectionism share a basic focus upon consciousness (a term which both behaviourists and neo-behaviourists have sought to expunge from psychological language).

That the principal subject matter of both approaches is conscious experience is not being denied; however, their purposes in engaging in such studies are markedly different. In introspectionist studies, well-trained observers focused upon their subjective reactions to external stimuli in order to note various characteristics in their impressions, and sought, ultimately, to reduce their subjective experiences to the simplest mental elements, that is, to sensations, feelings, images. They also attempted to examine certain attributes of their experiences, such as their quality, intensity and duration. In a phenomenological study, no assumption concerning the composition or attributes of impressions is permitted.

Moreover, whereas in an introspective report, objects and meanings were excluded, in a phenomenological study they are essential. The phenomenological psychologist is interested in the meaning that stimuli or situations have for the observer; introspectionists, on the other hand, primarily analysed impressions of various stimuli and provided reports which focused upon their sensory experiences.

The distinctions between the two approaches might perhaps be made more obvious to the reader by example. For instance, consider the notion of self, or 'I', which was discussed in Chapter 5. Introspectionist theorists studying the self typically began from the (arguably erroneous) assumption that there is a constant self (which might be divided into various components), and, through which, we experience the world. As such, the starting point of the introspective approach is the 'I'. The phenomenological approach, on the other hand, takes exactly the reverse position: the perceived 'I' is the product of experience, not its originator.

Such differing stances lead, as I have already argued, to quite different analyses and issues of concern. As such, though it is true to say that both introspectionism and phenomenological psychology are concerned with the nature of consciousness, it is, nevertheless, also important to understand that not only are the methods employed by each system vastly different, their scope and focus of investigation are clearly distinct from one another.

Phenomenological Psychology and Environmental Stimuli

Behaviourists stress environmental factors, as exemplified by cultural and social variables, as primary, even causal, stimulus determinants of human behaviour. Phenomenological psychologists also stress environmental variables as stimuli to behaviour, but insist that such stimuli are first *intentionally interpreted*. It is these interpretations of stimuli that initiate specific behaviour, not the stimuli in themselves.

Each of us develops more or less sedimented biases and outlooks which result both from the development of culturally sedimented schemata and from our unique experientially based interpretations of environmental stimuli. Our cultural, social and moral considerations are not simply due to socio-cultural environmental influences; they are also the direct results of this interpretative process. This perspective leads to the consideration of human beings as active constructors of their experience and not, as behaviourists suggest, as passive reactors to environmental stimuli.

The implications of the phenomenological argument can be seen to have immediate practical and social relevance. For, as active interpreters of our experience, we are led to acknowledge our experiential responsibility as beings-in-the-world. The acceptance of responsibility reorients one's *being* experiences; in turn, this new perspective may well allow for the alteration of one's behaviour.

Phenomenological Psychology's Stance on Interpreted Realities

A common critique of phenomenology questions the phenomenological conclusion that reality, as experienced by each of us, is a construct brought about by intentionality. For many critics of phenomenology, this idea seems to be patently absurd (Wann, 1964; Dreyfus, 1982) in its implications. They might argue that, on the basis of phenomenological theory, if, for example, someone were to decide that a brick wall before her no longer existed, she should be able to walk through it with no injury since it was not part of her constructed experience. Obviously, such critics point out, were such a person to

put this assumption to the test, she would quickly discover its fundamental error.

This criticism, rather than placing doubt upon the phenomenological argument concerning constructed realities, reveals the critics'
misunderstanding of the argument. Phenomenologists do not dispute
the existence of a physical reality separate from our conscious experience of it; their point is simply that we do not experience reality in its
'pure' state but, rather, we experience an intentionally interpreted or
phenomenal, reality.

With regard to the specific example employed above, phenomenological psychologists would argue that the object that has been
labelled as 'a wall' is an intentional construct. What that wall *actually*
is in its real state is unknown. However, that it exists, that it *is*,
regardless of what interpretation is made of it, is not in doubt.

The clarification of this basic misunderstanding of phenomenological theory once again brings to light the major divergence between
phenomenological psychologists and behaviourists. Where behaviourists speak of 'responses' to stimuli (thereby implying passive
reaction), phenomenological psychologists employ terms such as
'construction' or 'interpretation' in order to make explicit the mediative events that lie between stimulus and response.

Phenomenological psychologists hold that this interpretative
model of human behaviour is far more adequate than that proposed
by behaviourists. The behaviourist model is partially correct in stress-
ing the importance of environmental stimuli, but it is also naively
misguided in not realizing that our responses are not to the stimuli
themselves but, rather, to our current interpretations of them.

Phenomenological Psychology's Stance on the Experience of Unique Worlds

Related to the criticism just discussed is the equally misunderstood
argument concerning the phenomenological conclusion that each of
us experiences a unique perspective of the world. Experimentally
oriented critics (Gibson, 1950) have argued that this cannot be the
case since their results demonstrate that, for example, we perceive
the same things and can communicate quite clearly and (seemingly)
accurately with others about what we have perceived. If so, where is
the evidence of 'uniqueness' that phenomenological psychologists
take as being so central to their approach?

Phenomenological psychologists *do* argue that our assumption of a
shared reality is an illusion since what each of us perceives is the result
of a unique intentional construction of experience. While it is true
that there are certain biological invariants which bring species-based

limitations to the possibilities of perception (for example, ours is an object world), these invariants still allow a vast range of noetic possibilities. Experimental studies of ambiguous figures, for example, reveal this all too clearly.

Equally, those of us who share a similar language or cultural perspective may develop mental frameworks which, in influencing the labels we impose, and our general attitudes towards those labels, may lead us to assume that our perceptions are shared. Once again, phenomenological psychology does not reject this argument; however, it does point out that, nevertheless, our experience is not *solely* based upon these stated variables but is also the product of experiential variables unique to each individual. Phenomenological psychology stresses these latter variables not because they are seen as being more important than the former, but because the other systems of psychology either minimize or deny these variables in their studies.

Criticisms Concerning the Scientific Status of Phenomenological Psychology

The most vociferous critics of phenomenological psychology tend to be from the behaviourist-orientated schools of psychology (Shaffer, 1978). Such critics point out that any approach which turns our area of focus away from experimentally based studies relying upon conclusions derived from directly observable behaviour will only succeed in causing psychology to relinquish its 'scientific' status and return it to the morass of out-dated and dead-end speculations which characterized nineteenth-century psychology.

Phenomenological psychologists question the validity of the behaviourist argument by pointing out that, in order to understand any behaviour, that behaviour must first be seen within the context of a person's perceptual field or orientation so that we can be better able to see how that person interprets it and decides his or her place/role within it. The more data we have in this regard, the more adequate (and predictive) can our understanding of the person become.

The phenomenological method, which lies at the core of all phenomenological analyses, reveals an underlying scientific attitude to investigation and, either explicitly or implicitly, has been adopted (albeit under a variety of terminologies) by all other approaches which claim scientific status. Although this would at first suggest that the phenomenological method is no more than a basic 'truism' of science, I have shown that, at least in the area of psychology, this 'truism' has not been applied sufficiently even within 'hard' experimental psychology (for example, in the investigation of perception) with the result that numerous unnecessary sedimented assumptions have led investigators to form distorted and misleading conclusions.

The Problem of Objectivity

By far the most commonly voiced criticism of phenomenological psychology by representatives of experimentally based schools of psychology has concerned itself with the role of objectivity in science (Gibson, 1950; Wann, 1964). Such critics have argued that so long as phenomenological psychologists stress the study of subjective experience, the conclusions derived from their studies cannot be accepted scientifically unless they are put to some kind of objective test which is both repeatable and open to falsification and which allows for the generation of testable predictions.

This is a thorny issue. Certainly, there have been precious few phenomenologically based experimental studies that have been carried out (though not so few as critics would suggest; see, for example, Shaffer, 1978; Yalom, 1980; and Graham, 1986, for discussions of some of these studies). On the other hand, as I've tried to show, phenomenological psychology makes a great deal of use of the experimental findings obtained by the other approaches to accommodate and assimilate these findings into many of its conclusions and, also, in order to clarify the often disparate results obtained by experimental studies.

Nevertheless, it remains the case that phenomenological psychologists *do* reject the traditional stance of objectivity in that they argue that complete objectivity in any enterprise (including experimentation, of course) is impossible since all conclusions about the world are, by their very nature, *interpretative*. For example, they point out that psychological studies dealing with the effects of the experimenters's expectations concerning the results of a study demonstrate the error in assuming that one can obtain truly objective data.

But this is not simply a psychological issue. Since the beginning of this century, primarily as a result of the Einsteinian and quantum revolutions in physics, our understanding of objectivity has undergone radical change (Zukav, 1980; Capra, 1982). For instance, one central feature of modern atomic physics is the notion that 'we cannot talk about the properties of an object as such. They are only meaningful in the context of the object's interaction with the observer' (Capra, 1976: 144). As such, the role of the scientist is no longer that of the passive observer whose measurements reflect an objective reality; rather, the scientist is, more accurately, an active participator, who, through specific measurements and subjective interests or goals, sets temporary (and arbitrary) limits upon an uncertain universe.

This view, of course, alters the notion of 'objectivity' quite drastically. Rather than state 'facts' or 'final truths', physicists can only speak in terms of probabilities which allow for increasingly adequate theories and conclusions that *approach* 'truth' or 'objective reality' – but can never achieve such.

Along similar lines, both Bohm's (1980) and Pribram's (1971, 1976) corresponding theories positing a 'holographic' universe and Gleick's recent (though already highly influential) text entitled *Chaos: Making a New Science* (1988) reveal an indebtedness to phenomenological theory that the authors may or may not have been aware of. Though pursuing slightly different lines of enquiry, each author concludes that the 'real' world is ultimately never fully knowable nor predictable. Our species' attempts to understand and predict are, of necessity, partial and limited. Moreover, through our very attempts to know, we 'set', or define, these very limits of 'knowability' and objectivity.

Clearly, the phenomenological position reflects these current views on objectivity much more closely than does the traditional stance adopted by most experimental psychologists.

Final Comments

Having presented the principal critiques of phenomenology in general, and of phenomenological psychology in particular, I hope that I have succeeded in raising doubts about their strength. If readers have been sufficiently convinced by my arguments that they are willing to consider the phenomenological alternative more seriously and to weigh up its possible implications and benefits to psychology with greater accuracy and open-mindedness, then I think I will have been granted all that an author can reasonably expect from his readers.

As well as all the obvious limitations that are set within the writing of an introductory text on *any* subject area, a written introduction (indeed, any expository work) dealing with phenomenology suffers from the added burden that, ultimately, it is the *doing* of phenomenology that both clarifies its central ideas and removes much that at first appears to be obscure and difficult in its language and methodology.

As Ihde (1977, 1986) has pointed out, without *doing* phenomenology it may be practically impossible to gain a proper understanding of its most significant implications. This is not to say that one may not find it useful to learn about the history, concerns and methodology of phenomenology through the reading of its major hypotheses and conclusions. This is, of course, a standard element of any intellectual enquiry. Nevertheless, without initiating an 'experiential' attempt to understand the basic thrust of phenomenological enquiry, one runs the risk of both misunderstanding and failing to recognize its potential value to areas of scientific exploration such as psychology.

Like any other investigative science, phenomenological psychology relies upon observational and experimental data in order to arrive at its conclusions. However, the subject matter of its investigation – consciousness – requires phenomenological investigators to 'test' such findings (at least initially in order best to understand them), upon their own experience of the world. Phenomenological psychology is not 'merely' experiential, but its ideas are best clarified through experientially based investigations.

I hope that the various points raised throughout this text are intriguing enough for readers to initiate their own experientially oriented 'experiments'. On the basis of my own experience, I can report that such attempts are eminently worth the effort. For instance, as a psychologist, I find myself, today, amazed (and amused) that I have become intrigued by topics in psychology that I once found impossible even to feign any interest in. Similarly, whereas I was once dominated by outlooks and biases that essentially dismissed the findings and hypotheses of one approach, or overvalued those of another, I can now consider the various approaches far less defensively and, more significantly, all the more critically with regard to their theoretical and methodological assumptions.

These experiences, I believe, have led to my becoming a better lecturer in, and practitioner of, psychology and have convinced me of the significance of phenomenological theory.

Interestingly, since I began to teach an introductory course in this area almost a decade ago, it has become somewhat commonplace for students to approach me with enquiries as to where they can pursue further studies in phenomenological psychology since, as many of them have put it, it is this approach more than any other that they have taken that 'feels like what psychology should be' and which provides them with renewed enthusiasm for their subject area.

Though sympathetic to their requests, I have had to inform them that, unfortunately, phenomenologically oriented graduate programmes in psychology still remain relatively uncommon. Perhaps this will change. On the other hand, as I've tried to show, it is both possible and of great potential theoretical and practical value, to attempt a phenomenological 'input' into existing programmes and approaches.

Ultimately, on a broader level, the 'doing' of phenomenology must have significant impact on one's life in general and one's relationship to the world. It does not take much to realize that, although our age is characterized by its multiplicity of advances in science and technology, both nations and their individual members remain so divided by their beliefs and attitudes that the very existence of all living things has come under serious threat of annihilation.

If each of us were willing to apply the phenomenological method to the various private and social interactions in our lives, if we were all momentarily to bracket our sedimented outlooks and beliefs in an attempt to enter each other's frameworks of being with mutual openness and respect, we would be likely to find that highly similar elements of concern and fear underlie our separate and seemingly antagonistic actions. Under such circumstances, although the many and varied problems of the world would not be instantly resolved, we could at least begin to disassemble many of the barriers that stand in the way of such a goal.

In shifting from an 'I *or* you' position to one which provides for the consideration of 'I *and* you' options, we would set into motion a major revolution in all forms of social behaviour, ranging from small group interactions such as contained within the family and pair-bonding, to the workings of industry, education, welfare, government and, ultimately, to the interactions between nations.

Without doubt, such changes require us to shift our philosophical and psychological assumptions. My personal conviction is that, should it ever come about, this revolution would be, in its broadest sense, one dependent upon *phenomenological* insight.

References

Allport, G.W. (1955) *Becoming*. New Haven: Yale University Press.

Allport, G.W. and Cantrill, H. (1934) 'Judging Personality from the Voice', *Journal of Social Psychology*, 5: 37–55.

Asch, S. (1952) *Social Psychology*. New York: Prentice-Hall.

Bandura, A. (1974) 'Presidential Address' delivered at the meeting of the American Psychological Association, New Orleans, August.

Bandura, A. (1978) 'The Self-Esteem in Reciprocal Determinism', *American Psychologist*, 33(4): 344–58.

Bannister, D. and Fransella, F. (1971) *Inquiring Man: The Theory of Personal Constructs*. Harmondsworth: Penguin.

Baron, R.A., Byrne, D. and Kantowitz, B.A. (1980) *Psychology: Understanding Behavior*, 2nd edn. New York: Holt, Rinehart & Winston.

Barrett, W. (1958) *Irrational Man: A Study in Existential Philosophy*. New York: Greenwood Press.

Bartlett, F.C. (1932) *Remembering*. Cambridge: Cambridge University Press (1967).

Benoit, H. (1955) *The Supreme Doctrine: Psychological Studies in Zen Thought*. New York: Viking Press.

Berger, P. and Luckmann, T. (1966) *The Social Construction of Reality: A Treatise in the Sociology of Knowledge*. Harmondsworth: Penguin (1979).

Bergson, H. (1907) *Creative Evolution*, trans. A. Mitchell. London: Macmillan (1911).

Bergson, H. (1911) *Matter and Memory*. London: Allen & Unwin.

Binswanger, L. (1968) *Being-in-the-World*. New York: Harper Torchbooks.

Bohm, D. (1980) *Wholeness and the Implicate Order*. London: Routledge & Kegan Paul.

Bolton, N. (ed.) (1979) *Philosophical Problems in Psychology*. London: Methuen.

Boss, M. (1963) *Psychoanalysis and Daseinanalysis*, trans. I.B. Lefebre. New York: Basic Books.

Boss, M. (1979) *Existential Foundations of Medicine and Psychology*. New York: Aronson.

Brehm, J. (1966) *A Theory of Psychological Reactance*. New York: Academic Press.

Brentano, F. (1973) *Psychology from an Empirical Standpoint*. London: Routledge & Kegan Paul.

Brown, R. and Garland, H. (1971) 'The Effects of Incompetency, Audience Acquaintanceship and Evaluative Feedback on Face-saving Behavior', *Journal of Experimental Social Psychology*, 7: 490–502.

Cantor, J. (1976) 'Individual Needs and Salient Constructs in Inter-personal Perception', *Journal of Personality and Social Psychology*, 34: 519–25.

Capra, F. (1976) *The Tao of Physics*. London: Fontana.

Capra, F. (1982) *The Turning Point: Science, Society, and the Rising Culture*. London: Wildwood House.

Cherry, E.C. (1953) 'Some Experiments on the Recognition of Speech with One and Two Ears', *Journal of the Acoustical Society of America*, 25: 975–9.

Clifford, M. and Walster, E. (1973) 'The Effect of Physical Attraction on Teacher Expectation', *Sociology of Education*, 46: 248.

Cohen, J. (1958) *Humanistic Psychology*. London: George Allen & Unwin.

Collier, A. (1977) *R.D. Laing: The Philosophy and Politics of Psychotherapy*. Hassocks, Sussex: Harvester Press.

Cooper, D. (1967) *Psychiatry and Anti-Psychiatry*. London: Paladin (1970).

Coopersmith, S. (1967) *The Antecedents of Self-Esteem*. San Francisco: Freeman.

Coren, S., Porac, C. and Ward, L.M. (1978) *Sensation and Perception*. New York: Academic Press.

Crabtree, A. (1985) *Multiple Man: Explorations in Possession and Multiple Personality*. Eastbourne, Sussex: Holt, Rinehart & Winston.

Crider, A.B., Goethals, G.R., Kavanaugh, R.D. and Solomon, P.R. (1986) *Psychology*, 2nd edn. London: Scott, Foresman.

Davenport, W., Brooker, G. and Munro, N. (1971) 'Factors in Social Perception: Seating Position', *Perceptual and Motor Skills*, 33: 747–52.

Day, W.F. (1969) 'Radical Behaviorism in Reconciliation with Phenomenology', *Journal of the Experimental Analysis of Behavior*, 12: 315–28.

Deaux, K. and Emswiller, T. (1974) 'Explanations of Successful Performance on Sex-linked Tasks: What's Skill for the Male is Luck for the Female', *Journal of Personality and Social Psychology*, 29: 80–5.

Deaux, K. and Wrightsman, L.S. (1984) *Social Psychology in the 1980's*, 4th edn. Monterey, CA: Brooks/Cole.

DeJong, W. (1977) 'The Stigma of Obesity: The Consequences of Naive Assumptions Concerning the Causes of Physical Deviance'. Unpublished doctoral dissertation, Stanford University.

Deurzen-Smith, E. van (1988) *Existential Counselling in Practice*. London: Sage.

Diener, E., Fraser, S., Beaman, A. and Kelem, R. (1976) 'Effects of De-individuation Variables on Stealing Among Halloween Trick-or-Treaters', *Journal of Personality and Social Psychology*, 33: 178–83.

Dion, K. (1972) 'Physical Attractiveness and Evaluations of Children's Trangressions', *Journal of Personality and Social Psychology*, 24: 207–13.

Dion, K. (1977) 'The Incentive Value of Physical Attractiveness for Young Children', *Personality and Social Psychology Bulletin*, 3: 67–70.

Dreyfus, H.L. (1982) *Husserl Intentionality and Cognitive Science*. London: MIT Press.

Drosnin, M. (1985) *Citizen Hughes*. London: Arrow (1986).

Duncan, S. (1974) 'Some Signals and Rules for Taking Speaking Turns in Conversation', *Journal of Personality and Social Psychology*, 23: 283–92.

Duncan, S. and Niederehe, G. (1974) 'On Signalling that it's your Turn to Speak', *Journal of Experimental Social Psychology*, 10: 234–47.

Duval, S. and Wicklund, R. (1972) *A Theory of Objective Self-Awareness*. New York: Academic Press.

Ebbinghaus, H. (1964) *Memory*. New York: Dover.

Ekman, P. (1975) 'Face Muscles talk every Language', *Psychology Today*, Sept: 35–9.

Ekman, P. and Friesen, W. (1971) 'Constants across Cultures in the Face and Emotions', *Journal of Personality and Social Psychology*, 17: 124–9.

Ellis, A. and Whiteley, J. (eds) (1979) *Theoretical and Empirical Foundations of Rational–Emotive Therapy*. Monterey, CA: Brooks/Cole.

Erdelyi, M.H. (1985) *Psychoanalysis: Freud's Cognitive Psychology*. New York: Freeman.

Erikson, E. (1950) *Childhood and Society*, 2nd edn. New York: W.W. Norton (1964).

Erikson, E. (1968) *Identity: Youth and Crisis*. New York: W.W. Norton.

Evans, R.I. (1975) *Dialogue with Carl Rogers*. New York: Praeger (1981).

Evans, R.I. (1976) *Dialogue with R.D. Laing*. New York: Praeger (1981).

Eysenck, M.W. (1984) *A Handbook of Cognitive Psychology*. London: Laurence Erlbaum Associates (1987).

Fantz, R.L. (1961) 'The Origin of Form Perception', *Scientific American*, 204: 66–72.

Farber, M. (1962) *The Foundation of Phenomenology*, 2nd edn. New York: Paine-Whitman.

Ferrare, N. (1962) 'Institutionalization and Attitude Change in an Aged Population'. Unpublished doctoral thesis, Western Reserve University.

Festinger, L. (1954) 'A Theory of Social Comparison Processes', *Human Relations*, 7: 117–40.

Festinger, L. (1957) *A Theory of Cognitive Dissonance*. Stanford: Stanford University Press.

Filmer, P., Phillipson, M., Silverman, D. and Walsh, D. (1972) *New Directions in Sociological Theory*. London: Collier-Macmillan.

Follesdal, D. (1982a) 'Brentano and Husserl on Intentional Objects and Perception', in H.L. Dreyfus (ed.), *Husserl Intentionality and Cognitive Science*. London: MIT Press. pp. 31–41.

Follesdal, D. (1982b) 'Husserl's Notion of Noema', in H.L. Dreyfus (ed.), *Husserl Intentionality and Cognitive Science*. London: MIT Press. pp. 75–80.

Frankl, V.E. (1963) *Man's Search for Meaning: An Introduction to Logotherapy*. New York: Washington Square.

Frankl, V.E. (1967) *Psychotherapy and Existentialism*. New York: Washington Square.

Freud, S. (1960) *The Psychopathology of Everyday Life*. Harmondsworth: Penguin (1980).

Freud, S. and Breuer, J. (1955) *Studies on Hysteria*. Harmondsworth: Penguin (1971).

Friedman, M. (ed.) (1964) *The Worlds of Existentialism*. London: University of Chicago Press.

Fromkin, H. (1968) 'Affective and Valuational Consequences of Self-perceived Uniqueness Deprivation'. Unpublished doctoral dissertation, Ohio State University.

Fromm, E. (1956) *The Art of Loving*. New York: Harper.

Gay, P. (1988) *Freud: A Life for Our Time*. London: Dent.

Gergen, K. (1971) *The Concept of Self*. New York: Holt, Rinehart & Winston.

Gergen, K. and Wishnov, B. (1965) 'Others' Self-evaluations and Interaction Anticipation as Determinants of Self-presentation', *Journal of Personality and Social Psychology*, 2: 348–58.

Gibbins, K. (1969) 'Communication Aspects of Women's Clothes and their Relation to Fashionability', *British Journal of Social and Clinical Psychology*, 8: 301–12.

Gibson, E.J. and Walk, R.D. (1960) 'The "Visual Cliff"', *Scientific American*, 202: 64–71.

Gibson, J.J. (1950) *The Perception of the Visual World*. Boston: Houghton Mifflin.

Ginsburg, H. and Opper, S. (1969) *Piaget's Theory of Intellectual Development: An Introduction*. Englewood Cliffs, NJ: Prentice-Hall.

Giorgi, A. (1970) *Psychology as a Human Science: A Phenomenologically Based Approach*. New York: Harper & Row.

Gleick, J. (1988) *Chaos: Making a New Science*. London: Heinemann.

Goble, F. (1970) *The Third Force*. New York: Pocket Books (1972).

Goffman, E. (1959) *The Presentation of Self in Everyday Life*. Harmondsworth: Penguin (1972).

Goffman, E. (1961) *Encounters*. Indianapolis: Bobbs-Merrill.

Goffman, E. (1967) *Interaction Ritual: Essays in Face-to-Face Behavior*. Chicago: Aldine.

Gordon, C. and Gergen, K. (eds) (1968) *The Self in Social Interaction*. New York: Wiley.

Graham, H. (1986) *The Human Face of Psychology*. Milton Keynes: Open University Press.

Grant, E. (1988) 'A Pen by any Name?' *Psychology Today*, May: 16.

Greenberg, J.R. and Mitchell, S.A. (1983) *Object Relations in Psychoanalytic Theory*. London: Harvard University Press.

Gregory, R. (1981) *Mind in Science: A History of Explanations in Psychology and Physics*. London: Weidenfeld & Nicolson.

Grimsley, R. (1967) *Existentialist Thought*. Cardiff: University of Wales Press.

Grossmann, R. (1984) *Phenomenology and Existentialism: An Introduction*. London: Routledge & Kegan Paul.

Grunbaum, A. (1984) *The Foundations of Psychoanalysis: A Philosophical Critique*. London: University of California Press (1985).

Gurwitsch, A. (1966) *Studies in Phenomenology and Psychology*. Evanston: Northwestern University Press.

Gurwitsch, A. (1982) 'Intentionality of Consciousness', in H.L. Dreyfus (ed.), *Husserl, Intentionality and Cognitive Science*. London: MIT Press. pp. 59–71.

Haber, R.N. (1969) 'Eidetic Images', *Scientific American*, 220 (4): 31.

Haber, R.N. (1970) 'How we Remember what we See', *Scientific American*, 222 (5): 104.

Hall, G.S. (1904) *Adolescence*. New York: Appleton.

Hampden-Turner, C. (1981) *Maps of the Mind*. London: Mitchell Beasley.

Harré, R. and Secord, P. (1972) *The Explanation of Social Behaviour*. Oxford: Basil Blackwell.

Hawley, P. (1971) 'What Women think Men think: does it Affect their Career Choice?', *Journal of Counseling Psychology*, 18: 193–9.

Hebb, D.O. (1966) *A Textbook of Psychology*. London: Saunders.

Heidegger, M. (1927) *Being and Time*, trans. J. Macquarrie and E. Robinson. New York: Harper & Row (1962).

Heron, W., Doane, B.K. and Scott, T.H. (1956) 'Visual Disturbances after Prolonged Perceptual Isolation', *Canadian Journal of Psychology*, 10: 112–22.

Hilgard, E.R., Atkinson, R.L. and Atkinson, R.C. (1975) *Introduction to Psychology*, 6th ed. New York: Harcourt Brace Jovanovich.

Hilgard, E.R., Atkinson, R.L. and Atkinson, R.C. (1987) *Introduction to Psychology*, 9th ed. New York: Harcourt Brace Jovanovich.

Hochberg, J. (1970) 'Attention, Organization and Consciousness', in D.I. Mostofsky (ed.), *Attention: Contemporary Theory and Analysis*. New York: Appleton-Century-Crofts.

Hodges, H.A. (ed.) (1944) *Wilhelm Dilthey: An Introduction*. London: Routledge.

Holland, N. (1985) *The I*. London: Yale University Press.

Hubel, D.H. and Wiesel, T.N. (1962) 'Receptive Fields, Binocular Interaction and Functional Architecture in the Cat's Visual Cortex', *Journal of Physiology*, 195: 215–43.

Hughes, R. (1980) *The Shock of the New.* London: BBC Books (1981).

Hume, D. (1739) *A Treatise on Human Nature*, Book One, ed. D.G.C. Macnabb, London: Fontana (1967).

Husserl, E. (1929) *Formal and Transcendental Logic.* The Hague: Nijhoff (1969).

Husserl, E. (1931a) *Ideas: General Introduction to Pure Phenomenology*, vol. 1. New York: Macmillan.

Husserl, E. (1931b) *Cartesian Meditations*, trans. D. Cairns. The Hauge: Nijhoff.

Husserl, E. (1948) *Experience and Judgement.* London: Routledge & Kegan Paul (1973).

Husserl, E. (1965) *Phenomenology and the Crisis of Philosophy*, trans. with notes and an introduction by Quentin Lauer. New York: Harper Torchbooks.

Husserl, E. (1983) *Ideas Pertaining to a Pure Phenomenology and to a Phenomenological Philosophy*, trans. F. Kersten. Lancaster: Nijhoff.

Hyman, H. (1942) 'The Psychology of Status', *Archives of Psychology*: 269.

Ihde, D. (1977) *Experimental Phenomenology: An Introduction.* Albany: State University of New York (1986).

Ihde, D. (1986) *Consequences of Phenomenology.* Albany: State University of New York.

James, W. (1890) *The Principles of Psychology*, vols 1 and 2. New York: Holt.

Janis, I. and Feshbach, S. (1953) 'Effects of Fear-arousing Communications', *Journal of Abnormal and Social Psychology*, 48: 78–92.

Jaspers, K. (1964) 'Psychologie der Weltanschauungen', trans. M. Franck and A. Newton, in M. Friedman (ed.), *The Worlds of Existentialism.* London: University of Chicago Press.

Jones, E. and Nisbett, R. (eds) (1972) *Attribution: Perceiving the Causes of Behaviour.* Morrison, NJ : General Learning Press.

Jourard, S. (1964) *The Transparent Self: Self-Disclosure and Well-Being.* Princeton, NJ: Van Nostrand.

Kassajarjian, H.H. (1963) 'Voting Intentions and Political Perceptions', *Journal of Psychology*, 56: 85–8.

Kegan, R. (1982) *The Evolving Self: Problem and Process in Human Development.* London: Harvard University Press.

Kelley, H. and Stahelski, A. (1970) 'The Inference of Intention from Moves in the Prisoner's Dilemma Game', *Journal of Experimental Social Psychology*, 6: 401–19.

Keyes, D. (1981) *The Minds of Billy Milligan.* New York: Random House (1982).

Kleinke, C., Staneski, R. and Pipp, S. (1975) 'Effects of Gaze, Distance, and Attractiveness on Males' First Impressions of Females', *Representative Research in Social Psychology*, 6: 7–12.

Kocklemans, J.J. (1967) *A First Introduction to Husserl's Phenomenology.* Pittsburgh: Duquesne University Press.

Koestenbaum, P. (1973) 'Phenomenological Foundations for the Behavioral Sciences', in F. Severin (ed.), *Discovering Man in Psychology: A Humanistic Approach.* New York: McGraw-Hill.

Koestler, A. (1964) *The Act of Creation.* London: Pan (1975).

Koffka, K. (1935) *Principles of Gestalt Psychology.* New York: Harcourt Brace.

Kohler, W. (1929) Gestalt Psychology. New York: Liveright.

Kovel, J. (1976) *A Complete Guide to Therapy*, Harmondsworth: Penguin (1981).

Kuhn, T. (1962) *The Structure of Scientific Revolutions.* Chicago: University of Chicago Press.

Kvale, S. and Grenness, C.E. (1967) 'Skinner and Sartre: Toward a Radical Phenomenology of Behavior?', *Review of Existential Psychology and Psychiatry*, 7: 128–48.

Laing, R.D. (1960) *The Divided Self*. Harmondsworth: Penguin (1970).

Laing, R.D. (1961) *Self and Others*. Harmondsworth: Penguin (1971).

Laing, R.D. (1967) *The Politics of Experience and The Bird of Paradise*. Harmondsworth: Penguin (1968).

Laing, R.D. (1982) *The Voice of Experience*, Harmondsworth: Penguin (1983).

Laing, R.D. and Esterson, A. (1964) *Sanity, Madness and the Family*. Harmondsworth: Penguin (1971).

Laing, R.D., Philipson, H. and Lee, A. (1966) *Interpersonal Perception: A Theory and a Method of Research*. New York: Springer.

Langer, E. and Abelson, R. (1974) 'A Patient by any Other Name . . . Clinician Group Difference in Labeling Bias', *Journal of Consulting and Clinical Psychology*, 42: 4–9.

Lawson, E. (1971) 'Hair Color, Personality, and the Observer', *Psychological Reports*, 28: 311–22.

Leahey, T.H. (1982) *A History of Psychology*. London: Prentice-Hall.

Lee, N. and Mandelbaum, M. (eds) (1967) *Phenomenology and Existentialism*. Baltimore: Johns Hopkins Press.

Lieberman, E.J. (1985) *Acts of Will: The Life and Work of Otto Rank*. New York: Free Press.

Lucas, J.R. (1970) *The Freedom of the Will*. Oxford: Clarendon Press.

Luchins, A. (1957) 'Primacy-Recency in Impression Formation', in C. Hovland, W. Mandell, E. Campbell, T. Brock, A. Luchins, A. Cohen, W. McGuire, I. Janis, R. Feierabend and N. Anderson, *The Order of Presentation in Persuasion*. New Haven: Yale University Press, 33–61.

Luria, A.R. (1969) *The Mind of a Mnemonist*. London: Jonathan Cape.

MacLeod, R.B. (1964) 'Phenomenology: A Challenge to Experimental Psychology', in T.W. Wann (ed.), *Behaviorism and Phenomenology*. Chicago: University of Chicago Press, 47–74.

Macquarrie, J. (1972) *Existentialism*. Harmondsworth: Penguin.

Mannheim, B. (1966) 'Reference Groups, Membership Group and Self Image', *Sociometry*, 29: 265–79.

Manz, W. and Lueck, H. (1968) 'Influence of Wearing Glasses on Personality Ratings: Cross-cultural Validation of an Old Experiment', *Perceptual and Motor Skills*, 27: 704.

Marcus, M. (1976) 'The Power of a Name', *Psychology Today*, 10 (5): 75–6.

Marcuse, F.L. (1959) *Hypnosis: Fact and Fiction*. Harmondsworth: Penguin (1971).

Maslach, C. (1974) 'Social and Personal Bases of Individuation', *Journal of Personality and Social Psychology*, 29: 213–14.

Maslow, A.H. (1968) *Toward a Psychology of Being*, 2nd edn. Princeton: Van Nostrand.

Maslow, A.H. (1971) *The Farther Reaches of Human Nature*. New York: Viking.

Masson, J.M. (1985) *The Complete Letters of Sigmund Freud to Wilhelm Fliess, 1887–1904*. London: Belknap Press.

May, R. (ed.) (1958) *Existence: A New Dimension in Psychiatry and Psychology*. New York: Basic Books.

May, R. (1969a) *Existential Psychology*, 2nd edn. New York: Random House.

May, R. (1969b) *Love and Will*. New York: W.W. Norton.

May, R. (1983) *The Discovery of Being*. London: W.W. Norton.

Mazis, M. (1975) 'Antipollution Measures and Psychological Reactance Theory: A Field Experiment', *Journal of Personality and Social Psychology*, 31: 654–60.

McGrath, W.J. (1986) *Freud's Discovery of Psychoanalysis: The Politics of Hysteria*. Ithaca, NY: Cornell University Press.

McGuire, W. and Padawer-Singer, A. (1976) 'Trait Salience in the Spontaneous Self-concept', *Journal of Personality and Social Psychology*, 33: 743–54.

Medcof, J. and Roth, J. (1979) *Approaches to Psychology*. Milton Keynes: Open University Press (1984).

Mehrabian, A. (1968) 'Inference of Attitude from the Posture, Orientation, and Distance of a Communicator', *Journal of Consulting and Clinical Psychology*, 32: 296–308.

Merleau-Ponty, M. (1962) *The Phenomenology of Perception*, trans. C. Smith. London: Routledge & Kegan Paul.

Merleau-Ponty, M. (1964) *The Primacy of Perception*. Evanston: Northwestern University Press.

Merton, R. (1957) *Social Theory and Social Structure*. Glencoe, IL: Free Press.

Middlebrook, P.N. (1980) *Social Psychology and Modern Life*, 2nd edn. New York: Knopf.

Milgram, S. (1974) *Obedience to Authority: An Experimental View*. New York: Harper & Row.

Miller, J. (1978) *The Body in Question*. London: Jonathan Cape.

Mishkin, M. and Forgays, D.G. (1952) 'The Tachistoscopic Recognition of English and Jewish Words', *Journal of Experimental Psychology*, 65: 555–62.

Misiak, H. and Sexton, V.S. (1973) *Phenomenological, Existential, and Humanistic Psychologies: A Historical Survey*. New York: Grune & Stratton.

Moray, N. (1959) 'Attention in Dichotic Listening: Affective Cues and the Influence of Instructions', *Quarterly Journal of Experimental Psychology*, 11: 56–60.

Morris, B.B. (1971) 'Effects of Order and Trial on Necker Cube Reversals under Free and Resistive Instructions', *Perceptual and Motor Skills*, 33: 235–40.

Neirenberg, G. and Calero, H. (1971) *How to Read a Person Like a Book*. New York: Hawthorn Books.

Neisser, U. (1967) *Cognitive Psychology*. New York: Appleton.

Neisser, U. (1976) *Cognition and Reality: Principles and Applications of Cognitive Psychology*. New York: Freeman.

Nielsen, S.L. and Sarason, I.G. (1981) 'Emotion, Personality and Selective Attention', *Journal of Personality and Social Psychology*, 41: 945–60.

Nisbett, R. and Wilson, T. (1977a) 'Telling more than we can Know: Verbal Reports on Mental Processes', *Psychological Review*, 84: 231–59.

Nisbett, R. and Wilson, T. (1977b) 'The Halo Effect: Evidence for Unconscious Alteration of Judgement', *Journal of Personality and Social Psychology*, 35: 250–6.

Norman, D.A. (1969) *Memory and Attention: An Introduction to Human Information Processing*. London: Wiley.

Passini, F. and Norman, W. (1966) 'A Universal Conception of Personality Structure?', *Journal of Personality and Social Psychology*, 4: 44–9.

Penfield, W. and Perot, P. (1963) 'The Brain's Record of Auditory and Visual Experience', *Brain*, 86: 595–697.

Perls, F.S. (1969) *Gestalt Therapy Verbatim*. New York: Bantam (1976).

Perls, F.S., Hefferline, R. and Goodman, P. (1973) *Gestalt Therapy*. Harmondsworth: Penguin.

Polanyi, M. (1967) *The Tacit Dimension*. London: Routledge & Kegan Paul.

Popper, K.R. (1963) *Conjectures and Refutations*. London: Routledge & Kegan Paul.

Popper, K.R. and Eccles, J.C. (1977) *The Self and its Brain*. London: Routledge & Kegan Paul (1983).

Pribram, K.H. (1971) *Languages of the Brain: Experimental Paradoxes and Principles in Neuropsychology*. Englewood Cliffs, NJ:Prentice-Hall.

Pribram, K.H. (1976) *Consciousness and the Brain*. New York: Plenum.

Ray, M. (1946) 'The Effect of Crippled Appearance on Personality Judgements'. Unpublished master's thesis, Stanford University.

Rhinehart, L. (1976) *The Book of est*. London: Sphere Books.

Ricoeur, P. (1970) *Freud and Philosophy: An Essay on Interpretation*, trans. D. Savage. New Haven: Yale University Press.

Rock, I. (1984) *Perception*. New York: Scientific American Books.

Rogers, C. (1942) *Counseling and Psychotherapy*. Boston: Houghton Mifflin.

Rogers, C. (1951) *Client-Centred Therapy*. New York: Houghton Mifflin.

Rogers, C. (1961) *On Becoming a Person*. Boston: Houghton Mifflin.

Rogers, C. (1964) 'Toward a Science of the Person', in T.W. Wann (ed.), *Behaviorism and Phenomenology: Contrasting Bases for Modern Psychology*. Chicago: University of Chicago Press. pp. 109–40.

Rogers, C. and Stevens, B. (1967) *Person to Person: The Problem of Being Human*. New York: Real People Press.

Rosen, R.D. (1977) *Psychobabble*. New York: Avon (1979).

Rosen, S. (1984) private communication.

Rosenthal, R. (1966) *Experimenter Effects in Behavioral Research*. New York: Appleton-Century-Crofts.

Rotter, J. (1966) 'Generalized Expectancies for Internal versus External Control of Reinforcement', *Psychological Monographs*, 80(1): 609.

Rowan, J. (1976) *Ordinary Ecstasy: Humanistic Psychology in Action*. London: Routledge & Kegan Paul.

Ruitenbeek, H.M. (ed.) (1962) *Psychoanalysis and Existential Philosophy*. New York: Dutton.

Russell, B. (1946) *History of Western Philosophy*. London: George Allen & Unwin (1961).

Ryan, E. and Carranza, M. (1975) 'Evaluative Reactions of Adolescents toward Speakers of Standard English and Mexican–American Accented English', *Journal of Personality and Social Psychology*, 31: 855–63.

Ryback, D. (1972) 'Existentialism and Behaviorism: Some Differences Settled', *Canadian Psychologist*, 13: 53–60.

Sacks, O. (1985) *The Man who Mistook his Wife for a Hat*. London: Pan (1986).

Sakurai, M. (1975) 'Small Group Cohesiveness and Detrimental Conformity', *Sociometry*, 38: 340–57.

Sanford, R.H. (1935) 'The Effects of Abstinence from Food upon Imaginal Processes: A Preliminary Experiment', *Journal of Psychology*, 2: 129–36.

Sartre, J.P. (1943) *Being and Nothingness: An Essay on Phenomenological Ontology*, trans. H. Barnes. New York: Philosophical Library.

Sartre, J.P. (1948) *Existential Psychoanalysis*. New York: Philosophical Library.

Sartre, J.P. (1984) *The Freud Scenario*. London: Verso (1985).

Schachter, S. (1964) 'The Interaction of Cognitive and Physiological Determinants of Emotional State', in L. Berkowitz (ed.), *Advances in Experimental Social Psychology*, vol. 1. New York: Academic Press.

Schachter, S. and Singer, J. (1962) 'Cognitive, Social and Physiological Determinants of Emotional State', *Psychological Review*, 69: 379–99.

Schneider, D. (1973) 'Implicit Personality Theory: A Review', *Psychological Bulletin*, 79: 294–309.

Schreiber, F.L. (1973) *Sybil*. New York: Warner Paperback (1974).

Scott, N.A. (1978) *Mirrors of Man in Existentialism*. London: Collins.

Searle, J. (1982) 'What is an Intentional State?', in H.L. Dreyfus (ed.), *Husserl Intentionality and Cognitive Science*. London: MIT Press, 1982, 259–76.

Seligman, M. (1974) 'Submissive Death: Giving up in Life', *Psychology Today*, 7 (12): 80–5.

Seligman, M. (1975) *Helplessness: On Depression, Development, and Death*. San Francisco: Freeman.

Shaffer, J.A. (1968) *Philosophy of Mind*. London: Prentice-Hall.

Shaffer, J.B.P. (1978) *Humanistic Psychology*. Englewood Cliffs, NJ: Prentice-Hall.

Sherrington, C.S. (1947) *The Integrative Action of the Nervous System*, new edn. New Haven: Yale University Press.

Shoemaker, S. and Swinbourne, R. (1984) *Personal Identity*. Oxford: Basic Blackwell.

Sigall, H. and Ostrove, N. (1975) 'Beautiful but Dangerous: Effects of Offender Attractiveness and Nature of the Crime on Juridic Judgement', *Journal of Personality and Social Psychology*, 31: 410–14.

Siu, R.G.H. (1957) *The Tao of Science*. Cambridge MA: MIT Press.

Sizemore, C. and Pittillo, E. (1977) *I'm Eve*. New York: Doubleday.

Skinner, B.F. (1971) *Beyond Freedom and Dignity*. New York: Knopf.

Snyder, M. and Swann, W. (1978) 'Behavioral Confirmation in Social Interaction: From Social Perception to Social Reality', *Journal of Experimental Social Psychology*, 14: 148–62.

Sorokin, P. (1947) *Society, Culture, and Personality: Their Structure and Dynamics*. New York: Harper.

Sortie, J. (1988) private communication.

Speake, J. (ed.) (1979) *A Dictionary of Philosophy*. London: Pan.

Sperling, G. (1960) 'The Information Available in Brief Visual Presentations', *Psychological Monographs*, 74: 498.

Spranger, E. (1928) *Types of Men*, trans. P.J.W. Pigors. Halle: Neimeyer.

Sprigge, T.L.S. (1984) *Theories of Existence*. Harmondsworth: Penguin.

Steele, R.S. (1982) *Freud and Jung: Conflicts of Interpretation*. London: Routledge & Kegan Paul.

Steiner, G. (1978) *Heidegger*. Glasgow: Fontana.

Stern, D.N. (1985) *The Interpersonal World of the Infant: A View from Psychoanalysis and Developmental Psychology*. New York: Basic Books.

Stotland, E., Thorley, S., Thomas, A., Cohen, A. and Zander, A. (1957) 'The Effects of Group Expectations and Self-esteem upon Self-evaluation', *Journal of Abnormal and Social Psychology*, 54: 55–63.

Szasz, T. (1970) *Ideology and Insanity*. Harmondsworth: Penguin (1974).

Szasz, T. (1974) *The Myth of Mental Illness*, revised edn. New York: Harper & Row.

Taylor, G.R. (1979) *The Natural History of the Mind*. London: Granada (1981).

Tesser, A., Gatewood, R. and Driver, M. (1968) 'Some Determinants of Gratitude', *Journal of Personality and Social Psychology*, 9: 233–6.

Thorndike, E. (1920) 'A Constant Error in Psychological Ratings', *Journal of Applied Psychology*, 4: 25–9.

Tipton, S.M. (1982) *Getting Saved from the Sixties: Moral Meaning in Conversion and Cultural Change*. Berkeley: University of California Press.

Trusted, J. (1984) *Free Will and Responsibility*. Oxford: Opus.

Tugendhat, E. (1986) *Self-Consciousness and Self-Determination*. Cambridge, MA: MIT Press.

Valle, R.S. and King, M. (1978) *Existential–Phenomenological Alternatives for Psychology*. Oxford: Oxford University Press.

Van Kaam, A.L. (1966) *Existential Foundations in Psychology*. Pittsburgh: Duquesne University Press.

Verinis, J. and Roll, S. (1970) 'Primary and Secondary Male Characteristics: The Hairiness and Large Penis Stereotypes', *Psychological Reports*, 26: 123–6.

Vesey, G. (1971) *Perception*. London: Macmillan.

Walster, E., Aronson, V., Abrahams, D. and Rottman, L. (1966) 'Importance of Physical Attractiveness in Dating Behavior', *Journal of Personality and Social Psychology*, 4: 508–16.

Wann, T.W. (ed.) (1964) *Behaviorism and Phenomenology: Contrasting Bases for Modern Psychology*. Chicago: University of Chicago Press.

Warnock, M. (1970) *Existentialism*. Oxford: Oxford University Press (1979).

Watts, A.J. (1957) *The Way of Zen*. Harmondsworth: Penguin (1974).

Wells, G. and Harvey, J. (1971) 'Do People use Consensus Information in making Casual Attributions?', *Journal of Personality and Social Psychology*, 35: 279–93.

Wilber, K. (ed.) (1982) *The Holographic Paradigm and Other Paradoxes*. London: Shambhala.

Wilson, C. (1972) *New Pathways in Psychology: Maslow and the Post-Freudian Revolution*. London: Gollancz.

Wollheim, R. (1984) *The Thread of Life*. Cambridge, MA: Harvard University Press.

Wolman, B.B. (1981) *Contemporary Theories and Systems in Psychology*, 2nd edn. London: Plenum.

Woodside, A. (1972) 'A Shopping List Experiment of Beer Brand Images', *Journal of Applied Psychology*, 56: 512–13.

Wooler, S. (1981) 'est and Transference'. Unpublished report, archives of the Edale Research Group.

Wright, B.A. (1960) *Physical Disability: A Psychological Approach*. New York: Harper & Row.

Wylie, R., Miller, P., Cowles, S. and Wilson, A. (1979) *The Self-Concept: Theory and Research on Selected Topics*, vol. 2. Lincoln, NB: University of Nebraska Press.

Yalom, I. (1980) *Existential Psychotherapy*. New York: Basic Books.

Yandell, B. and Insko, C. (1977) 'Attribution of Attitudes to Speakers and Listeners under Assigned-behavior Conditions: Does Behavior Engulf the Field?', *Journal of Experimental Social Psychology*, 13: 269–78.

Young, J.Z. (1987) *Philosophy and the Brain*. Oxford: Oxford University Press.

Zimbardo, P. (1969) 'The Human Choice: Individuation, Reason, and Order versus Deindividuation, Impulse, and Chaos', in W.J. Arnold and D. Levine (eds), *Nebraska Symposium on Motivation*, vol. 17. Lincoln, NB: University of Nebraska Press.

Zimbardo, P., Haney, C., Banks, W. and Jaffe, D. (1972) 'The Psychology of Imprisonment: Privation, Power, and Pathology'. Unpublished paper, Stanford University.

Zukav, G. (1980) *The Dancing Wu-Li Masters: An Overview of the New Physics*. London: Fontana.

Index

Index compiled by Peva Keane